MW00861511

THE RACE TO RECRUIT

Strategies for Successful Business Attraction

edited by

Maury Forman
and
James Mooney

with a foreword by

Mike Fitzgerald
Director
Washington State Department of Community, Trade
and Economic Development
and
Paul A. Redmond
Chairman of the Board,
President and CEO
Washington Water Power

illustrations by

David Horsey
Editorial Cartoonist
Seattle Post-Intelligencer

KENDALL/HUNT PUBLISHING COMPANY
4050 Westmark Drive   Dubuque, Iowa 52002

Printed in the United States of America
10 9 8 7 6 5 4 3 2 1

CONTENTS

CHECKLISTS:

FOREWORD

This copy of *The Race to Recruit* is made available through a public/private partnership of the Washington State Department of Community, Trade and Economic Development and Washington Water Power. It is a primer written by some of the most highly regarded experts in the fields of marketing and economic development. Whether you're just starting out or are an old hand, we are certain you can use a new idea or two from the chapters in this book.

Working at both the state and community levels, we have observed an economic development industry that is ever-more competitive with recruitment packages that are more professional and creative. This is due in part to the utilization of new technologies. With the access to information and the speed of communication accelerating, it is critical that the profession incorporate these technologies in its process.

We have witnessed the successes brought about by teamwork as we strive to grow our local, state, and regional economies. That is why we are dedicated to working together in partnerships and to providing the future jobs for our citizens, our customers, and their children so that we may all prosper and enjoy living in this great Pacific Northwest.

Mike Fitzgerald
Director
Washington State Department of Community,
Trade and Economic Development

Paul A. Redmond
Chairman of the Board,
President and CEO
Washington Water Power

DEDICATION

We dedicate this book to those frontline people promoting growth, economic diversity, and wealth in their communities. They unite with the common goals of community betterment. Their work frequently goes unnoticed and unrecognized by their friends and neighbors. It is their commitment to change that creates the capacity for investment and employment opportunities in their community. These people are the economic development professionals working in communities throughout the world.

To these individuals, we dedicate this book. If it aids in the accomplishment of a single goal, it has been a success.

ACKNOWLEDGMENTS

We wish to acknowledge the contributions of the following key people who made this manuscript possible:

Cari Zuleger, who helped develop the checklists, format the text, and enter the data.

Russ Campbell and **Neal VanDeventer**, who provided technical support instrumental to the successful completion of the book.

David Horsey, editorial cartoonist for the *Seattle Post-Intelligencer*, for his insightful and artistic cartoons.

Mike Fitzgerald, Director of the Washington State Department of Community, Trade and Economic Development, for his support and funding of this project.

Evelyn Roehl, who polished and refined our initial work so that it could finally be submitted to the publisher.

The contributing authors who provided their knowledge, insight, and experience with this effort.

To all these people, we would like to say thank you very, very much. Your support and participation made this project possible, the dream a reality, and our goals accomplishable.

— *Maury Forman and James Mooney*

CHAPTER 1

WHY NEW INVESTMENT IS CRITICAL

Donna Batch

Director, Business Investment,
Washington State Department of Community, Trade and Economic Development

The air in the courtroom was thick with tension. The judge, a seasoned veteran of the bench, leaned forward to catch every word of the discussion. He wanted answers and he wanted them now! The prosecuting attorney had been questioning the local economic development official for two and a half hours. You could tell he was not happy with the evasive answers he was getting.

Drenched in sweat, the young economic developer sat on the witness stand. Who would have guessed that this position of seven months would have led so quickly to a defense situation? He knew the question would arrive eventually. Just how would he answer?

The prosecuting attorney ran across the room. His eyes focused on the witness as if he would burn a hole through his skull. He pointed, glared, and screamed, "So, just why are you attracting new investment to our community anyway?"

——— o ———

Most economic development practitioners will never experience a situation this intense. However, many can tell you of experiences when they had to defend a specific course of action or justify their reason for existence. Economic development, due to its wide reach, can be a nebulous service to many people in the community. A poorly focused effort can increase the probability for failure. For most practitioners, defining their work is paramount to defending what they do. Their work will always be questioned, evaluated and scrutinized.

You can keep your program on track by defining a course of action through a well-focused mission statement and performance objectives. Specific objectives are key components to any successful program. The mission statement summarizes the objectives. These initiatives become actions through the annual work plan. A well-thought-out mission statement will set the foundation for success and define the reasons for setting up an economic development program in the first place.

The justification for undertaking an economic development effort, as well as the actual strategies employed to implement an effort, varies from community to community. Some communities may define their economic development efforts as downtown revitalization, while others may focus on small business assistance or entrepreneurial development. Typical economic development programs contain one or more of the following elements: business recruitment, business retention, and business assistance activities. The underlying concept of creating jobs, increasing private investment and tax revenues, and providing stability and growth of the local economy are common threads among most programs. While it is important for a comprehensive economic development program to includes business retention and assistance in its strategies, the focus of this manual is on *business attraction.*

This aspect of recruitment as a component of economic development has come under intense criticism in recent years and is sometimes labeled "smokestack chasing." Yet attracting new companies and the jobs and revenue they bring can be an important part of growing and strengthening the local economy. What follows are reasons you may want to use in your defense of why new investment is critical to your community and why business recruitment efforts may be an integral part of your economic development program.

ECONOMIC DIVERSIFICATION

The economy of local communities can be described in three ways: economically concentrated, economically diverse, or economically deprived. In two of those three definitions—economically concentrated or deprived—a business attraction effort can be justified from the basis of trying to diversify the local economy.

Many communities find themselves tied to the cyclical swings of a single or predominant economic sector. Detroit, Michigan, has its automobiles; Pittsburgh, Pennsylvania, has its steel industry; Seattle, Washington, has its aerospace industry. When things are going well in these sectors, unemployment is down,

income is up, and everyone is (comparatively) happy. When the opposite occurs, elected officials scramble to find:

- ways to handle local revenue shortfalls,
- tactics to soothe disenchanted voters
- new economic development professionals

Your community may be highly focused on a single economy as well. An important reason for undertaking an economic development effort is diversification. The local economy benefits greatly through diversification: while one sector is experiencing a cyclical decline, the other sectors may remain stable or even expand. Diversification results in more resilience in the local economy and a greater ability to withstand outside economic influences.

The underlying concept of creating jobs, increasing private investment and tax revenues, and providing stability and growth of the local economy are common threads among most programs.

The Puget Sound region (Seattle, Washington) is an excellent example of an area that has recently turned the corner on dependence on a single industry. In the past, job growth in that region responded to the lead set by the Boeing Company, the area's largest private employer; growth declined whenever Boeing reduced employment. From the beginning of the jet age, that trend occurred in five of the six cyclical downturns at Boeing. Yet in the past three years, the Puget Sound region has weathered a significant reduction in the aerospace industry, with employment actually growing despite a layoff of nearly 35,000 workers by Boeing. Much of the growth is due to new and expanding companies in the high-technology industries. The region now appears to face a future in which no single industry has the power to tip it into recession.

INCREASE IN TAX BASE: REVENUE FOR LOCAL SERVICES

A good way for politicians to get themselves thrown out of office these days is to utter those two words no one wants to hear: "More taxes." Few people readily accept the payment of additional taxes in today's expensive living environment. However, everyone wants the streets paved, repaired, and safe from crime, their trash to be picked up, and fires extinguished quickly when they occur. The battle cry of the taxpayer has been "more service, fewer taxes." The first thing anyone learns when they are elected to office is how expensive it really is to run a community. The second thing they learn is that no one wants to pay any more for the services they are getting today.

Most communities get the bulk of their revenue from property taxes. Although the formula changes from state to state, it is usually a variant of "property-value-times-tax-rate-equals-revenue-available-for-services." In order for elected officials to hold the tax rate steady, they need to increase the value of the real assets in the community. Changing this value through increased assessments is possibly more volatile than raising the tax rate. Changing this value by adding new investment to the community is not only more palatable, but preferred by most communities.

New businesses spread tax-base wealth and its resultant benefits throughout the community. This provides additional revenue for the operation of the local government and schools while keeping taxes at a competitive rate. Spokane, a mid-sized city in eastern Washington, is a perfect example of this situation. This city was drastically losing population and business in the early 1980s. Over the past seven years, however, more than 80 companies have either expanded or totally relocated to Spokane, creating 4,000 new jobs and several million dollars in tax revenues for local services.

JOB CREATION

Probably the most common defense of the economic development profession has been job creation. However, most practitioners are quick to point out that not all jobs are created equal. That is to say, job quality—as measured by whether it provides family wages, benefits, some degree of permanence and opportunity for advancement—is an extremely important factor. The community that counts the loss of a permanent, family-wage job equally with several low-wage, minimum skill jobs has failed basic economic development math.

Seasoned practitioners generally believe that the most desirable industries to attract are those that demonstrate high employment multipliers. New industries moving into an area generate income which in turn supports additional jobs in that community. High employment multiplier industries are traditionally those that attract income from outside the area, both domestically and internationally. Manufacturing industries generally have the highest multipliers. This is not to say that service industries are not desirable; however, they have a multiplier only to the extent that they are able to export their services beyond the local area. If the service is only local, it essentially recycles existing income instead of generating new income. The result is that service industries will not create significant new employment or income unless they are "export-oriented."

The community that counts the loss of a permanent, family-wage job equally with several low-wage, minimum skill jobs has failed basic economic development math.

Much has been written about the field of job creation. It is a compelling and complex force in economic development. Use it in your justification for why new investment is critical, but be sure to be clear in your understanding of the type of jobs that your efforts are trying to attract.

DECREASE IN GOVERNMENT SUPPORT

If you look at the general fund budget of most communities, you will find many line items that reflect transfer payments from other units of government. A community may receive money from the county, and a county may receive money from the state. There was a time when the federal government transferred funds to the state. This trend has diminished while the responsibility for local implementation has increased rapidly. Regardless of the unit of government, there is always some level of interdependency on other, frequently larger, units of government.

While this interdependency increases revenue flows in the short term, it also increases dependency upon that unit of government. Just as a community may have its economy defined by a singe economic sector, a local unit of government can have a large portion of its revenues provided by another unit of government. This situation is most common in rural communities. It is also prevalent in communities whose major employer is strongly tied to the government, i.e., defense, space, and aeronautics facilities.

Think of your community as a business. If your business has one account receivable, it is totally dependent upon that account. When that customer is happy with your services they purchase them and your business prospers. If that customer becomes unhappy, or if a competitor enters the market and takes some business away from you, your sales will decrease and your business will struggle.

Conversely, if your business has multiple accounts receivable, it can build relationships with each account. Should one decide to purchase its services from another vendor, you can hopefully increase sales to the other ac-

counts to offset the lost revenue. This is the justification for decreasing dependence on intergovernmental transfer payments and promoting economic diversity in your community.

REPLACEMENT OF LOST JOBS

A business recruitment effort in some communities is established when a large employer in town decides to leave or closes down. At this point, the community realizes that something they have taken for granted for years will no longer be there. Businesses on Main Street may close, the schools may not have adequate funds, and dollars for municipal services may diminish.

This urgent situation is all too often the wake-up call that jump-starts a local economic development effort. Although it starts a program from a point of crisis, it is also the strongest motivator for bringing all of the players to the table and making things happen quickly.

One of the finest examples of where this scenario has developed is in Clark County, Washington. A little more than a decade ago, unemployment in the county was in the double digits. An aluminum factory closed and another major employer, a pulp mill, was struggling and threatening to close its doors as well. That's when local leaders formed the Columbia River Economic Development Council and charged it with the task of attracting new and diverse industry. Officials began an aggressive recruitment campaign and at the same time made necessary improvements to local infrastructure. The county focused its recruitment efforts, hoping to persuade foreign and domestic computer companies to cluster in southwestern Washington. Their strategy was a success. In the past decade, Clark County has attracted an all-star roster of high-technology companies including Hewlett Packard, SEH America, and Sharp Microelectronics Technology. Most recently, Taiwan Semiconductor Manufacturing Company chose the city of Camas as the site of its first U.S. joint venture manufacturing facility and will be investing $1.2 billion and creating a minimum of 800 new jobs in phase one of their development.

SUPPORT
EXISTING BUSINESSES

Within your community or region, companies may be purchasing supplies or services outside the region out of necessity, not necessarily out of desire. Attracting new businesses that serve as suppliers or provide support missing for an existing industry in your area can be good justification for a targeted business recruitment effort. Getting to know your local companies and finding out their needs are critical first steps in any business attraction program. Among the many advantages of this approach are:

▸ It can help you identify obstacles to doing business in your area. If an existing industry is having problems with permitting, the same problems undoubtedly will be encountered when trying to site new companies.

▸ A strategically focused recruitment effort can become an important marketing tool in this process. Having existing companies help identify suppliers or services they would like to have located nearby can be a tremendous start.

▸ As an advocate of your efforts, businesses can serve as important salespeople when you bring prospective companies to town. Gaining support of private industry in your recruitment program is critical for its success. As partners, they are also more likely to provide critical private dollars to supplement your recruitment activities.

Hopefully, the examples above will help you define and defend your business attraction strategies. Use these examples as explanations of why your services are vital to the community. You will undoubtedly be presented with many opportunities to explain your program to clients, constituents, and elected officials. Through clear definitions of the work that you do, you can increase your probability for success both in terms of program results and continued employment. Developing and implementing a successful business attraction program demands a big investment in time, effort, and capital. But winning programs can result in a healthy, diversified economic base that can weather local and national economic downswings, create long-term job opportunities for area residents, provide a tax base to support a strong physical and social infrastructure, and generally improve the area's quality of life.

About the Author.....Donna Batch

Donna Batch is the Director of Business Investment for the Washington State Department of Community, Trade and Economic Development. She began her 14-year career in this field managing the economic development efforts for an eight-county area in southern Idaho. For the past nine years she has worked for the State of Washington. Her most recent success in the area of recruitment was serving as lead state contact for a $1.2 billion investment by Taiwan Semiconductor Manufacturing Company in Camas, Washington. Donna is certified as an Economic Development Finance Professional through the National Development Council and is a member of the AEDC. She can be reached at 206.464.7143.

CHAPTER 2

THE DECISION-MAKING PROCESS
The Business Perspective

Mike Mullis
President and CEO, J. M. Mullis Inc.

A famous speaker once sought out a volunteer from the audience and posed the question, "If I were to place an I-beam on the floor in front of this podium, would you be willing to walk across it for $20?"

The person in the audience said that he would.

The lecturer continued. "If the I-beam was suspended high above the ground between the roofs of two 40-story buildings, would you walk across it for $20?"

The gentleman indicated that he would not.

The lecturer then asked the volunteer, "If I were on top of one of those buildings and was holding one of your children over the edge and you were on the other building and I said to you that if you do not come across the I-beam and get your kid, I'll drop him, would you then cross the beam?"

There was a moment's hesitation, after which the man in the audience inquired, "Which kid do you have?"

———o———

For the economic development professional, the same information may have different meaning to each and every prospect. If you understand the way they think, you'll be better able to meet their needs and compete for new investment. When you, as an economic developer, learn to think like your clients, you can utilize basic site selection principles to navigate through various perspectives of apparently diverse yet frequently similar decision-making steps.

The business location decision-making process often begins from a global perspective. In the early stages, companies identify those areas that give them the best market advantage. As the company identifies the best markets for the continued production of its products, it moves through the selection and elimination of continents, countries, regions, states, substate regions, counties, and ultimately communities. Once the decision advances to the state level, the priority changes to identifying the cost-of-doing-business factors. This moves the location decision-making process through increasing degrees of local control.

Site selection today is a process that requires balancing all of the costs and benefits associated with doing business in order to identify a best-fit situation for the relocating firm. As the decision-making process moves toward closure, the effective use of incentives may offset high operating costs and swing the location decision. However, market access and business cost considerations are far more important factors in the site selection process.

The typical site selection analysis involves four key steps:

- **Market Assessment**
- **Cost-of-Doing-Business Analysis**
- **Quality-of-Life Assessment**
- **Incentive Impact**

Each project will weigh these factors differently, and therefore each factor will have its own impact on the final decision.

MARKET ASSESSMENT

Market assessment involves all of the factors that affect getting the company's product into the marketplace. These include, but are not limited to: market size, the location of current production facilities, new market opportunities, distribution factors, and access to raw materials. These factors greatly influence the initial decision making about where to begin the site search. The management team often has a good handle on these factors from prior experience. They can focus on general regions to be considered in a short period of time.

As previously stated, the market factors and their priority will vary greatly amongst clients. However, it is beneficial to identify those factors here. Depending upon your source, the market factors identified will also vary. *Area Development Magazine* polls companies annually and produces a list of market factors that impact the site selection decision. A recent list identifies, in descending order of importance, the following:

- ▶ Highway accessibility
- ▶ Nearness to customers
- ▶ Nearness to suppliers
- ▶ Accessibility to a major airport
- ▶ Rail service
- ▶ Waterway or port facility

COST-OF-DOING-BUSINESS ANALYSIS

Assessing the cost of doing business in a specific market is more complex. Frequently, the management team will prefer a specific size or type of community. Personal desires for metropolitan communities, rural towns, or suburban communities all come into play here. Once identified, the analysis process begins to assess the cost of locating the facility in any one of many markets. This analytical effort is time-consuming and extremely important to the decision-making effort. Frequently, this work will produce the final analysis that identifies three to six communities with roughly comparable operating costs. These final communities advance into the next round of decision making; the assessment of quality of life factors.

Area Development Magazine also identifies key cost-of-doing-business factors considered by corporations involved in the site selection process. These factors include:

- ▶ Labor costs
- ▶ Availability of skilled labor
- ▶ Occupancy or construction costs
- ▶ Energy availability and costs
- ▶ Availability of telecommunication services
- ▶ Environmental regulations
- ▶ Low union profiles
- ▶ Availability and cost of land
- ▶ Availability of unskilled labor

QUALITY-OF-LIFE ASSESSMENT

To an increasing degree, corporations are taking a critical look at the quality-of-life factors expressed in a community. These will influence both the operating costs of the facility (crime rates, drug issues, etc.) and the home life of the people the facility will employ (quality of the schools, cost of housing, retail and recreation opportunities, etc.). Regardless of your source, the three most important quality-of-life issues become the local school system, the availability of executive housing and the local crime rate.

INCENTIVE IMPACT

The final step in the site selection process is identifying the incentives used to close the deal and site the new business. These have a short-term impact on the actual cost of doing business. However, they can have a powerful influence for a community that is willing to make a strong statement regarding its willingness to compete for and welcome new investment.

As may be expected, the most important incentives vary by client needs. However, in a national survey recently conducted by the National Development Council, the most important incentives reported were:

► Tax abatements
► Free or low-cost infrastructure
► Specially-tailored employee-training packages
► Free or below-market cost land
► Rent-free or below-market leased space
► Below-market loans
► State or local grants

The site selection process continues to be a mixture of science and art. In its early stages, as companies review the market opportunities and the costs of doing business associated with specific sites, it is every bit a science. Often, depending upon the scale of the project and amount of capital investment involved, the initial number of sites can exceed one hundred. It rarely focuses exclusively on one of the four stages. At any one point in time, your clients may place their priority on one stage. However, decisions made at each stage will directly affect the other three—thus, the fine line between art and science.

So why should you place such an emphasis on the decision-making process? Because many economic development professionals fail to understand what is going on in the mind of the prospect. When a firm enters the marketplace to gather data for a client search, it often sends a very detailed, very comprehensive questionnaire to the communities under consideration. It sends this questionnaire as the first encounter with the community for two reasons:

- First, the questions asked are the core, critical variables a company has to answer to make the initial evaluation on a community. Your community's ability to address its market and cost-of-doing business strengths head-on will quickly move it into the final round of potential sites for prospective clients. (Its inability to answer these questions will quickly get it eliminated from being a finalist as well.)

- Secondly, the economic development professional needs to focus on the issues a potential client is addressing. Approximately 50 to 60 percent of the cover letters and marketing pieces sent to economic development offices speak directly to the issue of incentives. In most projects, this is the wrong time to raise this issue. Your success as an economic developer will be contingent upon your ability to think like the prospect. Unfortunately, there have been many economic developers who failed to do so.

Meanwhile, back on Main Street, local officials are beginning the community marketing process from step three, quality of life. Many of these individuals are completely oblivious to the fact that their community is a product at some stage of market readiness.

You will increase your success rate considerably if you think more like your clients and less like your employers.

They are unaware that the community must have market presence. Its value will be determined by its proximity to major markets and the ability of companies to access these markets. Depending upon the company and type of market it represents, the relative value of this community will vary greatly.

If a misunderstanding of the market value of a community isn't enough, local officials also misunderstand the importance of competitive operating costs imposed by the community itself. Many times, communities have not come to terms with their excessive property taxes, utility costs, and location-imposed transportation expenses. The local officials are willing to extol the benefit of their peaceful little community and the reason for locating a company there, yet they don't understand why it must first see itself as a product ready to be taken to the marketplace. This misunderstanding eliminates many communities from the competition before they ever understand what hit them.

To succeed at business attraction, you must make every effort to think like your client. Understand the four-step process through which they move to make the site selection decision. Provide information pertinent to each stage of the site selection decision, and respond quickly and accurately to their needs. You will increase your success rate considerably if you think more like your clients and less like your employers.

*About the Author.....*Mike Mullis

Mike Mullis established the firm of J. M. Mullis, Inc. during the late 1970s to provide professional project location specialist services on an international basis for various private client groups. Today the firm does more than $1 billion annually in new project establishments. In addition to location analysis work throughout the United States, the firm also has affiliate representations in Canada, Mexico, and Europe where it does several projects annually. Mike is an active member of several state, regional, and international economic development organizations, as well as the Industrial Development Research Council and the International Facility Managers Association. He can be reached at 901.853.3740.

CASE STUDY:

A TALE OF EIGHT CITIES*

Jim Beatty
President, NCS International, Inc.

The following overview is intended to give economic developers a brief analysis of how location factors were determined and ranked according to relative importance by two companies conducting a site search. It is also intended to provide valuable insight into the timeliness of responses as well as lessons learned during the site visits to the local communities.

THE MAJOR FACTORS

Two firms wanted to develop site criteria and to specify a final location for their respective customer centers. Like most location analysis endeavors, these companies were interested in several key factors. At the top of both lists, however, were:

▶ **Labor Availability, Quality, and Costs**
While this was determined in part by the Census Bureau and Department of Labor statistics, the major information was provided by interviews and visits with similar companies in the finalist cities. This was crucial in both cases, as the workforce needs of the two companies were 1,000 employees.

▶ **Telecommunications**
Critical factors included the service reliability of the local exchange company and the specific long distance carriers serving those companies. Both clients were interested in what enhanced services were available, such as integrated services digi-

tal network (ISDN), call routing redundancy, and disaster recovery. Certainly, the location of the "point of presence" of the network carriers played a role.

▶ **Site Availability**
In one case, a facility of 20,000 square feet was required; in the other, a facility of 55,000 square feet was needed—both Class B+ or Class A with parking ratio of 1:100 square feet. Because of the narrow time frames involved (60 to 90 days in both cases), it was apparent that existing sites, with proper retrofit, would have to be found.

▶ **Incentives**
While incentives were evaluated, they were not the key factor for either company in choosing the final site, but certainly they could not be overlooked. Funds available through training grants, local funds, tax abatements, and low-interest items were reviewed, but only after the labor availability and quality issues were satisfied.

THE FUN BEGINS

Once the key executives were briefed and the reports accepted, the process moved from mach speed to warp speed—in other words, "Let's visit four to six cities within one to two days." Economic development officers from the finalist communities had to be called quickly (in less than 48 hours) to set up meetings, tours, lunches, etc. These phone calls are bittersweet for economic developers of the world. But isn't this the essence of their job?

---

*This report originally appeared in *Expansion Management's Inside E.D.*, February 1996. Reprinted with permission.

IF IT'S TUESDAY . . .

Five cities in two days, ending in Houston Texas. The visits were all informative and some were better than others. Little things—being met at the gate, personally driving four people around in a vehicle large enough to accommodate everyone in comfort, providing detailed agendas of the visit complete with names and telephone numbers of the involved parties—all enhanced the executives' first impressions, as well as their expectations of the communities. Even though these were both multimillion-dollar deals, the small details were just as important.

Other factors to note were the economic developer's knowledge of the area (questions invariably arise during the site visit), as well as their personality and ability to make the clients feel welcome, special, and important. Even though an economic developer may organize and attend the same types of visits and meetings 20 times a month, it is critical that he or she make this tour seem like the first and only one.

. . . IT MUST BE HOUSTON

Three cities in two days, starting in Houston, Texas. Same format, different company, but even more intense. Economic development people in Houston had only 12 hours notice but responded graciously and efficiently with key people from the community, key information, and site tours.

In both cases, the actual tour of the site took on greater significance as the client's desire to move more rapidly increased, in part due to the economic developer's excitement about the project. Never forget that enthusiasm is contagious.

AND THE WINNER IS . . .

Houston was selected for both projects because it met all criteria, but it must be noted that Houston's responsiveness, attention to detail, and willingness to pursue any question or issue made a significant impression on the two expanding companies. Final tally: 1,000 jobs.

*About the Author.....*Jim **Beatty**

Jim Beatty is President of NCS International, Inc., a site selection and economic development consulting firm headquartered in Omaha, Nebraska. Mr. Beatty has more than 25 years experience in the telecommunications field and is regarded as one of the nation's authorities on telecommunications and economic development. He has worked extensively with communities across the country in developing information-based industries and creating thousands of jobs. Jim can be reached at 402.453.9292.

SITE SEARCH CHECKLIST ✓

PROJECT TITLE _____ **PROJECT NUMBER** _____

General area of survey: _____
Countries/regions to be reviewed: _____
Proximity (mile/km) to: suppliers _____   customers _____
                          competition _____   major city _____
                          other company locations _____
Size of community desired: _____
Special amenities: _____

SITE

Required acre/ha: minimum _____   maximum _____
Optimum dimensions (a x b): _____
Which do you require: ☐ greenfield   ☐ present/planned industrial park
Access roads: _____
Parking requirements: _____
Which do you require: ☐ purchase   ☐ lease   ☐ either
If leased, on what terms? _____
Is location desired: ☐ within city limits   ☐ outside city limits
Special soil-bearing requirements?   ☐ yes   ☐ no
If yes, please explain: _____
Open-air storage needs?   ☐ yes   ☐ no
If yes, designate area required (sq m): _____
Is process sensitive to outside interference (electrical, radiation, vibration, etc.)?
                          ☐ yes   ☐ no
If yes, please specify: _____
Other special site requirements: _____

BUILDING

Will you: ☐ build to suit   ☐ purchase   ☐ lease/rent
If purchase or lease/rent, do you prefer: ☐ existing   ☐ new plant   ☐ either
Will the building be: ☐ single story   ☐ multistory
Projected floor space requirements (next five years) for:
      manufacturing _____
      warehousing _____
      office _____
      r & d _____
Total floor space requirements: _____
Initial building size requirements: _____
Dimensions (a x b): _____
Type of construction: ☐ brick   ☐ concrete block   ☐ metal   ☐ other
Number of floors: _____
Load-bearing capacity of floors: _____

SITE SEARCH CHECKLIST

Truss height: manufacturing _____ warehouse _____
Bay size (a x b): _____
Air conditioned? ☐ yes ☐ no
Intensity of lighting required: manufacturing _____ warehouse _____
Sprinkler? ☐ yes ☐ no   Cranes? ☐ yes ☐ no
If yes, number and capacity: _____
Special facilities/services required for this operation (e.g., tool and die shops, compressed air,
clean rooms): _____
Special fire protection requirements: _____
Date of required occupancy: _____
Time required for equipment installations: _____
Date of initial production: _____

TRANSPORTATION

Optimum transportation location: _____
Primary raw materials and commodities purchased: _____
Annual inbound tonnage: _____
Annual outbound tonnage: _____
% of raw materials received by: rail _____ road _____ water _____ air _____
% of products forwarded by: rail _____ road _____ water _____ air _____
RAIL
      Siding? ☐ yes ☐ no
      Depressed dock? ☐ yes ☐ no
      No. of products per month: by origin _____ by destination _____
ROAD
      Depressed dock? ☐ yes ☐ no
      No. of trucks per day: _____
      Proximity to motorway: _____
AIR AND WATER
      Commercial airline service?   ☐ yes ☐ no
      Proximity to site (distance/minutes): _____
      Deep water port?   ☐ yes ☐ no
      Special loading/unloading facilities required: _____

UTILITIES

ELECTRICITY
      Connected load (kW): _____
      Consumption average: kW/hour _____ kW/hour/year _____
      Power source (volts): _____
WATER
      Potable (gallons/24 hrs): _____ Process (gallons/24 hrs): _____
      % recirculated: _____ & make-up: _____
      Special properties: _____
      Describe use: _____

WASTE DISPOSAL
 Sanitary (gallons/24 hrs): _____   Process (gallons/24 hrs): _____
 Details of wastes: _____
 Predisposal treatment plan?   ☐ yes   ☐ no
FUEL
 Special heating: ☐ primary   ☐ alternate
 Process: ☐ primary   ☐ alternate
 Gas (million cubic feet/hr): _____
 Therms/month: minimum _____   maximum _____
 Gas required (mcf/day):   interruptible (standby fuel) _____
                  noninterruptible _____
 Special environmental or utility needs: _____
 Type of pollutant emissions: ☐ actual   ☐ potential
 Dedicated telecom lines required: _____

PRODUCT AND MARKET CRITERIA

Description and annual volume of products to be manufactured or distributed:
_____
Product shipment (tonnage/kg per year): _____
% shipments by: rail _____   truck _____   air _____   water _____
New products planned in next five years: _____
Prime market area: _____
Approximate location of market centers: _____
Key market constraints/requirements: _____
Impact of facility on competitive posture: _____
Significant market shifts expected in next five years: _____
Purchase materials required: _____
Source(s) of supply: major _____   alternate _____
Intentions or latitude to change current supply base: _____
Export volume (%): _____
Import volume (%): _____

TECHNOLOGIES

General technology level required at this facility: _____
_____
Design skills required now and next five years: _____
_____
Current and planned manufacturing technologies: _____
_____
Dependence on local university for design and/or staff development: _____
_____

SITE SEARCH CHECKLIST

MANPOWER

Length of working week required: basic _____
overtime _____
total _____

Projected manpower requirements for next five years and long-term (circle):

Year: 1   2   3   4   5   LT

Skilled: _____
Semiskilled: _____
Unskilled: _____
Salaried: _____
Managerial: _____
Professional: _____
Clerical: _____
Transferees: _____
New recruits: _____

BUSINESS CULTURE

Relationship to other company facilities: _____
_____
Relationship to government agencies: _____
_____
Intended public image: _____
Degree of visibility planned: _____
Desired fit to surrounding business types: _____
Intended management style: _____
Comparison with present management style: _____
Culture of desired workforce: _____
Comparison with present workforce: _____

ASSET VALUE BUDGET ESTIMATE

Land: _____
Land improvements: _____
Building: _____
Machinery and equipment: _____
Furniture and fixtures: _____
Finished goods: _____
Goods in process: _____

CHAPTER 3

EVALUATING THE COMMUNITY

Ken Wagner
President, Ken Wagner & Associates

A computer programmer died and found himself in front of a committee deciding whether he should go to Heaven or Hell. The chairman of the committee asked the programmer if he would like to look at each of those communities before stating a preference. The programmer said yes, and an angel took him to a great sunny beach filled with people playing volleyball, listening to music, and having a great time. "Wow!" the programmer said, "Heaven is a great community."

"This isn't Heaven," said the angel. "This is the community of Hell. Would you like to see Heaven?"

"Sure!"

The angel took him to another community. Here a bunch of people were sitting on park benches, playing bingo, and feeding pigeons. "This is Heaven?" asked the programmer.

"Yes," said the angel.

"Then I will take Hell."

Instantly he found himself engulfed in white hot lava, with the hosts of the damned in torment around him. "Hey, wait a minute!" he shouted, "where's the beach, the music, the volleyball?"

"That was just the demo," the angel said.

——— o ———

Before a community even decides that it wants to attract a business, it needs to go beyond the hype and do a self-examination of what it truly has to offer and what it needs to do to prepare for a successful recruitment. *More good marketing programs fail to produce results because of a lack of community preparedness than for any other reason.* It is therefore vital to evaluate your community and make sure it is ready for development, because communities that are not *fully* prepared can expect disappointment instead of success.

The good news is that you do not have to be perfect. To be fully prepared to market your area, you need to:

► know what needs to be done (plus and minus),
► have specific action plans to deal with each opportunity and problem—especially the problems.

A sophisticated marketing plan will include information on a community's problems, along with specifics on plans to deal with each problem. That approach enabled one community to site a 600-person manufacturing plant, winning out over 25 others. They learned after successfully winning the competition that six other cities achieved a better "point count" on the criteria the Fortune 500 company used. However, what impressed executives of the company was that the area's business leaders were fully aware of its problems. They liked how action teams were set up for each challenge area, headed by a local CEO, with a timetable and detailed costs required to deal with each problem. They decided they would be better off in the long term to locate in this area than in any of the six that outranked them.

Ignoring problems or trying to cover them up can be disastrous. An old saw still applies to economic development—and especially marketing—programs is: "For the lack of a nail the battle was lost." That "nail" is more likely than not to be crucial to the success of a community's marketing program. Here are some true examples:

Example #1: A community in a great vegetable producing area of south Georgia was courting a major frozen food processing company. Their preliminary communications had received highly favorable responses, so a tentative date for a visit by company executives was established. In a preparatory meeting with half a dozen key people, the mayor was very optimistic. He felt strongly about the possibility of getting a commitment from their frozen food prospect within the next four to six weeks. He reviewed the analysis they had completed. Everything looked fine—including the new waste treatment plant built just three years earlier.

More good marketing programs fail to produce results because of a lack of community preparedness than for any other reason.

But one of the people asked to review the facts had a funny feeling about the waste treatment situation. And the city engineer confirmed the economic developer's fears. "We do have a new waste treatment facility," he said, "However, the new industry we slated the year before last is using half the plant's capacity. When we add everything up, there is maybe 5 percent of the new plant's capacity left. There is no way we can handle another frozen food plant until we build additional capacity." A key location requirement overlooked in the enthusiasm to recruit new employers caused this project to fail. That community was quickly eliminated from the list of possible sites.

Example #2: A commercial developer from a metropolitan area in upstate New York had been wooing a Canadian manufacturer planning a $20 million production facility in the United States. After months of phone calls, visits, and transmittal of promotional materials, the developer finally persuaded the president of the company to come to his area for further discussion. The developer met the Canadian at the area's outmoded airport, expecting to rush him to his plush suburban office to start negotiations. He was stunned when the man told him there was no point in talking further. "Sorry," the manufacturer said, "but I could not bring my customers into an outdated, poorly managed airport like the one I have just flown into." (The terminal had no jetways; it was cold and raining when the man arrived, and he was forced to walk through chilling rain to get into the building. The nearly 30-year-old facility was dirty and poorly lit.) The Canadian declined even to go to the developer's office to further discuss the project. Instead, he took the next plane back to Canada.

Example #3: A northern manufacturer being shown possible sites in Mississippi shocked the man who had arranged meetings in four communities by instructing him not to stop in one of the towns where the developer had local officials and business leaders waiting. The prospect pointed to the condition of the main street and sidewalks along the route they were traveling and said bluntly, "This may sound like a superficial way to judge a town, but I've found that usually at least three and sometimes six or more of the communities we evaluate can meet all our primary needs. Then our decision comes down to factors other than available land, transportation costs, labor supply and skills or trainability, and the attitudes of local people. I have found over the years I've been locating new facilities that when the streets and sidewalks look this bad I'm in a community that doesn't have pride and positive work attitudes. So I just will not waste time meeting with local leaders. I'm sorry if not stopping creates a problem for you, but my time's too valuable to waste talking to people in an area that I know I'm not going to select. Maybe telling them what I've told you can get them moving in the right direction."

These examples make one point clear: the best marketing program in the world cannot produce results unless it is built on a strong community preparedness program.

These examples make one point clear: the best marketing program in the world cannot be expected to produce results unless it is built on a strong community preparedness program. That involves a great deal of systematic effort to make every facet of your community as attractive as possible.

A typical site selection analysis will identify certain factors as crucial to a new plant. In effect, the study will most always conclude that three or four factors were vitally important —access to markets, transportation resources and costs, and availability and cost of labor. However, these studies list many other factors corporate clients rate in importance.

Most company location studies identify at least three or four communities that meet all their major requirements. Then what happens? The fifth or tenth or fifteenth factor may become the deciding one. In effect, it becomes number one—the crucial one. So taxes may vault to the top, or the quality of elementary schools may become important. The appearance of the entrances to the city, zoning problems, the antibusiness attitudes of an extremist environmental group, or the quality of recreational facilities and programs can all become driving factors.

It is therefore vital to upgrade every facet of your community. What appears unimportant in initial discussions may become a major factor before a decision is completed. Successful economic development efforts involve only four steps:

- Inventory of an area's economic assets.
- An action plan to develop each of those assets, based on a systematic analysis of their specific job and income potentials.
- Inventory of an area's economic liabilities.
- An action plan to eliminate or reduce each liability as much as possible.

The preparation of asset/liability inventories is only one of several different ways to build a solid base for an effective marketing program. The first step, deciding how strong or weak a community is on each factor, provides useful information for the action plans that need to be developed. Rate each aspect of your community or area on a scale of 1 to 5 using the following ratings:

1—**SUPERIOR**: as good as an investor would expect to find in competitor cities. Example: An industrial or commercial park of 500 acres that not only looks like a park but has all utilities and services provided, access roads in, and provides land and buildings at reasonable cost.

2—**EXCELLENT**: well above average, but needing improvement and not up to your top competitors. Example: a solid waste disposal program that includes an approved landfill with capacity for at least five years, a comprehensive recycling program, and temporary arrangements to handle hazardous waste—not yet complete, but far above average.

3—**AVERAGE**: mediocre, nothing to be proud of, not appealing to investors. Examples: access routes that are unattractive—occasional trash; roads with dirt shoulders; a few vacant lots or abandoned buildings.

4—**BELOW AVERAGE**: requiring substantial improvement just to be acceptable. Example: streets in many areas have potholes, rough patches, or poor drainage.

5—**POOR**: so far below average you can count on investors to be turned away—unless you happen to have special assets (such as raw materials or unusually good market access) so important to some companies that they will be attracted despite your poor rating on other factors. To use this approach you need to know two things: (1) who your competitors are—especially for individual projects you consider particularly important, and (2) how strong or weak they are on each factor you need to compare.

The Available Buildings and Commercial/Industrial Sites section of the Checklist (page 29) provides background information and questions designed to help local leaders decide how they stand on key issues. Having attractive land available is not enough to do the job. You need high-quality sites that are ready to build on and that have all utilities and services in place and zoning and environmental studies complete. This allows an investor to start construction when possible on his or her terms and not have to wait for zoning changes or other state or local approvals.

Another important consideration is that 75 percent or more of the companies that come unsolicited to your area will be looking for available buildings. If you lack such buildings, you will lose out. Therefore, it makes sense for many areas to adopt a carefully planned speculative building program.

IS YOUR COMMUNITY PREPARED?

Now let's take a brief look at 23 community preparedness factors every marketing program needs to consider. They are listed in alphabetical order, and no effort was made to rank their importance. Some are clearly more basic than others; however, remember that

seemingly minor items may become key factors, as noted above.

APPEARANCE

Often overlooked. But first impressions sometimes make a big difference in a community's overall evaluation, largely because (as in the Mississippi example cited earlier) appearance may be considered a reflection of "care" or "don't care" attitudes. Poor appearance may represent poor worker productivity, as well as community leaders unwilling to deal with important community development challenges.

ASSETS AND LIABILITIES

Two of the essential and basic steps in evaluating a community involve completion of an inventory of economic assets and liabilities. It is important for local leaders to accept as reality that their community has problems and liabilities. No community is perfect. Some clearly are more attractive than others. However, communities that possess serious drawbacks or limitations may become quite marketable if local leaders make effective action plans part of their marketing plan.

Unfortunately, very few communities make a thorough inventory. Even fewer do the comprehensive analysis needed to identify the types of industries—and companies within those industries—whose location requirements their area can meet. Still fewer have action plans for dealing with each of their liabilities. Using the approach outlined above can make all the difference in the world in the amount of success a marketing program has—or doesn't have.

A vital initial question to ask is whether your community has any special assets to offer, such as a prime location with respect to major markets and excellent transportation resources. Your community may have a plentiful and unusually productive work force that established companies would hold in high regard, or an especially effective training program that would be highly valued.

If you do not have any special or outstanding assets, it is especially important to upgrade every aspect of your community. In other words, if you have no special attractions, you need to be able to show that you have in place a well-managed economic development business that offers unusual opportunities for companies to prosper in an especially healthy business environment.

ATTITUDES TOWARD GROWTH

In other words, "pro-business climate." Certain small towns in Nebraska provide an outstanding example of the most effective approach to convincing prospects they will be welcome. They hold a community-wide assembly at which a company executive receives a plaque plus leaders' expressions of appreciation for the jobs and payrolls the company has contributed to the area's economy.

AVAILABLE BUILDINGS

Since an estimated 75 percent of companies seeking new locations want to occupy available buildings, it is clear that an inventory of high-quality buildings can be a vital part of any community's marketing program. If no buildings are available, seriously consider creating a spec building program or having specific plans (including financing) on the drawing board to quickly construct a new building. That means having a site ready to build on—environmental permits in place, etc.

CHILD CARE

The rapid increase in two-paycheck families in recent years has made providing child care for workers an important part of marketing for many communities. Child care is especially important for prospects that employ a relatively high percentage of women, since the cost of such care can be quickly offset by reductions in absenteeism, sick leave, and turnover. Areas that have made plans to provide such care as part of their incentive package can therefore expect to have a significant advantage over their competitors when dealing with some prospects.

COMMUNICATIONS

These days, the term communications has become almost synonymous with having in place and operational the most advanced telecommunications equipment. Some communities are even providing free access to the Internet as part of their efforts not only to attract companies from outside but also as a key part of their internal marketing program. Being able to go to a local library to log onto the Internet, as employers and entrepreneurs can do in one community, may be a big help to established companies and especially to new companies that have limited capital.

COMMUNITY and/or AREA DATA SUMMARY

Depending on your area's demographics, especially whether your town or city is relatively separate or one of several in a large population area, it is important to have an accurate, up-to-date summary of data on your community's resources. Four pages of carefully selected material that concentrates on basics important to a prospect's evaluation of your area, or eight pages for a multi-county region, are all that are needed. But those pages can be vitally important to making a sale.

COMMUNITY FACILITIES

Community facilities can have an extremely positive effect on a prospect's attitude toward investing in one location as opposed to another. (Some of the more important facilities are discussed in the "Recreational and Cultural Facilities" section, page 25.) Larger areas often have a significant competitive advantage. They usually can afford physical facilities that enable them to produce outdoor musicals during the summer as well as do other things most prospects will find inviting. However, by joining with neighboring cities or towns, smaller communities often can jointly develop facilities and programs they could otherwise not afford—extras that will enable all participating local governments to compete more effectively.

EDUCATIONAL AND TRAINING SYSTEMS

As the shift from a manufacturing to an information-based economy accelerates, the availability of top quality educational and training programs will become increasingly important. Workers in telecommunications are educated and technically trained, and they demand quality educational programs for their children. In recent years more workers have refused to relocate to areas they felt did not meet their children's educational needs.

The availability of training programs for local workers assuming relatively high-tech jobs has become an important factor in attracting the companies that will be providing most of the high-wage jobs in the years immediately ahead. State and local governments are providing tens of millions of dollars in training subsidies for companies like BMW and Motorola. The State of Virginia, for example, plans to provide subsidies totaling over $85 million for the $3 billion Motorola semiconductor plant announced in the spring of 1995; $5 million of that total will involve technical training for area residents hired to work in the plant (at an average salary of $35,000 per year). An additional $16 million is earmarked for the development of an electronic manufacturing curriculum at one of the local universities.

It would be a mistake to overlook the importance of elementary and secondary systems, however. In recent years they have been rated among the top ten or twelve factors that have major impacts on location decisions.

ENVIRONMENTAL ISSUES

Increasing emphasis in recent years on maintaining environmental quality has given greater weight to the degree of influence environmental groups have on location decisions. A small group in one county, for example, delayed the construction of a distribution facility for over two years by filing an essentially frivolous lawsuit. The delay not only cost the company large sums but also cost the county an estimated $7 million in tax revenues. Perhaps more importantly, it raised a red flag to other potential investors, alerting them to the possibility that they might encounter the same type of costly opposition.

It is therefore highly desirable to have strong planning and zoning programs that clearly define areas that can be used without opposition for industrial, commercial, and other uses. Even where such well-thought-out programs exist, it is important for development professionals and local leaders to persuade developers to plan well-thought-out information programs that tell area residents what they can—and especially what they cannot—expect to happen when a particular construction project is approved.

75% of companies seeking new locations want to occupy available buildings

Example: One quality homebuilder, who asked for help in dealing with local officials who typically bent with the wind whenever local residents opposed a builder's request for approval of a construction project, reported a two-year delay was costing him $35,000 a month.

This brings up another important point: the need to have well-informed local officials who will support desirable growth based on the merits of each project, but not do as local officials were doing in the example just cited: playing politics at the expense of not only the builder but the community as a whole to placate a few uninformed or biased voters.

FINANCIAL RESOURCES

Two things are especially important to determining whether the funds your community is investing in its development efforts are likely to do the job that needs to be done. One is the investment a community makes to provide the facilities and services essential to attracting investors. The other is the amount of money local leaders invest in their economic development program. Frequently, both are seriously deficient.

The financial crunch local governments in many areas find themselves in as a result of federal and state cutbacks is resulting in two things, both of which negatively impact economic development: (1) reduced ability to maintain essential facilities and services, and (2) tax increases. If water and sewer systems and other facilities aren't maintained, it inevitably will become more and more difficult not only to market a community to outside investors but may result in decisions by established firms not to expand or even to move elsewhere.

However, another problem exists in most cities and towns. Most local development organizations are financially unable to do several things essential to compete in the 1990s and beyond, including three that are becoming increasingly important:

- They do not have enough money to do the in-depth market/feasibility analyses that are becoming increasingly important every year.
- They do not have the funds required to provide management and technical services to established companies—often their best short-term opportunity to add jobs.
- They have neither the funds nor staff they need to help start and then support new companies, the other major potential for new jobs in most areas.

When you evaluate your community's ability to compete for new jobs under the unique conditions that now exist, it is important to identify gaps in your existing development program that may be vital to whether your area succeeds or fails to create the jobs you need.

Another specific need that exists in many areas, already referred to, is the need to finance a spec building program or to develop a new industrial or commercial park. One or both of those are important missing pieces of many local development efforts.

GOVERNMENT

With an estimated 50 percent of local governments operating in the red, according to a recent national survey, government has become a major problem for economic developers. The lead article in the fall 1995 issue of *ED Review* points out that dealing directly with the inefficiencies of local government may prove to be one of the major challenges many professional developers face the balance of the 1990s and beyond.

Regretfully, most local governments are woefully inefficient. Many lack adequate planning and capital improvement programs. Developers have voiced lament for at least thirty years that, "Just about the time I get a mayor (or town or city council members) to a point where they understand what economic development is all about, they leave office and I have to start all over again with newly elected officials who think they know how to run my business."

What it amounts to is that most local officials have only vague and often mistaken ideas about the business of economic development. Most have no idea that they need to regard it as their local government's most important concern. Nor do they have any idea of its many facets and how important each of these can be to success. And to be blunt about it, most local governments are badly in need of being reorganized and downsized. Local and state governments alike need to do the same thing that so many corporations have accomplished when they faced financial crises: reorganize and downsize.

When a developer has to go to twelve different physical locations to clear all local governmental hurdles before he or she can get a permit to build, this clearly presents a difficult obstacle to professional developers who are trying to market their area, whether externally or internally. Government can be either a big help or a severe deterrent. When the latter is the case, local developers may need to enlist business leaders to take action to make important changes.

HEALTH CARE

Three things make the availability of quality health care important to marketing your area:

- The aging of our population and the additional medical attention we can expect older people will need.
- The steadily increasing cost of medical services.
- The steady decline in federal and, in many areas, state funding for medical programs.

It is therefore important to know whether your area can provide the kinds of medical and health services potential investors will expect to find.

HOUSING

Your area's housing can be either a significant plus or a serious deterrent to your marketing efforts. A factor often important to a company that wants to move quickly to bring in key personnel is the availability of high-quality housing for management level employees. If you don't have an inventory of such housing, it will be important to have one or more builders ready with land, financing, and the production capabilities needed to quickly construct it. More than one community has lost a good prospect because they weren't prepared to meet executive housing needs.

A company that wants to move quickly to bring in key personnel wants high-quality housing for management level employees.

On the other end of the spectrum are the positive values provided by attractive subdivisions and a strong low-cost housing construction program. If your community doesn't have the latter, you may want to encourage banks in your area to launch such a program. They can gain Community Reinvestment Act (CRA) credits important to their operations by strongly supporting low-cost housing.

INDUSTRIAL SITES

Since the subject of sites is treated in more detail in another chapter, comments here will limited to how they fit into community preparedness. In brief, they are absolutely vital. In fact, without at least one and preferably several different sites ready to build on, a community simply is not ready to even start a marketing program. Sites—commercial as well as industrial—are one of the basic products a community must be able to offer an investor. Without them you're just not in business.

"Construction ready" means that the area is zoned, all utilities, services, and access roads are in place, and environmental studies are completed. It also means that firm prices have been set. If subsidies of any kind will be offered, the conditions under which those will be available should also be clearly spelled out—whether the company must employ a specified minimum number of people before certain subsidies will apply, and so on.

LABOR FORCE AND CLIMATE

Having a surplus of even highly skilled workers is not necessarily an asset. A classic example exists in a Midwest community which had over 7,000 highly skilled and semiskilled workers who had been laid off by area farm implement manufacturers. The marketing strategy they were banking on to attract new employers to the area focused largely on the existence of this pool of experienced workers. But key local leaders refused to even consider a major liability—the area's reputation not only for frequent strikes but for strike violence. Instead of hitting the issue head on and at least making an effort to talk with union leaders to come to an agreement on worker behavior, community leaders shied away from the problem and insisted they could sell companies on coming in to use the skilled people the area had available. In the more than three years since starting their marketing program, they have had no success whatsoever.

Whatever your local labor situation, it is important to have current data on not just the numbers of workers available but on their experience and skills. Data on the underemployed in your area may be difficult to compile but extremely valuable if you can develop it. In addition to the availability of workers, information on their productivity (reflected in measures such as the value added to products made in your area), absenteeism, and strike records are important to your selling efforts.

It is important to recognize that unemployment data are often quite misleading. An acknowledged flaw is that only those actively registered with the Labor Department are counted. Workers who may have gotten discouraged and are no longer registered, therefore, aren't included in the statistics.

Even more important in some areas where large corporations have laid off thousands of workers is the number of underemployed people in the workforce. In many cases you can find people who were making $30,000 to $40,000 a year are working, but at jobs that not only don't use their skills but pay perhaps only half as much as they formerly earned. These people may be one of the most valuable attractions you have to offer potential investors. It would involve considerable work, but a special labor survey to collect data on the thousands who fall into this category could make a big difference in the results your marketing program produces.

MAJOR EMPLOYERS

Your area's major employers that have had good experiences with both labor and government can be a big help in your recruitment efforts. They can provide written or oral statements attesting to the productivity of their employees, to the positive political climate that exists, to the fair way they have been treated so far as taxation is concerned.

As you evaluate the many facets of your community that impact your marketing program, it is important to identify any employers who can make positive contributions when you get to the point of having a prospect actually on the scene. As an example, when a local commercial realtor brought a financial services company executive to one area, he also met with the manpower resource manager of a local company in the same business. When the prospect heard directly from the local manager, whose company also had offices in the city from which the visitor came, that two employees in the local area produced as much work as three in the other location, his eyes widened. And when he heard that the workers' attitudes were far superior, absenteeism was much lower, and turnover was relatively low, it was clear he was sold. The smaller company involved moved their entire company to the area to which the realtor had brought them. That kind of help from a major local employer can be a tremendous asset.

Questions you may want to ask are:

- Do any of our major employers now participate in our marketing efforts?
- Are they happy with our community's business climate?
- If we asked them to help sell other companies on moving to our area, would they tell a good story about how they have been treated and the favorable conditions they have found to make a profit?

If you get negative answers to any of these questions, it would be important to go to work immediately to make whatever changes may be needed to make present employers happy enough with their situation to encourage them to join your sales team in its efforts to attract new employers.

PLANNING
(City, Town, and/or County)

A community without an up-to-date planning and capital improvement program is in much the same straits as a community without a site ready to build on—just not ready to start marketing. Planning has always been a vital part of community and economic development, but has become even more important in the 1990s because of the rapid pace at which economic change has been taking place. A good city or county plan will target community development problems and determine the funds needed to solve those problems. It will also lay out action plans to deal with each. Few plans do even one of these three things, much less all three.

Zoning is also important as a way to protect property values and avoid losing jobs. The best way to protect property values is to make sure an undesirable or competitive land use doesn't encroach on valuable land. Zoning makes that possible. It prevents noisy commercial and industrial firms from doing business next to valuable residential property. But it also prevents the problem many communities without zoning have had—residential development building up next to a manufacturing plant after a manufacturer has been in business for years, with subsequent conflicts between residential property owners and the business. That type of problem not only may severely damage an existing employer but scare potential employers away. By setting aside land that is best suited for industrial, commercial, and residential use, zoning protects everybody's financial interests and encourages healthy economic growth.

RECREATIONAL AND CULTURAL FACILITIES

As we continue to move swiftly into the information age that's already upon us, recreational and cultural facilities and programs will become increasingly important. Because of the higher educational and technical levels of people in the information industry, they tend to demand both quality and variety in the recreational and cultural programs available in the areas where they live.

Of course, small cities and towns often simply do not have the financial resources required to support a symphony orchestra or local theater system. But they can do much in the way of amateur theatrical and musical programs, folk festivals, and other activities. A local college or community college can develop quality choral and orchestral groups. If a large corporation operates in your area, its executives can perhaps be persuaded to subsidize cultural activities that would otherwise be impossible. Occasionally, a major bank might assume that role.

Well-managed recreational programs can be important to your overall marketing program as well. Not too surprisingly, one of the prime requirements of a manufacturer from Detroit, where juvenile delinquency and drug abuse are common, was a well-planned and well-supervised recreational program for teenagers. Usually, recreational programs are a relatively minor consideration in investment decisions. Occasionally, however, they may take on special importance. But always, they are a part of the total economic development business.

SOLID AND HAZARDOUS WASTE

The steady increase in the problems involved in maintaining acceptable solid waste disposal sites as well as the regulations governing waste disposal have created serious difficulties for many communities. Communities that started to develop long-range plans four or five years ago tend to be in relatively good shape. But many communities lack approved landfills, while others lack effective plans for dealing with hazardous waste.

In one community, the lack of acceptable landfills nearby made it necessary for a large company to ship its solid waste more than 200 miles at an expense of more than $300,000 per year. The plant manager stated that if they hadn't had so much money invested in their manufacturing facilities, he would have recommended moving or closing the operation, because he was so exasperated with the lack of local and state cooperation on their waste disposal need. It is therefore important to know:

- Whether your local governments have approved sites.

- If not, what cost problems that may be creating both for the types of industries you hope to attract as well as for some of your established firms.

- What actions you may need to take to solve the problem.

TAXATION

Local tax structures and the way taxes are handled can be a decisive factor in whether a marketing plan succeeds or fails. As in the example given earlier, even if your tax system is equitable, it may become a decisive factor if other primary considerations balance out. But if your local government taxes industrial and commercial property more heavily than residential (as many do), or if reassessment and equalization have been ignored for many years, potential investors may shy away from your area because they know they would have to pay more than their fair share and would prefer to select a community that will treat them fairly.

For years one Fortune 500 company had paid excessive local taxes. It finally got tired of trying to negotiate a lower rate, went to court, and was awarded a multimillion-dollar judgment from the local government. In that particular community, property hadn't been reappraised and taxes hadn't been equalized for 30 years. As one result, new employees whom the company brought into their research center or manufacturing operations found themselves paying twice as much in local property taxes as their next-door neighbors. That's not a good selling point when you're trying to market your area.

It is therefore important for you to compare your tax system with that of areas with which you expect to be competing and make sure your taxes compare well. If they don't, this handicap could cost you one or more of your best prospects.

TRANSPORTATION

Since access to markets is often a primary cost consideration in location decisions, transportation resources—not just truck and rail but also air transportation—can be a deciding factor for many potential investors. Unless you maintain good, close contacts with established firms and are aware of any concerns they may have, it is easy to overlook a major transportation problem.

As an example, a manufacturer in the Midwest who had a major client in the Southeast was having to ship his products 60 miles in the wrong direction—away from the major

client—because his community did not have a long-haul trucking firm that shipped to the Southeast. As if that wasn't bad enough, at times his products sat on a loading dock one or even two days before a long-haul trucker could pick them up, so he not only had additional shipping costs but delivery delays as well. Needless to say, a high-priority task for that community was to persuade a long-haul shipper to move in to handle the business. Fortunately, enough additional business was found in nearby communities to make it worthwhile for the new trucking company to move in.

Air transportation continues to take on additional importance for two reasons:

- Executives increasingly need to travel quickly not only from one location to another within the United States, but often have to travel outside the country as well. It is therefore vitally important that they can readily fly wherever they need to go. Communities with limited airline service have a considerable handicap in their efforts to attract many companies that have such a need.

- Companies that make components for the many high-value-added products that go into electronic and telecommunications equipment also need regular air service for shipment of their products. The light weight and relatively high value make it economical to move such products by air rather than by truck.

If your community hasn't already done so, survey local companies to determine their transportation needs and, in particular, to learn whether they are satisfied with the services available to them. Such a survey can help you evaluate the transportation resources you have available. If local firms are having problems, it obviously would be important to learn precisely what those problems are and, where possible, take quick action to solve them.

UTILITIES AND SERVICES

The evaluation of infrastructure readiness is covered in a later chapter, so discussion here will focus mainly on the importance of having utilities and services available for development—industrial, commercial and residential.

In some parts of the country, local government planning goes so far as to require that utilities and services be extended to areas zoned for different types of development. The clear advantage this offers is that builders have no need to wait for the passage of a bond issue or the arrangement of financing before they can proceed with construction. Areas that require builders to pay for the construction of water and sewer lines to their property, or which impose high "impact fees" as a price for approval for construction, clearly are at a serious disadvantage as far as both cost and timing of construction are concerned.

Summing up, it is safe to say that 90 percent or more of the money now spent on marketing is wasted because the communities (and states) spending it haven't done their homework. They spend large sums trying to attract industries and companies that in many instances don't fit their area's resources at all. Many times they lack one or more of the key requirements of the companies they solicit. Since for public relations reasons most companies are reluctant to tell local leaders why their community lost out, they never learn specific deficiencies that disqualified them.

That doesn't mean some communities that aren't well prepared or that haven't cleared away most of their liabilities won't succeed in attracting new employers from time to time. Location decisions aren't always based solely on logic—or even on a company's best long-term interests. And some communities just get lucky and happen to deal with a company or an executive who goes against the apparent facts and selects a location that is perhaps not the best from a profit viewpoint, but will do well enough.

> *For public relations reasons, most companies are reluctant to tell local leaders why their community lost out, so they never learn specific deficiencies that disqualified them.*

For one reason or another, a community that quantitatively may not rate highest overall may be more attractive to the person making the location decision. One example was given of a community that rated sixth out of 26 yet was picked because of its leadership and well-planned actions scheduled to deal with each of its more than a dozen liabilities. Geographic location, climate, the availability of recreational facilities, the strength of a local university or college, or some other factor may tip the scales. The executive or company involved may be willing to forgo a percent or two of net profit in order to locate in an area they consider more attractive to key employees.

But for most communities, the four-step process described earlier is basic to building an effective marketing program. A community that identifies its assets, determines the industries and companies to which those assets will appeal, clears the way to success by upgrading as many of its facets as possible, and develops a businesslike plan to deal with the rest can be assured its marketing program will succeed.

About the Author.....Ken Wagner

Ken Wagner has 30 years experience developing and directing regional and state economic development organization. He has conducted hundreds of workshops for business and political leaders and has appeared on numerous television and radio interview programs across the U.S. Ken is also the author of the widely used *Economic Development Manual* and creator of the video *Growing*. His second book, *How To Create Jobs in the '90s*, was added to AEDC's Certification Exam reading list when it was published in 1992. His newest book is *How You Can Help Create Jobs in Your Area*. Ken Wagner can be reached at 518.426.8142.

COMMUNITY EVALUATION CHECKLIST ✓

PROJECT TITLE _____   PROJECT NUMBER_____

APPEARANCE

	YES	NO

How would the route from the airport into a meeting place in town look to an investor coming to your community for the first time?_____

_____

Would he or she get the impression that people have pride in your area?	___	___
Is the route well-landscaped?	___	___
Does the highway have dirt shoulders?	___	___
Is there litter along the way or ramshackle buildings that should be torn down?	___	___
Are the sidewalks downtown well-cared for?	___	___
Are the streets well-paved?	___	___
Are there trees or plants along downtown streets?	___	___
Are storefronts painted and well-kept?	___	___
Or does everything look bare, with broken curbs and sidewalks and trash along the way?	___	___
Are your parks and recreation areas inviting (landscaped, attractive, clean, well cared for)?	___	___
Are your central business district and shopping areas attractive (landscaped, free of trash, storefronts painted and in good repair)?	___	___

How would you rank your community's appearance:

☐ *Superior*   ☐ *Excellent*   ☐ *Average*   ☐ *Below average*   ☐ *Poor*

What would bring it up to the level you want it to be?

_____

_____

ATTITUDES TOWARD GROWTH (BUSINESS AND POLITICAL CLIMATE)

How will prospective business creators in your community be treated:

Will they be welcomed?		
Will local officials do their best to make it easy for them to get started?	___	___
Will they be given a checklist of the things they need to do and be shown how to quickly work through the list?	___	___
Do you have a one-stop place where they can go to get all the information they need to meet local planning and zoning requirements?	___	___
Will they be treated in a courteous, businesslike way?	___	___

How are people already in business in your area treated:

| Do they get the red carpet treatment they deserve as the people who produce the jobs, payrolls and taxes you need to maintain and improve your quality of life? | ___ | ___ |
| Do elected officials have a positive attitude toward healthy growth? | ___ | ___ |

	YES	NO

Do they support your development efforts?

Are your local taxes reasonable and fair?

How long has it been since property was reappraised? _____

Does your local government have an updated master plan?

Does it have a long-range capital improvement program based on recent
    engineering and planning analysis of infrastructure and other needs?

Are local business leaders actively involved in the governmental process and
    concerned with the efficiency of local government?

Do they act to correct political inaction on important issues as well as any excesses?

How would you rate your area's business climate?

    ☐ *Superior*   ☐ *Excellent*   ☐ *Average*   ☐ *Below average*   ☐ *Poor*

What steps can you take to improve that rating?

_____

_____

AVAILABLE BUILDINGS AND COMMERCIAL/INDUSTRIAL SITES

Do you have a good, up-to-date inventory of commercial and industrial sites
    and buildings?

Are those buildings of a quality and size that would appeal to most prospects?

Are your prices competitive?

Can you get a company into a building quickly?

Can you have a site ready to build on within 90 to 120 days?

Do you have at least one first-rate industrial or commercial park of at least
100 acres (preferably 500 for many areas) ready to go—that is:

    – utilities and services installed?

    – access roads built?

    – environmental studies completed?

    – ready to build on?

    – rail and interstate access in place?

Do you have a variety of quality sites and buildings in a variety of settings
    (rail and interstate access; interstate only; high, limited, or no visibility)?

How would you rate your area's available sites and buildings?

    ☐ *Superior*   ☐ *Excellent*   ☐ *Average*   ☐ *Below average*   ☐ *Poor*

How can you improve your site and building rating?

_____

_____

CHILD CARE

Are there adequate child care facilities available for parents who work?

Are the programs well-managed and highly rated by parents whose children
    participate?

COMMUNITY EVALUATION CHECKLIST

| | YES | NO |

If your community doesn't have such a program, what arrangements can you make?
_____

If your community already has an acceptable program, is it able to handle all
    the children that workers want to have participate?   —— ——

Does it need to be expanded?   —— ——

Can you offer the program to new companies that may want to consider
    locating in your area—that is, do you have additional capacity or plans
    to expand it if needed?   —— ——

COMMUNICATIONS

Is your area served by fiber optic cable?   —— ——
Do you have total digital switching?   —— ——
Do you have multi-media data service (MMDS)?   —— ——
Are E911 enhanced emergency services available in your area?   —— ——
Do you have central office-based PBX services?   —— ——
Do you have "SmartCall" services available?   —— ——
Are telemarketing circuits available?   —— ——
Do you have digital private line circuits?   —— ——

COMMUNITY and/or AREA DATA SUMMARY

Do you have a brief but complete local data summary that uses effective
    graphics to tell your basic data story?   —— ——
Are there other communities nearby that offer additional attractions that
    can at least help bring commuting jobs to your city or town?   —— ——
Do you also have an area or regional data summary that presents, in no more
    than eight pages, essential information on your area?   —— ——
Do you cooperate with nearby towns in an area or regional development
    effort that can benefit everyone in your area?   —— ——
If not, can you develop such a program to take advantage of the attractions
    offered by the total economic resources of the larger area, such as
    industrial sites, labor pool, and transportation resources?   —— ——

EDUCATIONAL AND TRAINING SYSTEMS

How do your schools compare with top-quality schools elsewhere?
    □ *much better* □ *a little better* □ *about the same* □ *a little worse* □ *much worse*
    Is the drop-out rate higher or lower? ___ *higher* ___ *lower*
    Are you spending as much per student?   —— ——
    Do your schools offer special courses that compare well with other schools? —— ——
    If not, can you persuade local school officials to review their present
        curricula and develop additional courses?   —— ——

YES   NO

How do your elementary and secondary schools rate in comparison to your
    state as a whole?
    □ *much better* □ *a little better* □ *about the same* □ *a little worse* □ *much worse*

Do your schools offer special courses for both underprivileged and outstanding
    students? ___ ___

Are your schools of sufficiently high quality to be acceptable to highly educated
    executives and managers who may move to your area? ___ ___

Do your counselors guide those not going to college onto career paths that
    will help them make the best use of their abilities and find available jobs? ___ ___

Can employers get the people they need from your vocational/technical schools? ___ ___

Are your vo-tech programs keyed to the needs of local firms? ___ ___

What special training programs do you now have that could benefit potential
    employers?

Do you need to develop additional training programs? ___ ___

If so, can one or more of your local universities, colleges or vocational/
    technical schools develop special training programs? ___ ___

If not, can you persuade their leadership to gear up to provide special training
    programs if you attract a company that requires them? ___ ___

Are state subsidies available? ___ ___

If not, what would you be willing to offer a major employer who would hire
    people from your local workforce only if they receive special training?

ENVIRONMENTAL ISSUES

Does your area have acceptable waste disposal programs in place and
    operational—solid waste, hazardous waste, recycling? ___ ___

If not, what do you need to do to be able to measure up to your likely competitors?

Do you need to persuade local officials to take action to develop new programs? ___ ___

If your local governments don't have the funds needed to develop essential
    programs, could you set up an action team to talk with local government
    officials about increasing its efficiency so that money can be reallocated
    for environmental and other projects? ___ ___

Do you know whether any of your established firms have waste disposal
    problems (e.g., spending substantial sums to dispose of waste because
    of local program deficiencies)? ___ ___

If you don't have such information, can you prepare a survey that will determine
    if you need to solve a problem in order to keep established companies from
    spending money for waste disposal that their competitors don't spend? ___ ___

Do your environmental programs create difficulties for you as you compete
    for new payrolls? ___ ___

	YES	NO

Do your local and state environmental review personnel provide quick and
   reasonable resolutions to environmental issues?   —   —
If not, what steps can you take to make sure they do?   —   —

FINANCIAL RESOURCES

Do you have the bonding capacity you need to finance major physical
   improvements important to adding new employers?   —   —
Does your community have a tax base large enough to make needed
   improvements?   —   —
Do your local governments have a strong enough budget to be able to finance
   special training programs if such programs are needed to attract a
   company you want to bring to your area?   —   —
Do local governments have the financial strength necessary to upgrade or
   replace, if necessary, outmoded and decaying water and sewer systems?   —   —
Or will they have to do what one community did—raise the sewer connection
   fee for new housing from $500 to $5,000 per house (thereby killing its
   chances of attracting new investors)?   —   —

COST OF LIVING

How does your area's cost of living compare with other areas?
   ☐ Superior   ☐ Excellent   ☐ Average   ☐ Below average   ☐ Poor
If it is above average, is so high that it discourages people from moving there?   —   —
Is there one cost category that is especially high?   —   —
More than one?   —   —
Is your high category important to the average worker?   —   —
Is there any way you can bring it down?   —   —
Does your area have an overall quality of life, amenities, and attractions that
   make it attractive enough to offset a higher cost of living?   —   —
If so, do people outside the area know that?   —   —
What can be done to reduce the cost of one or more factors?   —   —

_____

_____

GOVERNMENT

Have local officials been able to maintain balanced budgets?   —   —
Have they done so at the expense of maintaining roads or water and sewer
   systems, recreational facilities, or other services important to your
   economic development marketing?   —   —
Do they have sound, problem-oriented planning programs?   —   —
Are capital improvement programs based on realistic assessment of needs
   and on realistic numbers?   —   —

	YES	NO

Is property reassessed on a regular basis? ___ ___

Do severe disparities exist in the taxes paid by some homeowners because of failure to reassess?

Are assessments on commercial and industrial property excessive? ___ ___

HEALTH CARE

Do you have one or more hospitals that can provide tertiary medical services, or are such services available at a hospital in a nearby community? ___ ___

Do your hospitals offer special emergency care for cardiac patients? ___ ___

Are your hospitals highly rated for the quality of the care they provide? ___ ___

Does at least one of your local hospitals have the latest diagnostic and treatment equipment available, such as LLLT (low level laser therapy) equipment that has been developed for industrial problems such as carpal tunnel syndrome? ___ ___

HOUSING

Does your community have a good supply of moderately priced and low-cost housing? ___ ___

How do housing prices in your area compare with other areas with which you compete for jobs?

Are housing prices in your area relatively stable? ___ ___

If not, have they gone up rapidly in recent years?

Do you have a good variety of available housing—different styles and different locations? ___ ___

Do you have an adequate supply of quality housing for incoming executives? ___ ___

Do you have an inventory of executive type housing available? ___ ___

If not, do you have one or more builders capable of quickly constructing the quality housing you may need on relatively short notice? ___ ___

Are your builders considered reliable and fair? ___ ___

Does your local government or any of your banks have a vigorous low-cost housing program?

Do attractive subdivisions dominate your housing market and give the kind of impression you want to give potential employers? ___ ___

If you have one or more slum areas, do you also have an active cleanup or improvement program? ___ ___

If you do not have such a program, can you get one under way in the near future so that you can tell prospects such a program is planned? ___ ___

Overall, how would you rate your area's housing?

☐ Superior ☐ Excellent ☐ Average ☐ Below average ☐ Poor

What specific steps could you take to improve that rating?

_____

_____

COMMUNITY EVALUATION CHECKLIST

	YES	NO

IMAGE

Does your community have a well-known image outside your immediate area? ____ ____
    Is that image favorable? ____ ____
    Or unfavorable? ____ ____
If you believe it has some negative characteristics, are there ways you can
    change those? ____ ____
How? _____
How would you rate your area's image?
    ☐ *Superior*   ☐ *Excellent*   ☐ *Average*   ☐ *Below average*   ☐ *Poor*
What specific steps do you need to take to improve your area's image? ____ ____

_____

_____

LABOR FORCE AND CLIMATE

Do you have an ample supply of professional, skilled and trained labor? ____ ____
If not, can you attract the types and numbers of people you need from other
    areas? ____ ____
What percentage of your high school graduates who are not going on to
    college stay in your area? ____ ____
Are your schools a good supply of human resources? ____ ____
What is the current percentage of unemployed people in your area? ____ ____
How does that compare with other areas that might attract the same types of
    companies you would like to attract? ____ ____
How many people with various skills and experience are currently available
    to work in a new firm? _____
How many underemployed do you have—people who have been displaced
    from higher paying, higher skilled jobs who could take new positions
    if they become available? _____
How many more people not now employed—including housewives and early
    retirees—do you have in your area? _____
Can you develop reliable data on the additional dozens, hundreds, or thousands
    of people who could make a significant addition to your workforce? ____ ____
If so, how? _____
How much retraining would some of these people need to be able to work
    effectively in the types of companies your marketing program seeks to
    attract? _____
Do you have a recent survey of your labor supply and human resources? ____ ____
Can you get your state labor department or some other state or local
    government agency to do a special survey to compile such information? ____ ____
If not, could one of your local colleges conduct such a survey? ____ ____

	YES	NO

How do your employers rate their employees:
    Do they consider them productive?   —— ——
    Do they believe them to have good attitudes?   —— ——
    Is absenteeism low?   —— ——
    Is their sick leave record low?   —— ——
    Are their training costs high?   —— ——
    Do they think turnover is high?   —— ——
What percentage of your employees are unionized?   —— ——
Are strikes frequent?   —— ——
How militant are your unions? □ very   □ moderately   □ minimally
What is their strike record?   average days on strike ____
    – any record of violence?   —— ——
How does your labor force compare to that of your competitors?
    □ much better □ a little better □ about the same □ a little worse □ much worse
How do you rate your labor supply?   —— ——
    □ Superior   □ Excellent   □ Average   □ Below average   □ Poor
What steps could you take to raise that rating?

_____

_____

MAJOR EMPLOYERS:

SUPPORT FOR EXISTING COMPANIES

Do your companies have problems you can help solve?   —— ——
Are any of them in serious trouble?   —— ——
Do any need capital?   —— ——
Do any need to find ways to cut costs?   —— ——
Do you have a local group or project to support the companies that now
    provide vital jobs?   —— ——
Do you have an active and effective team that can help them deal with:
    – cash flow?   —— ——
    – marketing?   —— ——
    – financial needs?   —— ——
    – plant layout?   —— ——
    – recruitment?   —— ——
    – training?   —— ——
Does your labor supply meet their needs?   —— ——
Do local schools provide satisfactory technical training programs?   —— ——
Are college level (including graduate) programs available to train and advance
    their people?   —— ——
Has the cost of solid waste removal become a major problem for them?   —— ——
Can you help them work out a solution?   —— ——

	YES	NO
Do they feel they get the support they want from local government?	___	___
Do you believe they pay more than their fair share of taxes?	___	___
Do they think they pay more taxes than they should?	___	___
Can they get the raw materials or component parts they need within your region?	___	___
Would it help them if you developed a local supplier?	___	___
Do they have capacity or other problems you can help them solve?	___	___
If they need to expand, can they do it where they are?	___	___
Will they need help to find a suitable building or construction site?	___	___
Will local officials make it easy for them to expand or relocate if that becomes necessary?	___	___
Does your community support them?	___	___
Do they generally feel appreciated by local business organizations, local government, and citizens?	___	___
Do you have an annual appreciation day or some other program that shows your support for local businesses?	___	___
How well do you rate the way you support companies you now have?	___	___

☐ Superior   ☐ Excellent   ☐ Average   ☐ Below average   ☐ Poor

What specific actions can be taken to correct existing problems?

_____

_____

NEW COMPANY START-UP PROGRAM

	YES	NO
Do you have an effective program to help new companies start up?	___	___
Do companies that request help from existing organization(s) in your community get the help they need?	___	___
Can your local group give practical help—quickly—on:		
– business plans preparation?	___	___
– funding needs?	___	___
– recruiting or training people?	___	___
– layout for a new manufacturing operation?	___	___
– cash flow needs review?	___	___
– marketing and selling?	___	___
Can you provide quick emergency service if companies get into trouble in their early months?	___	___
Do you have a systematic program to check on their progress regularly to see if they need help before they get into serious trouble, such as a financial or other crisis?	___	___
How do you rate your new company start-up support:		

☐ Superior   ☐ Excellent   ☐ Average   ☐ Below average   ☐ Poor

What specific actions can be taken to correct existing problems?

_____

_____

YES   NO

RECREATIONAL AND CULTURAL FACILITIES:

RECREATIONAL RESOURCES

How do your recreational facilities and programs compare with national standards?
    □ *much better*   □ *a little better*   □ *about the same*   □ *a little worse*   □ *much worse*
How do they compare to the areas with which you must compete for jobs?
    □ *much better*   □ *a little better*   □ *about the same*   □ *a little worse*   □ *much worse*
Do you have an ample supply of:
    – public parks?
    – playgrounds?
    – tennis courts?
    – golf courses?
    – swimming pools?
Do you have supervised programs for both younger children and teenagers?
Are your facilities of high quality?
    Are they well-maintained?
    Are they safe?
Do you have excellent and varied resources and programs for the elderly?
How does the variety of your resources compare with competitor areas?
How do you rate your recreational resources:
    □ *Superior*   □ *Excellent*   □ *Average*   □ *Below average*   □ *Poor*
What can be done to improve this rating?

CULTURAL AMENITIES

Do your cultural facilities offer a variety of high-quality programming for
    different ages and income levels?
Does your community have an adequate number of or top-quality:
    – theaters?
    – art galleries?
    – symphony orchestra?
    – museums?
Do you offer not only entertainment but training for those interested in:
    – music?
    – theater?
    – dance?
    – art?
How would you rate your cultural amenities?
    □ *Superior*   □ *Excellent*   □ *Average*   □ *Below average*   □ *Poor*
What specific improvements would you like to see in this area?

	YES	NO

SOLID WASTE

How does your community rate on the following solid waste questions:
    Are present landfills adequate? ___ ___
    If not, have plans been made to meet landfill needs? ___ ___
    Are recycling programs in effect? ___ ___
    Are they being maximized? ___ ___
Is your local government working with other local governments to find solutions
    to solid waste problems none of them can work out alone? ___ ___
How do local companies feel about present facilities and plans?

_____

Have their costs escalated to a point where they might seriously consider
    moving to an area where those costs are much lower, and where effective
    plans exist to deal with future needs? ___ ___
How do your local solid waste programs and plans rate?
    ☐ *Superior*   ☐ *Excellent*   ☐ *Average*   ☐ *Below average*   ☐ *Poor*
What can be done to correct existing problems?

_____
_____

TAXATION

How do your tax rates compare with competitor cities? ___ ___
Can newcomers expect to pay the same property tax rates as older residents? ___ ___
    Or do they pay a much higher rate? ___ ___
Do you have considerable bonding capacity? ___ ___
Are your tax rates actually quite low, and do you consequently have
    inadequate facilities and services? ___ ___
Are your tax policies keyed to current conditions: lack of federal and state
    funds, need to maintain infrastructure and quality of life with local tax
    revenues? ___ ___
Are you unable to compete for desirable payrolls because water, sewer, street,
    and other needs haven't been budgeted for? ___ ___
Is information on local government budgets readily available to citizens' groups
    for evaluation and comment? ___ ___
 How would you rate local taxes and financial management? ___ ___
    ☐ *Superior*   ☐ *Excellent*   ☐ *Average*   ☐ *Below average*   ☐ *Poor*
What specific actions would correct these problems?

_____
_____

YES   NO

TRANSPORTATION SYSTEMS

How good is your transportation system of highways and streets?
    ☐ *Superior*   ☐ *Excellent*   ☐ *Average*   ☐ *Below average*   ☐ *Poor*

Can people move readily about without long traffic delays?   ___ ___

Do you have community-wide or county-wide systems that are not only up to
   date but able to handle anticipated growth?   ___ ___

Does your local or state government have specific plans to upgrade existing
   roads and add new streets and highways?   ___ ___

How does your transportation infrastructure (air, rail, road) rate?   ___ ___
    ☐ *Superior*   ☐ *Excellent*   ☐ *Average*   ☐ *Below average*   ☐ *Poor*

What can be done to raise this rating?

_____

_____

UTILITIES AND SERVICES

Are essential utilities and services already provided to your most marketable
   sites?

If not, are they readily accessible so that a prospect would not have to wait
   a long time to have them installed where he or she needs them?   ___ ___

Do your local governments have a reasonable and relatively low-cost system
   for providing utilities and services to your best sites?   ___ ___

Do they have exorbitant impact fees or other costly penalties built into development (like the $5,000 per house sewer connection fee cited earlier)?   ___ ___

Are your utility rates competitive, especially for large power users?   ___ ___

Are your utility companies willing and able to provide services quickly and
   at competitive costs?   ___ ___

Do employers in your area have problems with power interruptions?   ___ ___

If so, can action be taken to eliminate that problem by improving present
   services?   ___ ___

Are your water and sewer systems in good condition?   ___ ___

Do you have community-wide or county-wide systems that are not only up to
   date but able to handle anticipated growth?   ___ ___

If your present facilities are near capacity, does your local government have
   specific plans to add new facilities or upgrade and expand the old?   ___ ___

Can a company that wants to locate in your area tie into an existing water
   and sewer system without delay and get the services it needs?   ___ ___

Can utility companies provide service quickly and efficiently?   ___ ___

How do your utilities and services rate?   ___ ___
    ☐ *Superior*   ☐ *Excellent*   ☐ *Average*   ☐ *Below average*   ☐ *Poor*

What can be done to raise this rating?

_____

_____

CHAPTER 4

PREPARING THE SOIL

Susan Lackey, CED
Executive Director, Washtenaw Development Council

Not many years ago I began to play the cello. Most people would say that what I am doing is "learning to play" the cello. But these words carry into our minds the strange idea that there exists two very different processes: learning to play the cello vs. playing the cello. They imply that I will do the first until I have completed it, at which point I will stop the first process and begin the second. In short, I will go on "learning to play" until I have "learned to play" and then I will begin to play. Of course, this is nonsense. There not two processes, but one. We learn to do something by doing it. There is no other way.

— John Holt

———— o ————

Preparing product in economic development is very much like John Holt's situation. It is a continual process that must be nurtured and developed by the economic development professional. Anyone who has worked in economic development for any amount of time also knows how challenging getting product ready can be. And anyone who has tried to present undeveloped farm land in a misguided effort to be competitive knows the value of having construction ready sites available.

You can assume the private sector will step forward and develop the sites upon demand. With site options an early-on request from consultants and companies, you then face the possibility of being left out of the hunt entirely. You could try to encourage a totally private speculative solution. In the 1990s that's a tough one, as experienced developers still bear scars from the fallout of the past decade. You may be faced with only one alternative.

Developing your own product and bringing into the market as developer and economic developer.

This chapter explores the greenfield development of business and industrial parks. It won't give you all the answers. It will pose the questions you need to answer if you intend to go forward. Hopefully, it will help ensure that your community has sufficient product to be competitive in the business of business attraction.

GETTING STARTED

You may see the need for a diverse inventory of sites as self-evident. However, no matter how sparse you may see that inventory, your stakeholders can probably name a dozen vacant parcels they believe are suitable for occupancy. Some people may believe that a proposal to construct a new facility is an excuse for an inadequate marketing effort. Some may believe this is a private enterprise function that will happen if and when the market demand exists. Private property owners may see this project as undercutting the value of their property or artificially depressing property values.

If the project is to be successful, you must address these issues up front. The following research approach focuses on the information required to report to the board and stakeholders.

REVIEW CLIENT AND LEAD FILES

Review these files for the past 12 to 18 months to get an overview of the types of buildings and sites requested. You may glean key information from this process, such as the frequency with which a lead failed to become a prospect because a building or site request couldn't be filled, and comments on the diversity and quality of sites made during site tours.

INVENTORY EXISTING BUILDINGS AND SITES

Review the existing site and building inventory, and make an effort to ensure that it is comprehensive and up to date. What insights do owners and realtors provide? Are many buildings older construction, multi-storied, limited in parking, located in residential areas, requiring substantial renovation or suspected of contamination? Are sites fully served with a broad range of utilities; were prior uses "clean"? Are there a variety of stand-alone sites and planned industrial areas? Do the available parks offer lot sizes that meet the needs of current prospects? Are covenants and restrictions in place to adequately protect future property values?

INTERVIEW LOCAL COMMERCIAL AND INDUSTRIAL REALTORS AND REAL ESTATE APPRAISERS

What constraints do they find in locating acceptable sites in the service area? Are they able to find adequate comparable properties in the market area? How do real estate values in the area compare to neighboring areas, and what are the factors that are impacting that value?

ASSESS THE COMPETITION

Are neighboring areas utilizing a similar program to attract economic development activity?

SETTING THE BOUNDARIES

In many ways, the board may be the easiest "sell" on a project of this nature. Already conditioned to economic development as a goal, the ability to stimulate a project through providing real estate is a short leap. Other allies have different agendas. As indicated above, the real estate and development community may feel threatened by a nonprofit or publicly supported project. If the economic development service area includes more than a single municipality, issues of "steering" and "favoritism" may arise. The answers to a series of questions help address these concerns while defining your project goals more clearly.

Who is your end user?

Is the purpose of this project to attract a specific targeted industry? Are there uses that you will prohibit in the park by policy rather than by covenant (e.g., a major distributor may be desirable, while a local warehouse be seen as undesirable)?

Many communities have constructed parks targeted to new specific research or high-technology uses in the hopes of stimulating a market. In other instances, the purpose is a more general interest industrial park. In either case, it is important to define the size of the ideal candidate facility, as well as the types of jobs to be created and the type of company to be targeted. Defining these factors up front can build up front support and guide your site location and construction decision. Existing property owners and realtors may see less competition for their projects if the project targets an untapped market.

What inducements are available in the project?

Federal and state enterprise zones offer reasons to locate in otherwise undesirable areas. You, too, may wish to provide certain inducements to locate in your park. These benefits may be tied to an existing development zone or developed specifically for your project.

How will you price the real estate?

Will you establish the land value at market rate? If so, do you intend to discount land value in order to stimulate desirable investment? If you do, what are the guidelines that will guide the decision? What if the cost of development exceeds the market value of land? (This may be the reason a private market hasn't developed.) Is your organization willing to absorb the subsidy between market value and cost? Are there grants or public loans that an assist in reducing this gap? Are you willing to live with the terms and conditions applied to these projects? (See "A Few Words on Financing," below.)

How will you work with the realty community?

The relationship between economic developers and realtors is, at best, love/hate. Entering the real estate market yourself can exacerbate that problem unless you handle it gently.

Do you intend to select a broker to list your property or handle the up-front marketing yourself? A listing broker may remove some of the burden from your marketing staff, but this also results in commission splits and other complications which impact costs. If you

A FEW WORDS ON FINANCING

Once upon a time, financing for industrial parks was relatively simple. Federal grants from the Economic Development Administration, Urban Development Action Grants, Community Development Block Grants, and Farmers Home Administration loans were fairly easy to come by and financed the majority of the project costs.

Over the past decade, these sources have become less reliable. Moreover, they may come with "strings" attached that limit your ability to freely respond to market conditions. This forces you to become more creative in the financing process. Use the grants where you can to supplement other, more innovative, financing strategies.

Alternatives may include the following:

- Tax Increment Financing Districts: Use the captured taxes as a revenue stream to pay off either bonds or traditional financing.
- Conventional financing with a favorable rate from local lenders.

- Private/public partnerships with for-profit investors.
- Land contributions for tax benefits; use the land as collateral for infrastructure construction.
- Traditional local government infrastructure bonds.
- Establishment of utility districts to bond for infrastructure, spreading the costs across the entire district.

The point of this list is not to be exhaustive. It is to stimulate you to be creative in your approach. Look at your costs not as a single project, but as a variety of smaller projects, and attack them on a piece-by-piece basis. Consider phasing your park into smaller projects. Consider build-to-suit buildings to develop a profit and revenue stream. Consider a series of smaller parks as a long term goal. Begin today with a light industrial park with quick build out, and use the proceeds to leverage future development.

choose this route, you must determine an appropriate level of commission, as well as establish parameters for dealing with prospects that you generate through traditional economic development efforts.

On the other hand, you may choose to "protect" all realtors. Working without a listing agent, any realtor who brings a project to your park would receive the pre-established commission. This should keep your commission costs lower and make your project attractive, as it ensures that the selling realtor will receive 100 percent of the available commission.

Other communities opt not to protect realtors in any way. These communities prefer to rely on their own economic development efforts to bring prospects to their facility. Several pitfalls are inherent in this approach. Realtors may be reluctant to cooperate with your organization on any project for fear that their clients will be "steered" to your real estate, depriving the realtor of a commission. Your community may even miss the opportunity to compete for good companies because the proper real estate or inducements weren't presented due to the realtor's reluctance to contact your office.

Each of the questions above addresses issues that you, as the local professional, need to answer for your own use in crafting the best possible project. But each serves an additional goal as well. By choosing the right answer to each of these questions, you have the opportunity to increase the commitment behind the project. While the "right" answer may vary significantly from case to case, solutions that provide a "WIFM" (What's in it for me?) for key players will increase support or, at the very least, decrease opposition.

It may also be appropriate to establish a special task force to guide this project. While not a substitute for paid professionals (see below), a well-developed task force can lend credibility to this effort. Respected business leaders, developers, community activists, and others can be your sounding board in the development of the project parameters. They may even assist in identifying the location of specific parcels of property, setting design guidelines, providing negotiating parameters,

and choosing the professional team. In addition to providing excellent advice and serving as a sounding board, this task force can assist you in selling the project to the community at large.

Define the size of the ideal candidate facility, as well as the jobs to be created and type of community to be targeted.

Finally, although it is instinctive to handle all real estate issues as top secret, confidential proceedings, you will build additional support for your project by discussing it with the community at large in the formative stages. Press releases, newsletter items, and public meetings may all be appropriate consensus-building methods. Explain to the neighborhood the benefits of additional job creation and tax base. Ask them what they like or don't like about the proposed plan. Identify steps to meet their concerns in the planning and development process.

As many private developers have discovered in recent years, these extra steps, although time-consuming and frustrating to people with the urge to build, can ultimately reduce the amount of time necessary to complete a project. You may also discover that these efforts will result in an even better project, thanks to the collective input of stakeholders from across the community.

GOING FORWARD

Once you've set the parameters for your project, it is time to proceed with the real work at hand: what you wanted to do when you started this project. Although your interest and goals in development may be different from those of the private sector, the process is similar.

MARKET ANALYSIS:

A conventional market analysis undertaken at this time is designed to discourage you from pursuing your project. Conventional market analysis focuses on defining the unfilled need in an existing market. Typically, economic developers enter the real estate market because there is no existing market. Thus, by definition, no market gap exists. A number of conventional market analysis tasks can, however, provide valuable insight into the real estate development process, and make your project more successful.

What are the real estate needs of your targeted audience? Lot size, project amenities, locational factors, and utility loads will all be determined by the needs of this target. These factors are particularly crucial if you intend to use this project to "make" a market for companies that haven't previously found your community attractive.

Some community-based industrial parks have failed because stakeholders neglected to determine how long they would have to hold property for sale.

This analysis should also examine land absorption for similar uses in your community. This number is likely to appear anemic. However, when taken with an estimate of the percentage of this market you are likely to capture, it provides valuable information. In the event you chose to borrow money to complete your project, this information will help you understand a reasonable repayment period.

Even if you don't have to secure conventional financing, a realistic understanding of land absorption patterns will aid you in under-

standing the task you face. More than one community based industrial park has been called a failure because stakeholders neglected to educate themselves as to the length of time they would likely have to hold property before sale. Most importantly, such a market analysis will help determine what inducements or other programs are necessary to "make" a market where none currently exists.

FINDING A LOCATION:

In some ways the toughest part of this process is finding a site for your project. This process requires that you pick "winners" and "losers" among your community stakeholders. As if this wasn't enough of a challenge, it also requires that you be sensitive to neighborhood concerns and respectful of long-term planning and zoning requirements. Few economic development organizations are willing to expend the political capital or time involved in negotiating protracted community conflicts, so the site selection process becomes particularly crucial. At the same time, you must remain conscious of market driven location factors such as infrastructure, visibility and access.

If your goal is to stimulate development within a specific community or zone, you may have yet another set of considerations. While the issues of "winners" and "losers" may be moot, your real estate choices may be limited as well. (See "A Few Words on Brownfields," page 46.)

PRELIMINARY PLANNING:

After you have selected a site, but prior to public announcement, you may wish to undertake some preliminary planning. This process entails a review of developmental constraints in the area. Are there known sources of contamination? Wetlands or endangered species issues? Is the infrastructure in the area adequate to handle industrial/commercial loads? If not, is the condition adequate to allow for reasonably priced enhancements? Will the property allow for appropriate lot configuration?

A private developer would not typically do this work until he or she obtained site control. However, an economic development project will take on added public dimensions at the time you take real estate options. As a result, negative findings on such basic due diligence issues can lead to public perception of project "failure" or failure of the organization to "do its homework."

SITE CONTROL / LAND ACQUISITION:

Unless the economic developer is a licensed and experienced real estate professional, it is wise to obtain the services of a realtor, real estate attorney, or other real estate advisor for this process. This is particularly true if the site under consideration isn't listed on the open market.

Again, there are some subtle differences between public and private negotiations at this stage. A private developer might choose to approach property owners anonymously. However, an economic developer must remember that his or her public responsibility extends to dealings with private individuals. In this climate it is generally preferable that your representative be open and honest about the purchaser and its intended use. This maintains your credibility while reducing rumors of the "big project" that is coming to and will occupy a large tract of land in your community.

In spite of your intention to be public-spirited, some landowners will see this as an opportunity to inflate land prices, believing you have limited options. Here you can learn a lot from your private developer colleagues. Set a maximum price and instruct your representatives that you will not exceed that limit. Then stick to it. Remember, it is likely that the economics of this project are suspect. A big run up on the front end is likely to leave you with a project that exceeds your ability to finance and develop.

As with any real estate deal, option periods should be sufficient to allow you to complete environmental studies, title searches and planning/preliminary engineering.

PLANNING / PRELIMINARY ENGINEERING / ENGINEERING:

Here, for the first time, your project really begins to come together. Your preliminary report to the board on prospect needs, the

market analysis, the constraints imposed by the real estate and infrastructure, your own knowledge of economic development, and all the creativity of your land planning/engineering team comes to bear on something really concrete—dirt!

▶ *Infrastructure Analysis*

A review of existing infrastructure was completed prior to this time. At this point, serious flow calculations, capacity analysis and other related items will be accomplished by your engineers. The obvious infrastructure needs are storm and sanitary sewer, water, natural gas and electric service, and roads. But we are entering an age where connectivity impacts far more than just Internet providers. You should also consider an analysis of anticipated telephone and cable needs.

Consideration of off-site infrastructure may also be important. Will truck routes be required? Will your project impact the load on roads or utilities in nearby communities? Examination of these issues up front will reduce negative community opinion in the future. You may even wish to consider whether you can design infrastructure improvements to address challenges in nearby neighborhoods. Special assessment districts or other partnerships may be developed that more broadly spread the cost of community improvements. This may make your project more welcome in the neighborhood, while spreading your costs across more users.

Real estate option periods should allow you to complete environmental studies, title searches, and planning/preliminary engineering.

A FEW WORDS ON . . .

Much of our discussion has assumed the availability of greenfield areas for the development of new industrial parks. If you are developing in an older community, this may not be possible. Moreover, with the advent of enterprise zones, empowerment zones, and the like, your mission may be to redevelop those most difficult areas.

Many of the concerns about infrastructure and contamination are magnified in older industrial areas. Several other factors must be considered as well. Unfortunately, these special concerns nearly always serve to move the cost of development substantially higher.

Most businesses seek to balance cost/quality/location factors in their site decision; few are tied to established community locations. It is important, therefore, that you seriously consider ways to make these sites financially competitive. This can be done through special inducements, indirect subsidy through unrecovered development costs, or a combination. In either event, these considerations are an important part of your up-front goal setting.

Land Assembly:

In greenfield areas it may be possible to assemble an entire park with acquisition from only one or two landowners. In a more highly developed area the number of land owners may be in the dozens. Moreover, if these individuals have hung on in the community through bad times, they may demand a premium for real estate sales.

In these instances a close working relationship with the municipality is imperative. Ideally, the municipal planning officials can identify areas within the city where much land is publicly owned, holding relocation to a minimum. If this is not possible, the municipality has a variety of condemnation techniques at their disposal.

Condemnation is a very costly process, which can push the cost of land up by five to ten times its market value. It can also add long delays to the process if legal challenges are brought. Seldom will you be able to fully recover these costs in the price of the land.

Even after land control has been achieved, you may face other costly site preparation challenges. The demolition of buildings has become increasingly difficult as landfill space is rarer and more expensive. Even vacant ground can provide unpleasant surprises when you discover the residential block that was demolished in 1968 was pushed into basements and covered with dirt, requiring re-excavation and new fill.

These added costs may encourage you to become a "landlord," focusing on land leases and build-to-suits, rather than outright sale of the real estate. This allows you to hold the property until the market matures, recouping additional value by sale at that time.

Infrastructure:

While greenfield sites may require the installation of new infrastructure, there are particular problems with existing infrastructure as well. Utilities installed a century before may require costly repairs and upgrading to meet modern standards. Streets developed on a grid system may not accommodate heavy truck traffic. Inconsistent zoning patterns may have residential areas abutting your industrial area, with accompanying noise and traffic concerns.

Contamination:

While a Level I environmental review may be adequate when developing a greenfield site, a redevelopment project places the burden of cleanliness on you, as the developer. Potential purchasers and occupants will be doubly concerned about contamination in previously

... BROWNFIELDS

developed sites. This includes everything from industrial tailings to fuel oil drums used for home heating.

The quality of fill dirt used in earlier demolition projects may also be questionable. It is money well spent to contract for a Level II assessment and bearing analysis. The environmental consultant will take soil borings from a number of areas in your site. This analysis will provide an estimate of the type and quality of the fill material, along with a screen for materials deemed "toxic" or "hazardous" by state and federal officials. While not a substitute for specific site-by-site testing prior to sale, it provides an additional level of assurance for potential buyers, who have been conditioned to expect the worst.

Design:

The design of a redevelopment project will particularly challenge your development team. Working within an already built environment, you must strive to create a project that has the open appeal of a greenfield site. Adjacent residential neighborhoods may have both current residents and potential tenants seeking physical barriers between business and home.

Ensuring both a familiar environment and a sense of security will challenge the

---

Most business seek to balance cost/quality/location factors in their site decision. . . . Seriously consider ways to make these sites financially competitive.

---

design team. As the leader of this group, you must strike a balance between these goals. Landscaping elements may be particularly critical in this regard.

Neighborhood Involvement:

When discussing conventional greenfield development, we touched briefly on forging partnerships with the neighborhood to reduce development costs. When developing in an existing community, "neighborhood" takes on more traditional connotations. As a public or quasi-public official, you must be conscious of these issues.

Existing residential neighborhoods may have a legitimate concern about additional traffic and noise. Fears may arise about environmental degradation. At the very least, issues of residential property values and community cohesiveness will be raised.

Address these issues at the beginning and on an ongoing basis with neighborhood leaders and the public at large. Don't assume that "jobs in the neighborhood" will be an adequate rallying cry. Many residents will assume that these jobs will go to people living outside the area, leaving them with only the negative spinoff.

Integrate the neighborhood residents into your design process, asking them what their concerns are and addressing them in the final plan. Keep them posted on progress. Identify other benefits, such as better street lighting, blight removal and improved infrastructure. Above all, keep talking and don't assume that the neighbors share your goal or your vision about what the community should look like. Brownfield development is the most challenging and difficult development you can undertake. It can also be the most rewarding. Stick with it, and keep remembering why you got into this business in the first place!

► *Lot Sizing and Configuration*

The most important thing to remember in determining lot sizes and configuration is flexibility. An appropriately designed plan will allow lot splits and combinations in a number of workable configurations. In this way you can offer maximum flexibility to your customer, while still maintaining the usability of all available land.

► *Phasing*

Engineers and planners should consider phasing development of costly infrastructure. If land absorption is likely to be slow, this will minimize your initial expense. Land sales can then help support expansion activities. A good phasing plan will allow the park to open in stages, providing full service to each phase on an ongoing basis.

There are also distinct marketing advantages in a good phasing plan. A fully developed park is likely to attract scattered facilities throughout the park. More concentrated clusters of buildings in the early years will lend an air of success to the project. And don't underestimate the benefits of being able to tout that "phase one is sold out."

► *Amenities*

Amenities are an important consideration in real estate development. As with everything else, you must tailor your amenity package to your intended audience. A park targeted toward research and development, high technology or office users will demand and support a higher level of physical amenities than one targeted to light manufacturing.

What might some of those amenities be? A highly wooded site might include picnic areas or hiking trails. Storm water and drainage retention areas might become water amenities. Depending on the activity in the surrounding neighborhood, sites may be reserved for day care centers, banks, service stations, or restaurants.

► *Landscaping / Signage*

Development of a landscaping and signage plan will help establish the quality of the project. It is easy, however, to go overboard in providing for landscaping in particular. Specify that all landscaping and signage be designed for minimum maintenance, using materials that take into account the local weather.

CONSTRUCTION:

Once planning and engineering have been completed and property acquired, you're ready to turn dirt. For most economic developers this will be the most exciting and the most frightening time. An industrial park can be the most permanent thing we have to show for our careers. At the same time, once the first bulldozer shows up there is no turning back.

There are two major guidelines for managing the construction process. First, hire someone to manage construction. Second, stay involved. Whether you choose to hire your engineer to manage construction or seek an independent professional, this will be money well spent. Construction management is a complicated task requiring the balancing of many separate interests. Change orders are inevitable, as are conflicts with vendors, questions over construction liens, requests for materials substitutions, permitting hassles, and a host of other issues. Few economic development organizations have the staff capacity to assign someone full time to this effort. Moreover, unless you are fortunate enough to have an engineer or other design professional on staff, few of us have the technical capability to understand the issues that arise. A trusted advisor with responsibility for this task can save time, energy, money, and sleepless nights.

At the same time, you do not want to forget that you are ultimately responsible for the success of this project. Your attention to weekly construction meetings, the details of change orders and other construction management activities will provide you with necessary answers when questions arise. Additionally, you will have received an invaluable education that will assist you in working with future prospects involved in site development or building construction.

ONGOING MANAGEMENT:

It is often overlooked that, once constructed, your organization has acquired a capital asset and you are now in the asset management business. Up front attention to this detail can make your life substantially easier.

How will you structure long-term management? Will you hire a firm to handle landscape management and snow removal or do it yourself? Will the roads and utilities be public or private? If private, how will long-term upkeep be managed—through a property owners' association? Or will you retain ownership of all land and finance maintenance through land leases?

If utilities are public, what priority will your project have in a community that potentially has miles of public arterials to maintain?

How will you manage the quality of buildings and their long term upkeep to ensure a quality image tomorrow and into the next century? Will there be covenants and restrictions? How restrictive will the CCRs be? Increased restrictions may make the facility more attractive and raise values, but they may also impede the speed of land absorption. Again, a consideration of your development goals should help you make this determination.

Will there be a property owners' association? What will its role be in relationship to you, the developer? What about the relationship with you, the economic developer? Are there potential conflicts in goals and roles? At what point will you be relieved of responsibility? At what point do you want your responsibility relieved?

You must have an aggressive plan for marketing not only your community, but your park.

Will you continue as landowner, making land leases with prospective tenants? Will you construct buildings and serve as landlord? (See "Adding Value—the Spec Building," page 50.)

Regardless of the answers to these questions, you must establish an adequate budget to maintain the common areas, public and private infrastructure and amenities. Failure to do so may have legal implications. More importantly, the image of your community and your organization become inextricably tied up with the quality and image of the real estate you own.

MARKETING:

You must have an aggressive plan for marketing not only your community, but your park. While marketing is covered in greater depth elsewhere in this publication, you must remember that you now have two products to market. One is your overall community, while the second is a specific piece of real estate.

WORKING WITH PROFESSIONALS

A good team of development professionals cannot be underestimated. Extensive value added is provided by assembling this team early in the process. In order to reduce costs, you may wish to identify a volunteer task force of realtors, builders, appraisers, and others to assist in preliminary site identification. However, there is no substitute for paid professional staff.

At a minimum you will want to contract with a market specialist, engineer, environmental expert, surveyor and land planner or landscape architect. These services should be contracted through the use of a Request for Proposals (RFP) which allows a number of firms to submit bids. In order to expedite the bidding process, a limited number of firms should be invited to bid.

The RFP itself should be clear on the goals of the project and the outcomes desired. The level of detailed supplied in the RFP will vary depending on the project. If you believe there

ADDING VALUE —

The real estate downturn of the past decade resulted in the elimination of for-profit spec buildings. Banks and developers decreed that never again would they bring product to market without an end user. Unfortunately, many manufacturing companies reached a similar conclusion. As a result, many companies find themselves running far in excess of current manufacturing capacity and in immediate need of buildings. Those businesses that lead the recovery absorbed the remaining "good" buildings, resulting in a building shortage with no speculative market to fill the void.

Finding yourself the proud owner of a new industrial park, you may want to enter the spec building business yourself. Whether you have immediate prospect needs, or view the new building as a "model home" for the park, a spec building is a logical outgrowth of an industrial park building program. As it is unlikely that your venture into industrial park construction has left you with much borrowing capacity, you may want to seek a partner for such a venture. Your approach to this project will look familiar.

- Using your existing marketing information and analysis of your prospect needs, determine the optimum size for your spec building.
- Select a site within your industrial park. Your biggest asset in this project will be

the ability to "bring the land" to the deal. Nearly every park has a less than desirable lot. Many economic developers choose this site for their spec building, as it minimizes the value of the land that is tied up in a project.

- Establish development goals for your organization. What return do you want to receive on your investment? Is this financial return, number of jobs created, types of jobs or a combination of the three? Is this building going to serve an immediate need, or be your "model" to lure prospects into a build-to-suit opportunity? How reliable is your market model? Do you trust it enough to build a fully fitted spec building, or is a shell building* more appropriate? Are you seeking an active partner in the project? If so, how much control are you willing to give to your partner?
- Develop a request for proposals for architectural services based on the above. If you are planning to seek an active partner, the plans should include working sketches and a preliminary budget

▶

---

*A shell building consists of walls and ceilings, with minimal lighting and heating and no flooring or interior finish. The building is finished to tenant specifications at time of lease and/or purchase.

are specific variables that will affect the project (potential for endangered species, unusual infrastructure needs), these factors should be identified in the RFP. Failure to draft a clear RFP will result in inconsistent proposals and unanticipated cost add-ons.

A good RFP should also provide bidders with an understanding of the intended evaluation criteria. Not only will this help the company present itself in the best possible light, but it will help ensure that your needs are met by the proposal. If experience with similar park

Whether you have immediate prospect needs or view a new building as a "model home" for ▶

THE SPEC BUILDING

suitable for review by bidding partners. If you are pursuing this project on your own, have a more fully developed set of construction drawings and bid specifications prepared. A number of partnership options may be available to you.

Local banks or utility companies may agree to participate, either through low/no interest financing or by assuming a portion of the equity risk in the project. This leaves full project control in the hands of the local economic development group. Such participation is limited. If the building does not move quickly, you may find yourself in the position of having to develop alternate sources of refinancing. (At this point you will understand why private developers have given up on this type of development.) Private partnership alternatives may also exist. If you wish to pursue this alternative, an additional request for proposals is in order. This RFP is presented to qualified developers and may take one of two forms:

- Considering your previously established goals, you may seek a specific risk/reward structure. This provides you with maximum control, but it limits the creativity of private investor/developers and may result in fewer interested parties.

- Invite the creativity of the private development community, asking them to propose a structure that meets your goals while ensuring their profitability.

Some typical results from a proposal of this nature may include:

▶ Private financing for construction, utilizing the real estate as community equity in the project.
▶ Shared risk, with greater risk accruing to the community the longer the property is held before lease or sale.
▶ Up-front private developers' fees, with proportionately greater ownership by the local economic development group.
▶ Pre-identified marketing strategy focusing specifically on the building.
▶ Private developer marketing initiatives.
▶ Economic development group veto power over specific sales or leases, based on job creation and business type.

This process is also used to solicit private investment in industrial parks. Because the time to sale for an industrial park is likely to be many years, private developers will view this as more risky. More aggressive terms will be required to attract this investment.

▶ *an industrial park, a spec building is a logical outgrowth of the park building program.*

projects is a priority, indicate this. Similarly, involvement of local firms may be politically important. You will no doubt have several evaluation criteria. It is helpful to provide a relative weighting to the major criteria.

Bids may come from "dirt-to-deed" real estate advisory firms, from multidisciplinary teams or from individual firms seeking to undertake a single segment of the work. It may be tempting to try to manage costs by hiring the various skills individually and as needed.

> **A good RFP provides bidders with an understanding of the intended evaluation criteria.**

This requires that you attempt to forge a team from various firms, and may result in a gap between, for example, market factors and design interests.

Establish your role as team leader early. Don't expect your team to understand the subtle differences between economic development goals and more traditional market goals. Without your ongoing guidance, market constraints may result in a final product that fails to meet your goals for quality development.

A WORD IN CLOSING

There is no risk-free way to stimulate economic development, and industrial park development certainly wouldn't be a contender for the list. Nor can you rely solely on your park to draw new and expanding business to your community. The lists of site selection criteria grow annually, and you have to develop strategies to address them all. Yet, one thing remains constant. Your community can have all the available human, financial, cultural and other resources to make a location work. But if there are not attractive, reasonably priced sites available to meet the demands of new and growing companies, they simply cannot make a decision in your favor. To paraphrase, "If you don't build it, they sure won't come."

■

*EDITORS' NOTE: For additional and more detailed information on the industrial park development process, see **Business and Industrial Park Development Handbook** (Urban Land Institute, 1988).*

*About the Author.....*Susan Lackey

Ms. Susan Lackey is Executive Director of the Washtenaw Development Council in Ann Arbor, Michigan. Prior to taking this position in 1994, she was senior vice president for economic development at Cornerstone Alliance in Benton Harbor, Michigan. While serving in this capacity, she was responsible for the initial development of two business/industrial parks.
In addition to being a Certified Economic Developer, Ms. Lackey is a member of the American Institute of Certified Planners (AICP). She can be reached at 313.761.9317.

CASE STUDY:

CORNERSTONE INDUSTRIAL PARK

In 1989, the Cornerstone Alliance undertook the construction of a light industrial park to attract appropriate job creating opportunities to residents of the Benton Harbor Metropolitan Area. Few planned industrial areas existed in the community, and those that were generally suffered from aging facilities, poor access, and other constraints. An attempt to create an in-town park to attract more suburban industrial development had been hampered by land acquisition issues. In short, the climate seemed ideal for such a project.

This case study explores some of the steps taken to bring this project to fruition and place what the Alliance's Chairman described as the "first stake in the ground in the areas redevelopment."

CONDUCT INITIAL REVIEW

A task force was initially established to guide the project. Consisting of elected officials from the city and an adjoining township, a builder/developer, a realtor and a local business person, the task force was charged with finding a site that would allow the Alliance to meet its mission of developing jobs with an emphasis on the City of Benton Harbor.

Immediate challenges to be addressed included the bankruptcy of a similar initiative in the 1970s and the lack of property within the city limits for development. The former concern was addressed to establishing an aggressive financing strategy which maximized the use of state and federal grants, and established firm goals for land acquisition costs. Additional support was provided by site visits to a nearby community with an extensive network of community-owned industrial parks. The latter was resolved by establishing a tax base sharing agreement between the two units of government, allowing for land transfer from the township to the city.

DEVELOP POLICIES AND GOALS

The task force established a variety of policies. Land would be priced at market rate, with write-downs allowed to make deals workable. Land sales would be made only to Cornerstone clients, and only to those companies with the ability to create substantial goals. All land acquisition would be completed in the public view.

COMPLETE MARKET STUDY

Staff undertook an informal market study, which established a need for high-quality, modestly priced light industrial property for small- to medium-sized businesses. Ironically, the first project in the park was a joint venture of Ford Motor Company and Rockwell International.

IDENTIFY SITE

Only one site was identified—a parcel in the township adjoining the city and adjacent to an abandoned landfill. While hardly an ideal site, it was the only property where a tax base agreement could be applied under the conditions of state law at that time. Several landowners were involved, and the site was reconfigured after some real estate prices exceeded the guidelines established by the task force.

PRELIMINARY PLANNING

Preliminary planning identified several major challenges. The adjacent land fill had resulted in some contamination on the subject property. This was resolved through extensive environmental testing to describe the contamination, and the drafting of site boundaries to avoid contaminated areas. A bisecting stream was established as a natural area, providing a site amenity. Finally, in an effort to hold down costs, the organization had contracted with a neighboring university to perform required archaeological reviews. Student identified pottery shards and arrow heads threatened the project briefly, until these were identified as typical of west Michigan farms.

More seriously, infrastructure costs were identified as being cost prohibitive. Several strategies were developed to address this. First, a series of state and federal grants were targeted, with the understanding that no development would take place until such grants were assured. Second, additional land was identified and acquired. The location of this land within the township itself allowed additional benefit for a community which might otherwise have been perceived as "giving up" revenue to the city. Finally, redesign of the water system allowed a portion of the cost to be defrayed by an extension to a neighboring residential area which had not previously been served. An additional grant designed to assist distressed residential neighborhoods supported this effort.

LAND ACQUISITION

As noted, some landowners took advantage of the perceived deep pockets of the Alliance to inflate land costs. While this might have been avoided had the Alliance approached property owners anonymously, community cooperation and support was the key to reasonable costs on other parcels.

PLANNING / ENGINEERING / DESIGN

A Request for Proposals was issued to local engineering and design firms to complete work on the project. The accepted proposal included a phased approach, which allowed the Alliance a variety of "out points" in the design process. This meant that the Alliance could cancel the process if, at any time, it proved infeasible. The firm selected had extensive experience in similar private projects, and has leveraged the Alliance activity into a new specialty working with economic development projects.

CONSTRUCTION

Phasing ultimately resulted in Phase II construction taking place prior to Phase I. However, the timely receipt of grants ultimately allowed both phases to be fully completed. Daily site visits by both Alliance staff and the engineer/construction manager ensured that very tight time frames were met.

Time frames tightened considerably when Ford Motor Land placed an offer on 20 acres in the second phase of the project, provided construction timetables could be met.

MARKETING

In addition to the usual marketing efforts of the Alliance, specific fact sheets and brochures had been developed to serve the needs of the Cornerstone Industrial Park. These were provided to prospects which meet the parameters originally identified in the policies established by the task force.

NOTE: By 1995, the Cornerstone Industrial Park was approximately 45 percent sold, including a build-to-suit facility owned by the Alliance and leased to a minority-owned auto supplier. Nearly 400 persons were employed in the park. The Alliance's experience with this park was seen as sufficiently successful that, in 1993, they began a second park, a high quality, amenity driven technology and business park known as the Elisha Gray Commerce Park. Whirlpool Corporation is the anchor tenant in this new facility.

— Susan Lackey

PROFESSIONAL TEAM CHECKLIST ✓

PROJECT TITLE _____   PROJECT NUMBER_____

MARKET RESEARCHERS

Experienced in "making" a market. The best market research professionals will have worked on economic development projects and understand how to create a market where none exists.

*NAME:*_____   *PHONE:* _____

ENVIRONMENTAL TESTERS

Diverse. In addition to experience with contamination issues and soil-bearing capacity, you should ensure that your environmental team includes people who understand wetlands, endangered species and related issues. Make certain, as well, that your professionals are on good terms with the regulatory colleagues. This doesn't mean they have to always have agree on definitions and solutions, but that mutual respect exists.

*NAME:*_____   *PHONE:* _____

PLANNERS / LANDSCAPE ARCHITECTS

Experienced in planning similar projects in the private sector. Firms with private sector experience will understand the need to provide flexibility and be familiar with existing market conditions. Thus, they can become active partners in converting the market research to design.

*NAME:*_____   *PHONE:* _____

ENGINEERS

Knowledgeable about state/local permits and current conditions in area.

*NAME:*_____   *PHONE:* _____

SURVEYORS

A good survey team can do much of the "leg work" for the engineers and planners, resulting in reduced costs.

*NAME:*_____   *PHONE:* _____

REAL ESTATE DEVELOPMENT CHECKLIST ✓

PROJECT TITLE _____   PROJECT NUMBER_____

	PLANNED DATE	ACTUAL DATE
CONDUCT INITIAL REVIEW		
Review client and lead files	_____	_____
Inventory existing buildings and sites	_____	_____
Interview allies	_____	_____
Assess competitive communities	_____	_____
DEVELOP POLICIES AND GOALS TO GUIDE IMPLEMENTATION		
Identify target industries	_____	_____
Establish inducements	_____	_____
Establish pricing policy	_____	_____
Establish realtor policy	_____	_____
COMPLETE MARKET STUDY		
Identify market requirements	_____	_____
Estimate land absorptions	_____	_____
Identify any special inducements	_____	_____
Revise policies if required	_____	_____
IDENTIFY POTENTIAL SITE		
Access issues	_____	_____
Visibility	_____	_____
Infrastructure availability	_____	_____
Special zones/districts	_____	_____
Community concerns	_____	_____
COMPLETE PRELIMINARY PLANNING		
Contamination	_____	_____
Wetlands/endangered species	_____	_____
Infrastructure	_____	_____
Site configuration	_____	_____
Reconsideration site selection if necessary	_____	_____
LAND ACQUISITION		
Obtain impartial advice	_____	_____
Be open	_____	_____
Set top end on terms and price	_____	_____
PLANNING / ENGINEERING / DESIGN		
Infrastructure analysis	_____	_____
Flexible lot configurations	_____	_____
Phasing plan	_____	_____
Amenities	_____	_____
Landscaping/signage	_____	_____
CONSTRUCTION		
Hire a construction manager	_____	_____
Celebrate	_____	_____
Stay involved	_____	_____
MARKETING		
Ongoing management	_____	_____
Special materials and campaigns	_____	_____

CHAPTER 5

ZEN IN THE ART OF TARGETING

Eric P. Canada
Partner, Blane, Canada Ltd.

A young developer walking down the road approached a crossroad. In each direction was a town offering opportunity for the traveler. One path appeared more warn and rutted. Another path appeared straight and unbroken to a distant mountain ridge. The final path was shrouded in the silent matte of a bamboo forest. Along which path, thought the young developer, is the opportunity I seek? Stopping to consider this, the young developer sat beneath a tree, promptly falling asleep to dreams of success and riches waiting down the road. Waking sharply to the sound of heavy foot-falls, the young developer looked up to see a little man bent over his walking stick approaching. Stopping the old man, the young traveler asked, "Which way should I go to achieve my success?"

"Which fruit do you seek, the easiest to pick or the juiciest?" asked the old man.

Seemingly ignoring the question, the young man went on, "This path has more ruts. Opportunity must be ripe in that town."

"Do many people know what is right for you?" queried the old man.

Without looking at the passerby, the young developer added, "I see distant mountains that must be crossed if I take this path."

"Are you intimidated by the effort required to cross?" asked the little man.

"Along this last path lies a great bamboo forest posing questions of the unknown."

"Is it risk you fear?" asked the old man.

"Along which path is the opportunity I seek?" concluded the young developer.

"What reward makes you happiest?" asked the man.

"The path into the forest it will be."

"Ah Grasshopper, it is so."

———— o ————

Economic development is about choices. It is about seeking harmonic balance among varied interests and wide-ranging needs found in every community. Deciding what to target is a different question for every community. Industrial development is not the only form of economic development as tourism/convention advocates are happy to argue. Development strategies take on many forms. A remote community has different options than a rural, suburban, or urban community. The economic development marketing strategy must fit circumstances, interests, and needs of the community. The art in economic development is in matching the development to the community and its people. For example, following is a random selection of development strategies:

- Dubuque, IA...*dog racing and river boat gambling*
- Indianapolis, IN...*amateur sports events*
- Lemont, IL...*antique shops*
- Littleton, CO...*growth in existing businesses*
- Ludlow, CA...*a combination gas station and restaurant*
- Memphis, TN...*distribution companies*
- Mt. Horeb, WI...*a mustard museum*
- State of North Dakota...*cooperative food processing businesses*
- St. Paul, MN...*entrepreneurship*
- Trenton, GA...*retail*

Not every development strategy is forever. Dubuque's dog racing strategy came during a period of severe unemployment. At that time, the gaming strategy helped rebuild the economy, however, Dubuque's leadership never intended to supplant Las Vegas as the gaming capital of the United States. Today, the successful gaming strategy continues as an element of the economy, but it is not the cornerstone of the community's future. Their future is anchored on diversifying the industrial base with white-collar, distribution, and other primary jobs.

Most economic development begins with some form of business attraction. The goal of a business attraction strategy is to bring new investment and jobs from outside the community be they manufacturing, tourism, or retail. Then potential investors from corporations, private individuals, or government can be approached by development organizations to solicit their expansion project, relocation, or formation of a new business unit in the community.

STRATEGY

Selecting a development strategy usually begins with an inventory—formal or informal—of strengths, weaknesses, and available resources. Business attraction has a variety of substrategies related to product strengths.

Some of these substrategies are also important to expansion and retention of the existing business base.

RESOURCE BASED

Although becoming less of a factor, access to a raw material or a critical resource can provide the competitive marketing strategy. The historic concentration of steel manufacturing around the Great Lakes is such an example.

MARKET BASED

A market strategy builds on the size of the available market for a given product or service. The market demand created by a large company or cluster of companies using similar components is the basis of a supplier or market-based strategy. The just-in-time inventory management technique of some manufacturing companies increases the opportunity for a market-based strategy. A market-based strategy can also be applied to demand for consumer products, especially those high-volume/low-weight consumer products that have a large transportation cost, i.e., potato chips.

LOCATION

Memphis' successful warehouse/distribution marketing is based on its strategic location. Suburban communities focus heavily on a location strategy that borrows heavily on the name recognition of the core community, i.e., Vaughan, Ontario, Canada, "The City Above Toronto."

EXISTING BUILDING

As every state and utility development representative points out, the majority of industrial suspects are primarily interested in available buildings. A suitable building can save the company three to six months of start-up during the development phase. A shell building strategy is a powerful employment generator when properly executed. Sioux Falls, South Dakota, Litchfield, Illinois, and the State of Virginia have successfully used this strategy. This strategy entails a high level of financial risk for the development organization, unless executed by a private sector developer.

PERSONAL PREFERENCE

People make the decisions about where businesses will locate. The personal preference strategy is based on offering a significant life style advantage: if the decision-maker will reside there. Typically these advantages relate to a hobby, sport, or cultural interest of the target decision-maker. Close proximity to golf, skiing, hunting, retirement, or a vacation home are examples. Wisconsin Public Service in Green Bay is an example of working to attract investment through vacation homes to nonresident owners.

After a strategy is selected, the next step always entails finding potential investors—corporate, private, government, or a combination. Decision-makers invest the money necessary to make something happen.

The discussion that follows centers on targeting primary jobs in manufacturing, processing, or white collar operations. The principles and practices described can be applied to any economic development marketing strategy.

WHERE IS THE TARGET?

Michael Porter of Harvard Business School argues in his book, *Competitive Advantage*, that as consumers gain expertise, they gain bargaining power. They become an increasingly difficult market demanding higher quality products and an increased level of service. Porter states, "Products have a tendency to become more like commodities over time as buyers become more sophisticated, and purchasing tends to be based on better information."

This evolution has already occurred in economic development. Company executives and site selection consultants now demand lower prices, ask for more incentives, and expect additional services. There are frequent examples where the location prospect "plays" one community against another, driving up the total cost of being successful for state and local development organizations.

Yet, the *all too common* practice in economic development is to target the most demanding prospects: corporate real estate executives. The Industrial Development Research

Council (IDRC), International Association of Corporate Real Estate (NACORE), and site selection consultants represent the most advanced consumers of economic development's products and services.

> *The developer's mind-set has been to chase deals, do deals, and push on to the next chase. This attitude ignores the potential for repeat business.*

Why target the toughest buyers? In part, because targeting corporate real estate executives and site selection consultants is easy. The lists are easily acquired. Events are open to anyone willing to pay the price. The audience is obviously involved in the corporate decision loop. The activity is highly visible to the board and, finally, less sophisticated buyers are much harder to identify. Yet, under Porter's premise, *development professionals would be smart to target companies with little or no site selection experience.*

In business marketing the accepted rule of thumb suggests:

- 70% of all business comes from repeat clients
- 15% comes from referrals
- 15% comes from new client development

While there is no hard evidence to support the application of this rule to economic development, the anecdotal evidence of many communities suggests it is a reasonable yardstick. "The developer's mind-set has been to chase deals, do deals, and push on to the next chase," points out Roy Williams, former EVP/COO of the Greater Phoenix (AZ) Economic Council. "This attitude ignores the potential for repeat business." In other words, development professionals have been deal-driven. As such, they ignore 85 percent of the market.

Deal-driven simply means a supply-side orientation. This is what we have available. Take it or leave it. Ryans and Shanklin noted the same problem in both their book, *Guide to*

Marketing for Economic Development, and their 1985 research of economic development marketing. They concluded, "Marketing is an increasingly important element in effective economic development efforts, but not marketing as it is viewed by many in the economic development field today. Rather, we are talking about marketing founded on a *marketing or demand orientation*—one that puts the prospect, the relocating or expanding firm, and its needs *first* in priority. Too often state or city economic development groups focus on what they are willing to 'give' or 'concede' to the prospect, that is, they adopt a supply-side orientation."

CUSTOMER SERVICE ORIENTATION

To access the upper 85 percent of the development market without giving up opportunities in the lower 15 percent, a fundamental change must occur in the practice of economic development. Development organizations must begin to aggressively adopt the Total Quality Management (TQM) principles developed in the business world. They must place a true customer orientation and relationship building in the center of their economic development strategy.

Development strategies must work to build trust and confidence within clients. It must communicate the desire to help solve problems, not just push product. Economic development must become a value-added service in site selection. Professionals must learn more about issues affecting prospect companies and their bottom line. As Robert Koepke, Ph.D., CED, and editor of American Economic Devel-

opment Council's *Economic Development Review* put it, "If an operative in the CIA wants to be a Russian specialist, he first has to think like a Russian. He has to immerse himself in the Russian's world." *Development professionals must immerse themselves in the world of their business prospects.*

There is evidence of a growing awareness of need for a client-driven environment in economic development. For instance, the Greater Phoenix (AZ) Economic Council has conducted a customer service survey to help evaluate their performance. Working with the North Dakota Department of Economic Development and Finance, Blane, Canada, Ltd. conducted an extensive customer use and preference survey of development professionals. The purpose was to set benchmarks to rationally align services with the needs of the department's primary partners in development and local development professionals in North Dakota.

While this growing awareness is very encouraging, recognition of the need for customer orientation in economic development is in an embryonic stage. Much work still must be done to bring the tools and techniques to the majority of development organizations.

THE PRACTICE OF TARGETING

Creating a marketing strategy always encompasses analyzing and selecting one or more target markets. A target market is simply an identified group of companies the development organization wants to reach. In economic development, the ultimate target should be companies with needs and preferences that match the community's resources.

Development organizations must adopt TQM principles and must place a true customer orientation and relationship building in the center of their economic development strategy.

A target market is simply an identified group of companies the development organization wants to reach—ultimately those with needs and preferences that match the community's resources.

The purpose of targeting is to eliminate wasted effort.

Targeting separates a general universe into desirable and undesirable categories. The marketing message is then directed at the desired audience which may include subgroups. Ideally, marketing should be a rifle shot at a specific company, not a shotgun blast in the direction of an industry group. In economic development, targeting exploits opportunities by identifying companies that have growth potential. The assumption is that growing companies will need the product offered by development organizations.

Targets represent the best opportunities for development and/or opportunities to diversify a local economic base.

The five general industry sectors targeted by economic development programs are:

- distribution
- office/service
- tourism
- manufacturing/processing
- retail

Targeting has implications for promotional planning and product improvement. Once a target audience is identified, trade shows or conferences can be selected where members of the target audience are likely to be found. When Sioux Falls, South Dakota, wanted to diversify its economy in the early 1980s, a decision was made to target back office operations. Sioux Falls and state development officials crafted a special package of incentives designed for financial back office operations. The combination of Sioux Falls' low-cost environment, infrastructure, and incentives resulted in the decision by Citibank to relocate a credit card operation to the city.

An audience designated for target marketing can be identified by using any shared characteristic. Historically, economic development targeting has relied on Standard Industrial Classification (SIC) codes because of convenience and availability. The SIC system is a ready-made tool that allows industrial marketers to divide industrial firms into market segments based mainly on the types of products produced or handled.

A target audience may be a large or small group. For example, a community could target SIC Major Group 30—Rubber and Miscellaneous Plastic Products as shown in Figure 1, or a target audience can be SIC 308, Miscellaneous Plastic Products, a subgroup of SIC 30. A narrower target, SIC 3086, includes only companies manufacturing Plastic Foam Products. But even at this four digit SIC level, there are eight diverse industry subgroups including plates and cups, carpet foam, insulation, and shipping pads. Subgroup detail has been eliminated from each industry category except for the example in Figure 2. At each successive level of the SIC code the type of firm becomes more similar. To identify a significantly homogeneous target audience, it is frequently necessary to reach the six- or seven-digit SIC level.

Flipping through the SIC code directory at the public library will quickly show the complexity of SIC codes. This complexity creates significant problems for development marketers.

TRADITIONAL TARGETING CRITERIA

The following list indicates the type of criteria used in economic development targeting. These are used in combinations of two, three, four, five, or even six characteristics. Sometimes it is only a single factor like capital expenditure. Seldom would more than six

▼ **Figure 1**

Industry Group No.	Industry No.	The Major Group as a Whole
MAJOR GROUP 30.-RUBBER AND MISCELLANEOUS PLASTIC PRODUCTS		
301		**Tires and Inner Tubes**
	3011	Tires and Inner Tubes
302		**Rubber and Plastics Footwear**
	3021	Rubber and Plastics Footwear
305		**Gaskets, Packing, and Sealing Devices and Rubber and Plastics Hose and Belting**
	3052	Rubber and Plastics Hose and Belting
	3053	Gaskets, Packing, and Sealing Devices
306		**Fabricated Rubber Products, Not Elsewhere Classified**
	3061	Molded, Extruded, and Lathe-Cut Mechanical Rubber Goods
	3069	Fabricated Rubber Products, Not Elsewhere Classified
308		**Miscellaneous Plastics Products**
	3081	Unsupported Plastics Film and Sheet
	3082	Unsupported Plastics Profile
	3083	Laminated Plastics Profile Shapes
	3084	Plastics Pipe
	3085	Plastics Bottles
	3086	Plastics Foam Products
	3087	Custom Compounding of Purchased Plastics Resins
	3088	Plastics Plumbing Fixtures
	3089	Plastics Products, Not Elsewhere Classified

characteristics be used. However, computers make it easier to increase the number of the following characteristics considered in the targeting process:

- growth in employment
- growth forecast
- presence and location patterns within the state/region
- growth in the state/region
- resource needs
- energy consumption
- Standard & Poors or value line ratings
- location
- ownership
- employment
- sales growth
- supplier links
- wage rates
- labor skill requirements
- technology
- company size

Once the target industry is identified, the marketer's first question is, "Which companies?" Identifying the target industry allows the development marketer to begin the marketing process. With this limited information, it is possible to identify advertising mediums such as trade publications to reach companies that may be expanding. It is also possible to identify trade shows or conferences where executives from the industry will gather. To expand marketing further, especially with a limited budget, it is necessary to identify specific companies to target within that industry.

A few of the commercial industrial resource materials used by development professionals to create company lists for marketing include: *Dun & Bradstreet's Market Identifiers, Middle Market Directory* or *Million Dollar Directory, Sales and Marketing Management's* "Survey of Industrial Purchasing Power," *Standard & Poor's Register*, and state commercial and industrial directories. In most cases, lists are available directly from the publisher in a variety of formats including CD-ROM, and electronic access.

Computer technology has simplified the tedious process of list development and also allows for use of a greater number of qualifying criteria. New technology in computers and information technology is creating new opportunities for segmentation.

INDUSTRY CLUSTERS

Historically, economic development organizations have targeted individual firms within a select industry sector sharing a common array of products and SIC codes. Now there is a trend to target industry clusters. Industry clusters are concentrations of competing, complementary, and interdependent firms crossing several industries including suppliers, service providers, and final product manufacturers. Cluster participants develop and maintain strong linkages with other firms that support the production or distribution of their goods and services. Cluster groups incorporate companies with a wide range of SIC codes.

SRI International, a California research firm, has been heavily promoting this concept. They define a cluster as:

- a geographic concentration of interdependent firms
- sharing production technologies, suppliers, materials and resource needs
- selling into similar markets
- relying on the same economic foundations
- the core product sold outside the region

Cluster-based economic development targeting works with both retention/expansion and attraction strategies. Targeting by cluster takes into consideration the supplier-buyer-server linkages important to business. It is

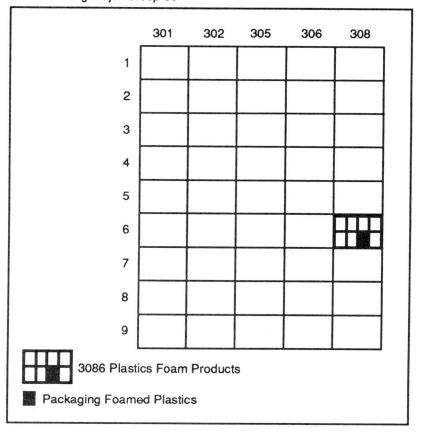

▼ **Figure 2**

Manufacturing Major Group 30

3086 Plastics Foam Products

Packaging Foamed Plastics

Cluster participants develop and maintain strong linkages with other firms that support the production or distribution of their goods and services.

---

broader than a supplier strategy because it can involve competitors using the same business infrastructure.

Clusters encompass both large and small firms sharing a common labor pool, information and technology. They are much broader in scope than target industries. Every cluster has a core industry. For example, a manufacturing cluster might be comprised of fabricated metal parts, machine tools, plastics, paperboard, and paint firms (Figures 3 and 4). The core company might manufacture tractors.

The concept behind cluster targeting is to identify companies that fill a gap, vertically or horizontally, within the cluster. This is accomplished by identifying companies to contribute a needed product or service or use similar business inputs. As shown in the example in Figure 4, a seat frame maker and upholsterer would fill a gap. A lawn tractor manufacturer

ILLINOIS ECONOMIC REGIONS: WHICH CLUSTERS ARE MOST IMPORTANT AND WHAT ARE THE LINKAGES? (% of Total Employment) (Figures may not sum to 100 due to rounding)							
	North East	North West	North West Central	East Central	West Central	South	Total State
Coal	0	0	0	0	2	4	1
Ag. & Food Processing	2	3	2	4	4	2	2
Industrial Machinery	2	9	7	3	2	2	3
Telecomm. Equipment	0	0	0	0	0	0	0
Electrical Equipment	2	4	1	2	1	1	2
Manufactured Inputs	3	7	4	3	1	7	4
Transp. Equipment	0	7	1	2	1	2	1
Consumer Appl./Electronics	0	0	1	1	0	0	0
Health Services & Biomed	9	8	11	11	14	11	9
Transp. & Distr.	4	2	3	3	3	3	4
Export Services	21	14	16	19	20	16	20
Business & Personal Travel	9	8	10	11	11	11	9
Non-Cluster Employment	47	38	45	41	42	42	45

Source: SRI International and DRI-McGraw Hill, April 1992

might share similar inputs (machine tools or fabricated metal parts). Attracting companies using these inputs help to diversify the existing cluster. Cluster targets are identified by their relationship to the cluster, not SIC code.

The implicit risk in a cluster strategy is the potentially negative impact of economic cycles. Economic downturn in one industry impacts the entire cluster. Hence, the community is increasing its dependence on a specific industry. Los Angeles' experience with defense industry cuts is an excellent example of the potential consequence of this strategy.

WHITE-COLLAR / BACK OFFICE

Large service firms generally divide their labor force into two sections—the headquarters with skilled workers who control the functions of the corporation, and back offices whose unskilled to semiskilled workers perform routine clerical functions.

One of the new challenges today for economic development marketers is the oppor-

tunity that is presented by the relocation of back offices. As site selection experts point out, back office operations do not generate revenue for a company because of intensive labor and real estate costs which can make up 85 percent of the total operating cost. These facts frequently support the need to consider alternative locations.

Historically, back offices were typically adjacent to the headquarters. However, advances in telecommunications and computer systems have allowed for the unbundling of headquarters and back offices, moving back offices from downtown areas to suburban locations with lower rent and wages, new labor pools, and improved productivity. As noted in the article, "Back Office Dispersal," CUED's *Commentary* (Winter 1993), "In the process of vertical disintegration—separating relatively routinized, capital-intensive, unskilled functions and moving them to peripheral areas, while retaining skilled, labor-intensive administrative functions in downtown areas—service firms follow much the same trajectory as many manufacturing companies before them, which sent waves of branch plants to the suburbs and beyond."

This vertical disintegration provides economic development opportunities for communities outside of the traditional urban/suburban corridors. Yet, for the development marketer interested in back office attraction, the target is no longer the headquarters or even a division. The target is the back office operation performing internal corporate function secondary to the primary product/service. Examples of these internal functions include:

- claims processing
- collection centers
- credit processing
- customer service

- data entry
- mail order processing
- order processing
- purchasing
- reservation centers
- technical support
- telemarketing
- warranty registration

SICs are not appropriate for identifying all back office opportunities as they are limited to a few broad business categories such as Finance (SIC 60), Insurance (SIC 63), Investment (SIC 67), and Data Processing (SIC 73). Targeting only these select industries would eliminate the majority of the back office industry found in other business sectors including retail, travel, lodging, manufacturing, and public utilities.

▼ **Figure 4**

Clusters in Illinois - Working Profiles

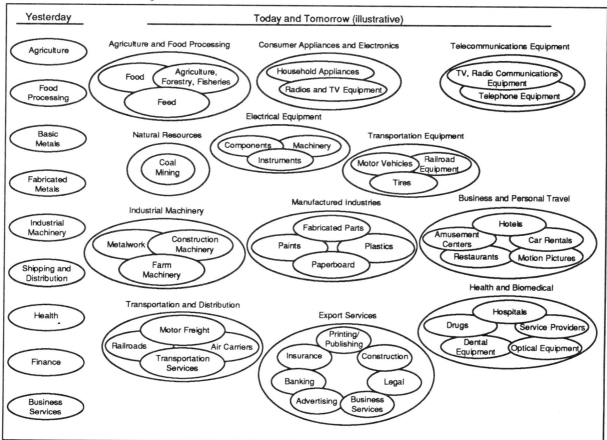

Source: SRI International and DRI-McGraw Hill, April 1992

The target is no longer the headquarters or even a division. It is the back office operation performing internal corporate functions. . . . The relocation of back offices is a new challenge for economic development marketers.

Primary relocation factors considered during the initial back office site selection process differ slightly from those used in selecting a manufacturing or headquarters facility. Relocation factors for back offices include:

- quality and size of the semiskilled workforce
- level of sophistication for telecommunications infrastructure
- quality of mail service
- available package and express package service
- existing Class A and B office space
- reliability of electric power system

DEVELOPMENT MARKETING EXPERIENCE

The consensus among development professionals interviewed by Blane, Canada Ltd. is that marketing to the back office industry is still an experimental process of trial and error. There is no proven pattern. The primary means of marketing is through relationships.

The Greater Des Moines (IA) Chamber of Commerce Federation has been successful at targeting back offices with SICs. David Maahs, executive director of the Ames (IA) Chamber of Commerce (formerly vice president of marketing with the Greater Des Moines Chamber), noted that an extensive public relations campaign targeting Chicago and other major insurance centers has been an important part of Greater Des Moines Chamber's back office attraction effort. Yet, once they have targeted back office industries with SICs, there is no easy way to target those without. According to Maahs, the best advice for targeting back offices is to work through contacts from area companies who identify back office opportunities within their own company. After the insurance industry, Des Moines targeted their existing retail companies and banks.

Fargo, North Dakota, has had success with back office attraction even though they have an unemployment rate of 3.2 percent. Their strategy is to offer a lower cost of living, and a unique selling proposition capitalizing on Fargo's under employment within their labor force. Through a telephone survey conducted by area universities, Fargo-Cass County Economic Development Corporation has been able to identify an estimated 44,000 underemployed workers within their multi-county labor shed.

Documenting the available workforce has been a powerful selling tool for Fargo resulting in a number of success stories. "Marketing to the back office segment has been very challenging," according to John Kramer, president of marketing for Fargo-Cass County Economic Development Corporation, "because industries have so many layers. It is hard to know where to focus a marketing attack. The president is still our primary target. Yet, in back office location decisions, we know the decision-maker is frequently not the president. We just don't know who else to go after."

ALTERNATIVE BACK OFFICE TARGETING STRATEGIES

What other alternatives exist for targeting the back office industry? Consider the possibility of using professional associations. Operators for telecommunications and management information systems become involved in back office relocation, consolidation, and reorganization decisions because of their job responsibilities. Many of these same individuals belong to metropolitan and/or national associations specifically for professional development and networking. These professional associations have membership lists that can be used for direct mail marketing and offer conferences for personal contact. These conferences provide an opportunity to learn about the needs and trends that affect their profession. The Chicago Industrial Communications Association and the International Customer Service Association are just two examples. Identifying potential target companies using specific criteria such as a job function is the essence of prospect profiling.

The principle behind the professional association strategy is similar to joining and participating in the IDRC or NACORE. The advantage is that the competition (other development professionals) is not in the room, or at least they don't outnumber the prospects (IDRC Gold Cards).

Another targeting option is to work through a contact associated with one of the major management consulting firms. These firms can be leading edge indicators because they assist companies in formulating reorganization strategies. They keep track of corporate reorganization activities for their own interests and also track the reorganization assignments of their competitors. With the right relationship, it would be possible to identify specific companies in a reorganization mode.

SMALL BUSINESS

Target marketers sometimes use "size" as a criteria. Small businesses as a target are a challenge to manage. The assumption is that they are similar because of their size. However, "small" businesses are not just little "big" businesses. This common assumption can have a negative impact on working with small business prospects. For example, consider sales

and distribution. Both are more challenging for small businesses because they lack the resources to build the distribution system enjoyed by big businesses. They also frequently lack the resources to develop sophisticated market research; consequently, their expansion plans are more tightly aligned with existing demand not anticipated demand. As a result, the site selection schedule is more likely to be shorter or more erratic reflecting the behavior of the market they serve.

Cash flow in a small business is king. Big business operates for profit; small business operates for cash flow. It is more difficult and more costly for small business to finance sales growth. At the same time, debt financing for small business is frequently a personal as well as a business risk. Financing is more elusive because small loans are more costly for financial institutions to service and accordingly less profitable than larger loans. Dealing with small companies requires different sensitivity by the development professional and different qualifying questions than when dealing with big companies.

CRITICAL QUESTION

Regardless of the industry segment, the critical question in targeting is, "What common characteristics define the company or unit you want to reach?"

Changing technology, along with a growing variety of databases and better sampling techniques, now allows development organizations to do a much better job of targeting. Unfortunately, many communities still rely on the old economic development research methodology using SIC codes.

The missing link from many targeting exercises is matching resources with the needs and preferences of the prospect. You need to identify companies with needs that may fit the product they have to offer.

No matter how good the specific targeting technique, one of the biggest challenges in economic development, especially at the community level, is the inelastic product. Each community is a very specific bundle of features, attributes, benefits, and weaknesses: location is fixed, the state legislative climate is outside of your control, and the size and skills of the workforce are given. A development organization can be 100 percent accurate in its forecast of expanding companies and still not succeed at attracting new jobs.

The missing link from many targeting exercises is matching resources with the needs and preferences of the prospect. This is one of the greatest weaknesses observed in current economic development targeting methodology (Figure 5). This weakness leads directly to the failure of many marketing initiatives to understand the target industry's needs and preferences. Without this information, target selection becomes an intuitive decision. Some development organizations conduct industry-specific studies. Unfortunately, this research as practiced in economic development is often oriented to determining the comparative operating cost. This orientation misses the opportunity to gather the "market intelligence" needed to refine targets and shape a marketing direction.

Development organizations really want to target those companies with active projects. Unfortunately, there is no "active projects" list. Every development professional has wished for such a list; however, since it does not exist, professionals work to find other ways to get close to company executives who may have projects. Therefore, development professionals must identify companies with needs that may fit the product they have to offer.

Industry research for economic development needs to be redefined. For example, a few years ago a client expressed an interest in a specific industry. Industry trends looked very good for continuing growth, and the region had a base of existing companies within the industry as well as related suppliers. On the surface, the industry appeared to be a very logical target. Blane, Canada Ltd. was hired to create a multi-year marketing plan toward which the client was ready to devote major funding. After the necessary background research on the industry, Blane, Canada Ltd. began interviewing top industry executives in management, real estate, product design, production, research, and planning. What was found did not support the common view of the industry's potential. Contacts related that the industry was loaded with overcapacity, and that global competition was rampant in pushing margins down. Sources revealed that a shakeout was eminent. The client was advised not to pursue targets within this industry. Within 12 months, the industry was making headlines daily with news of reorganizations and layoffs.

The point is that historical facts and trends only tell part of the story. Too often economic development targeting is built on this weak foundation. As currently practiced, industry research does not look for critical marketing intelligence such as needs, preferences, forecasts, outside influences, research and development, and other critical factors which will determine

▼ **Figure 5**

Win-Win Targeting

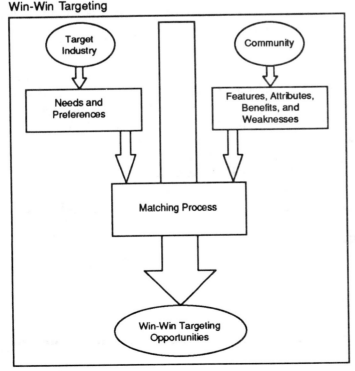

▼ Figure 6

```
                            TARGETING

Do ─────────────────          Don't ─────────────────

Match your product with your        Don't assume all companies within
target market's needs (or           a segment have the same needs.
perceived needs) using the
potential user's perspective as     Don't ignore your competitors'
the benchmark.                      actions in different market
                                    segments.
Define a segment broad enough to
provide adequate potential within   Don't forget that markets change
the segment.                        requiring adjustments to define
                                    targets.
Track successes and failures of
each target segment.                Don't concentrate only on actual
                                    buyers and ignore those who may
Make sure you have adequate         influence decisions.
resources to go after a target
segment.                            Don't assume that all your market
                                    segments cost the same to reach
Qualify your market target with     and offer the same potential.
sound research.

Continually look for ways to
pinpoint the needs of the target
audience.
```

the industry's future needs. Targeting opportunities for economic development professionals is much more accurately defined by these other needs.

FAILURE OF SIC TARGETING

By using SIC growth characteristics, development professionals hope to segment the enormous number of industrial companies into manageable units. Units are selected on an above average growth rate and forecast. The assumption is that growth will force facility consideration. The theory is that pinpointing opportunities in this manner will provide a starting point for marketing.

Unfortunately, SIC targeting produces a false sense of security among development marketers. SIC targeting is a *superficial segmentation*. Why has SIC code targeting become the dominant market segmentation concept in economic development marketing? There are six reasons:

- ▶ Experts tell us we have to target our marketing effort.
- ▶ SICs are easily accessible.
- ▶ SICs are easily defended as an approach.
- ▶ SICs were the best available technology of its day.
- ▶ SICs are easy to use in a marketing strategy.
- ▶ Experts have built models using SICs and defend their techniques vehemently.

In short, SICs have been the easy route to market segmentation. If SIC codes are the best tool for identifying targets, then:

— Why is there so much frustration with SIC marketing?
— Why have development organizations not produced better results using SIC marketing?

— Why are so many prospects outside of the targets identified?
— Why do industrial and service marketers not rely on SICs?

Problems with SIC targeting in economic development include:

- too broad at the four-digit level, requiring seven or eight digits
- lack of data at the seven- and eight-digit level
- driving factor of industry growth is sales and employment
- ignores nature of growth in the economy
- forecasts based on government surveys
- data sometimes too old to be reliable
- target industry studies lack inclusion of marketing information
- weak connection between targets and differential advantages

Many of the answers to these questions are in a better understanding of SIC and the dynamics of a free market economy. Economist Joseph Schumpeter first articulated the theory of "creative destruction" as a principle of economic growth in his 1934 monograph, *The Theory of Economic Development*. Under Schumpeter's theory of creative destruction, the economy grows through innovation and entrepreneurship. As some companies grow, others are contracting.

Schumpeter's definition of entrepreneurship differs from the dominant contemporary reference to small business. Schumpeter's entrepreneurship refers to the forces of change which induces modernization within industry. He argues that by destroying old methods and practices, industry frees itself from constraints thus allowing the opportunity for growth. Within any industry sector, firms are growing and replacing old firms which are declining.

As entrepreneurial companies seize new opportunities, they grow and increase their influence within the industry. Other companies bound by tradition and holding fast to old methods begin slipping, resulting in declining influence within the industry. In reality, every industry is comprised of growing and dying companies as shown in Figure 7.

Traditional economic development targeting relies on the overall industry average being greater than zero. Therefore, a growing SIC may encompass 60 percent growing companies and 40 percent declining industries, producing the desired positive average. Yet, another industry may encompass 40 percent in growth companies and 60 percent in declining industries, resulting in a net negative growth average for the industry. Since current targeting

▼ **Figure 7**

Target Industry Selection

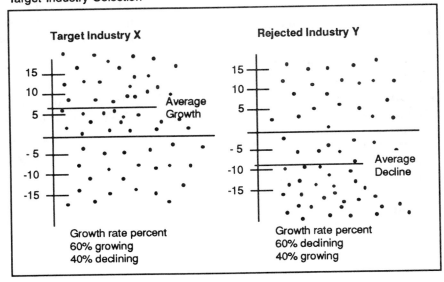

> *In the end, after extensive computer analysis of the results, target industries produced the same hit rate as randomly selected industries.*

methodology focuses on net growth industries, as shown in Figure 7, a traditionalist would automatically select industry X because it has an average growth rate of approximately 7 percent. Industry Y, with an average growth rate of minus 8 percent, would not be quickly discarded as a potential target. Looking closely again at Figure 7, is Industry X the best target for marketing?

The answer is in Schumpeter's theory of creative destruction and the truism taught in basic economics, "distribution is not equal to the mean." Schumpeter tells us that every industry has companies moving up and down even during a period of growth. So, by targeting Industry X we merely guarantee that over 40 percent of our marketing effort will be wasted on companies that are dying—companies slipping out of one market position into a new lower market position. Secondly, economics teaches us that an average growth rate does not mean every company in an industry is growing at that average rate. So how does the informed development professional decide where to focus marketing resources. Should the focus be on Industry X or Industry Y? Neither, because neither Industry X or Y are appropriate target audiences for economic development.

Development professionals, backed up by researchers and consultants, have been fighting reality by arguing that a growing industry means growing companies. Hence, frustration is brought on by results equal to those produced by random selection when target industries identified through traditional targeting methodology are used as the platform for a marketing campaign. For example, a two-year telemarketing test conducted by Tom Gulbranson, vice president of community development for Northwestern Public Service Company, produced 158 leads representing a 2 percent hit rate. To keep the test going, industries selected at random were used to generate telemarketing lists. During the first six months, identified targets were pursued and, Gulbranson said, "We went through the target industries very quickly. In the end, after extensive computer analysis of the results, targets industries produced the same hit rate as randomly selected industries."

Where is the target? A company's position in Industry X or Industry Y—above the zero line or below—is irrelevant to economic development marketing. In reality, the concern is not with the industry average but with the individual firm. What is important is the direction of change and rate of change of the individual company. The best development opportunities may well be companies below the line that are moving up and growing quickly. SIC codes are not a means of identifying specific growing companies.

Two examples will help illustrate this principle. The first example is the automotive industry. This industry does not show up on any list of growth industries. Targeting methodology would not conclude any community should target automotive manufacturing. Eight years ago in an automotive parts industry study for a client, Blane, Canada Ltd. found industry movement was being driven by a decentralization trend within the industry and the replacement of outmoded facilities. While researching development trends, the emerging technology for automatic braking systems (ABS) just appearing on luxury import automobiles was noted. Expert sources predicted a strong demand by American consumers. Within the last decade, ABS began to be offered as an option on American cars. Today, an ABS is standard equipment on a growing list of American models. As predicted, in a flat market where auto makers are dramatically working to cut overhead and consolidate suppliers, ABS manufacturing was a growth business opportunity.

The second example is general aviation. General aviation was in a depression created by onerous product liability laws. As a result, the General Aviation Manufacturers Association (GAMA) reported that the number of aircraft produced plummeted by 95 percent from a peak of 17,000 in 1978 to 899 in 1993. While investigating trends and developments, Blane, Canada Ltd. discovered that corporate aircraft manufacturers were drawing up plans to include global positioning systems (GPS) in the cockpit instrument cluster for corporate aircraft. The huge installed base of corporate and private aircraft, and lack of new aircraft available for purchase, creates pent up demand among pilots hungry to upgrade their current aircraft. Therefore, avionic companies with GPS technologies and GPS software companies represent a growth opportunity in an otherwise stagnant industry.

The point is that within any industry, regardless of the average rate of growth or decline, there will be pockets of opportunity. Identifying these pockets of opportunity will increase the demand for better development research. This research will benefit attraction efforts as well as retention and expansion of existing companies. Development professionals need to think less like economists and more like stock analysts.

A BETTER ALTERNATIVE FOR TARGETING

Using the terminology of Cognetics, Inc.'s founder, David Birch, development professionals want to pick the gazelles out of the crowd of elephants and mice. To accomplish this, Steve Buttress, president of Community Networking Institute, believes new economic development organizations will be comprised of equal parts, research and sales. He believes economic development cannot afford to continue its sales-driven mentality. Wayne Sterling, director of the Virginia Department of Economic Development and former director of South Carolina Development Board agrees. He invested heavily in research for every industry segment in which South Carolina had an interest. South Carolina's research staff included Ph.D.s, MBAs, librarians, and marketers. All are trained to be specialists in economic development. Sterling attributes South Carolina's successful marketing trips (one trip turned 40 percent of the attendees into prospects) to their

research-heavy approach to profiling companies for targeting.

TARGET AUDIENCE PROFILE

Since SIC code targeting is out of sync with the needs of economic development organizations, what does work? Development marketers are better served by the technique of profiling. Target audience profiling is a technique proven successful by industrial and consumer marketers alike. The target audience profile evolves from a string of characteristics. Each characteristic is general in nature, i.e., ages 25 to 35. When used in combination with another characteristic, i.e., married, the two characteristics combined reduce the size of the initial group population. Each successive characteristic, i.e., children, homeowner, can further reduce the group until all that remains are those with the greatest potential. In this example, candidates with the greatest potential would be those buying life insurance. Savvy insurance agents have learned from experience what characteristics are shared by their best prospects. They focus their marketing energies on these prospects rather than the broader class.

Profiling works like the childhood game Guess Who?™ where a player tries to guess the identity of a mystery person on an opponent's card by asking questions and eliminating faces on a game board that don't fit the mystery person's characteristics. A succession of questions, i.e., "Does your person wear glasses?" quickly eliminates characters from the possible suspects. Eventually, everyone is eliminated except the one pictured on the opponent's card.

Development professionals want to pick the gazelles out of the crowd of elephants and mice.

The skill in profiling is posing the questions which eliminate suspects most quickly, leaving behind prospects. In economic development, a target audience profile can be built from national trends, regional location experience, types of companies in the economic base, company management practices, resources, types of firms the leadership seeks to add to the community, or dozens of other factors. By using a succession of characteristics, the technique narrows the full universe of suspects into a manageable target audience. It defines a specific set of companies with the greatest potential for a location in the community.

Even though prospect profiling is a proven business marketing practice, the transition to prospect profiling will not be easy for development professionals. In part, development professionals have been conditioned to demand SICs as the output of a targeting exercise. Recently when discussing a draft marketing report with a client, the client's comment was, "It's real general." Although the report identified a number of specific target opportunities, the core of the report focused on structuring a prospect profile to be used to identify target companies for a planned marketing campaign. No SIC codes were used to identify these targets because the target audience shared a business practice preference—not an industry. After further discussion, it became clear that the client felt uncomfortable defending the concept of profiling to his constituents. What the comment actually implied was "where are the SIC codes?" Once identified, the problem was resolved quickly by significantly expanding the rationale for profiling in the report. This showed how the profile characteristics were to be used and how specific companies would be identified for the campaign.

Another challenge to the widespread use of profiling in development is the need to organize and maintain marketing databases. Historically, development organizations have been careless with documenting and maintaining marketing strategies and results. Consequently, critical information is lost. Since past successes and failures provide the best clues to success in the future, gathering, organizing, and analyzing market intelligence from each of our successful as well as unsuccessful prospects is an important role of the development marketer. By gathering this type of information, every community can identify its own unique prospect profile characteristics.

USING A PROSPECT PROFILE

In many cases, the target audience is not restricted to a type of product or a specific industry, which are the characteristics easily identified by SICs. For example, many back office opportunities as discussed earlier, are operational units such as:

- customer service
- claims processing
- report processing
- order processing
- telemarketing
- accounting

These operational units are found in all types of business, including finance, manufacturing, publishing, insurance, software development, and government. Some have SIC codes and many others do not.

Sample Prospect Profile

- ❑ privately held
- ❑ employs 50-400 workers
- ❑ pays above average wages
- ❑ makes regular investments in new products (R&D) or new markets
- ❑ desires to control production in-house
- ❑ has a large regional market

The practice of prospect profiles seeks to group the market into clusters sharing common characteristics. Again using the example of a back office operation, a few of the common characteristics shared by these operations include: sophisticated, telecommunications-intensive demands, extensive computer support systems, inbound 800 numbers, outbound WATS lines, and labor-intensive operations. Each of these characteristics offers clues as to how to locate companies sharing these variables.

Depending on the marketing technique to be used, these characteristics can be used individually or in combination to identify specific companies. As the marketing process evolves, other characteristics identified through feedback from the marketing effort can be added to refine the focus of the marketing activities.

More time is required to construct a marketing database from a prospect profile than from simply ordering a SIC list from a vendor. Using existing database research tools, the individual companies sharing these characteristics can be identified for the marketing effort. This will take a number of steps. The reward for the investment is reduced marketing costs and a dramatic increase in quality.

The prospect's characteristics with the strongest connection to the development organization become the focus of the marketing message and the central theme of the marketing promotion effort.

REAL WORLD PROFILING IN AN ECONOMIC DEVELOPMENT ENVIRONMENT

When the focus shifts from a product (SIC code) to a use, how can prospects be identified? The following example resulted from this case study research for a client's airport industrial park. The profile is designed to identify companies with a management preference for the use of corporate aircraft in the business.

GOAL: Target potential airpark tenants.

OPTIONS:
- Companies with aviation related products (SIC codes)
- Companies performing aircraft related maintenance, retrofitting, etc.
- *Companies with a management preference relying on corporate aircraft*
- Express shippers, freight forwarders, and air cargo operators

CHALLENGE:
Identifying companies that have a management preference for location near an airport

PROSPECT PROFILE:
Management preference for corporate aircraft

AIRCRAFT CRITERIA:
- Registered aircraft
- Fleet aircraft
- Business uses
- Aircraft type
- Effective service range

BUSINESS CRITERIA:
- Sales minimum
- Number of employees

Each of the factors listed in the profile is very general. Yet taken as a group, they describe a very limited number of companies with a preference for using corporate aircraft within range of a given airport industrial park. In this case, to apply this profile, the marketer begins with the Federal Aviation Administration's (FAA) aircraft registration.

APPLYING THE AIRCRAFT CRITERIA

All aircraft owners: The FAA contracts with a company in Colorado to maintain, manage, and make available the ownership records of every registered aircraft in the U.S. The company will sell this list to anyone. But the list contains approximately *192,000 aircraft registration numbers.*

Corporate aircraft: Eliminate commercial service aircraft, i.e., Delta Airlines, and personal aircraft registered to individuals — *46,000 registered aircraft remain.*

Business operators: Eliminate non-business fleet users, i.e., the State of Arizona's government aircrafts and other government fleet operators — *21,500 registered aircraft remain.*

Aircraft type and service range: Select only aircraft of a certain type, i.e., twin turboprop, and select registrations within a 4-hour flight range of the airpark — *3,800 registered aircraft remain.*

APPLYING THE BUSINESS CRITERIA

Sales over $3 million: Eliminate small companies — *2,500 registered aircraft remain.*

Number of employees 100 to 1,000: Eliminate small, one-facility companies — *2,100 registered aircraft remain.*

Ownership: eliminate duplicates caused by multiple aircraft ownership — *1,400 registered owners remain.*

Target companies — 1,400

As the FAA database is maintained on computer, this sorting and screening of aircraft criteria can be completed very quickly. Applying the business criteria requires merging the aircraft database with a corporate database to access the needed sales and employment records. Again, computers make this step much easier than a similar manual process. As can be seen in Figure 8, each additional criteria reduces the general population to a more specific group of individuals or, in this case, companies.

One of the tremendous benefits of profiling is the end product—a list. In the FAA example, the original list of aircraft owners included addresses and phone numbers. The end product was a target list of 1,400 aircraft owners. This list is merged with another list of businesses that adds further information such as CEOs, CFOs, sales, and products. At the end of the pipeline, the development marketer is in an ideal situation. Not only are the targets identified, but they are in list form on computer and available for immediate implementation.

Once a profile is created, it can be used as a screen to qualify prospects brought in by allies. Through the experience of matching a prospect's needs, interests, and characteristics, the profile can be refined.

▼ **Figure 8**

Prospect Profile Targeting

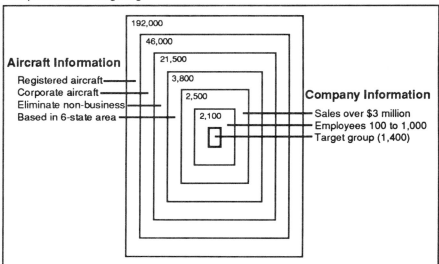

SUMMARY

Based on its resources and interests, every community must determine what type of economic development strategy is appropriate. Industrial development in only one of the options suitable for some communities. To implement the strategy, a development organization must identify individuals, companies, or units of government willing to invest in the community making the strategy a reality.

Identifying those investors, the targets, has produced tension between researchers and development marketers. This results largely from a failure of understanding. Detail oriented economic researchers live life like their orderly tables and numbers but do not really understand the dynamics of marketing. Marketers eschew detail and seek the creative, innovative, and the novel. These differing personality types have created tension between the marketer and the researcher, frustrating both sides. Traditional economic development targeting has come to represent the gorge between the two.

The target audience profile technique is a powerful tool for development marketers. Using this tool eliminates much of the battle between research and marketing, producing harmony. As in the principles of Zen, the quest is to eliminate disharmony to achieve a personal state of marketing nirvana.

About the Author..... Eric P. Canada

Eric P. Canada is a psychologist by training, an entrepreneur at heart, and an economic developer by choice. Mr. Canada has more than 20 years experience in economic development including managing local development programs. He has successfully adopted business-to-business marketing techniques to economic development marketing challenges. A few examples of these adaptations include client contact research, prospect profiling, predictive retention tools, and direct response advertising. Mr. Canada can be reached at 630.462.9222 (e-mail: ecanada@ix.netcom.com).

INDUSTRY PROFILE CHECKLIST ✓

(This Checklist was provided by Audrey Taylor of Chabin Concepts.)

PROJECT TITLE _____   **PROJECT NUMBER**_____

Industry Name: _____   SIC Code: _____

Product(s):_____

ACCESS TO MARKETS:

Does this industry tend to locate within a geographic proximity of its major markets?
□ YES   □ NO

For this product, is it better for this company to be situated close to raw material/supplies or markets?   □ YES   □ NO

How important is a transportation network so that markets and resources are easily accessible, i.e., open roads all year?

	VERY	SOMEWHAT	NOT
– trucking (what type: _____)			
– air	___	___	___
– bus	___	___	___
– railroad	___	___	___
– port	___	___	___
– overnight air	___	___	___
– mail	___	___	___
– highway/freeway/interstate systems, etc.	___	___	___

How do transportation costs affect the product/service cost?

_____

Is it important to reach markets within a certain time, i.e., overnight?   □ YES   □ NO

Are convenient people-transport services (primarily airports and freeways) a concern for this industry in order to bring customers, suppliers, business associates to the companies, or for sales travel to customers?   □ YES   □ NO

RESOURCES:

Does this industry buy raw materials, resources, or intermediate manufactured goods from a specific portion of this country?   □ YES   □ NO

Where? Why? Please classify raw materials and goods purchased.

_____
_____

INDUSTRY PROFILE CHECKLIST

How do transportation costs affect the resource(s) cost?

_____

Do companies within this industry consume large quantities of energy (gas, electric or a combination) for plant operations?   ☐ YES   ☐ NO

If so, what is the average consumption rate per day? _____

What type of energy is needed? _____

What would the average company pay for energy each month, as a percentage of expenses?

_____

Is energy dependability a concern for the industry?   ☐ YES   ☐ NO

Do companies within this industry consume large quantities of water for plant operations?
   ☐ YES   ☐ NO

If so, what is the average consumption rate per day? _____
Type of water is used? _____

On average, what are the waste disposal needs of companies within the industry for the following:
   – water effluent? _____
   – toxic waste? _____

Does the industry situate itself within areas that offer a high quality of business, professional, and technical services?   ☐ YES   ☐ NO

If so, give specifics please: _____

_____

Please list the type(s) of communication network systems that companies within this industry tend to want nearby.

_____

Are earthquake-proof areas attractive to this industry? (For example, information processing companies need to locate in earthquake-proof areas so that their services are not interrupted.)
   ☐ YES   ☐ NO

What type(s) of support companies are critical to this industry's efficiency and cost effective operation?

_____

INDUSTRY PROFILE CHECKLIST page 3 ✔

FINANCIAL NEEDS:

What type of financing structure is usually needed by this industry? Please circle, rank (1–9), and explain the appropriate choices:

	RANK
– working capital	____
– lines of credit	____
– long-term land and building	____
– equipment	____
– inventory	____
– seed fund	____
– R & D	____
– letters of credit (export)	____
– v.c.	____

Are seed equity funds, debt funds, and venture equity funds demanded by companies within this industry on a regular basis? (For example, high-technology companies must devote huge sums of money for research and development (R & D) so that they can produce new, technologically advanced products as often as possible, satisfying market(s) that put pressures on them to produce such products.)

☐ YES   ☐ NO

What percent of financial assistance is desired? _____ %

QUALITY OF LIFE:

How important are the following quality-of-life issues to this industry and its workforce?

	VERY	SOMEWHAT	NOT
– Number of hospitals/health care facilities	____	____	____
– Area's image, recreational activities, and cultural diversity	____	____	____
– Physical environment and climate	____	____	____
– Sense of physical stability	____	____	____
– Housing quality and cost, including number of subdivisions, both existing and proposed	____	____	____
– Rent comparisons for homes and other dwellings	____	____	____
– Transportation (including accessibility to public transportation) and commuting stage	____	____	____
– Living costs other than for housing	____	____	____
– Child care facilities for employees who are parents	____	____	____
– Quality and number of postsecondary/vocational colleges or universities	____	____	____
– Metropolitan amenities	____	____	____
– Airport facilities (within one, two, or three hours)	____	____	____

INDUSTRY PROFILE CHECKLIST

SPACE:

Does this industry prefer to locate within: ☐ R & D/business parks   ☐ industrial parks
☐ industrial/warehouse buildings ☐ commercial office space

Which does the industry require: ☐ build-to-suit facilities   ☐ shell (warehouse) design

Please list the typical acreage requirement: _____

Is it typical for this industry's companies to own unutilized acreage ready for expansion?
☐ YES   ☐ NO

Are company facilities typically: ☐ owned   ☐ leased
☐ leased with option to purchase

Do other industry-types locate adjacent to this industry? (For example, a wholesale hardware store may locate next to a wholesale store such as Price Club.)   ☐ YES   ☐ NO

Are the companies within this industry beginning to relocate outside of high-cost (primary land and workforce) areas such as the Bay Area and Los Angeles Basin?   ☐ YES   ☐ NO

If so, please explain the critical issues causing the move.

_____
_____

Does this industry require outside storage?   ☐ YES   ☐ NO

REGULATIONS AND TAXES:

What regulatory agencies monitor the products/services offered by companies within this industry?

_____
_____

How do these agencies and their regulations affect the industry as a whole, i.e., product/service cost(s)?

_____
_____

What state regulations affect the industry, and how do they affect its companies and their ability to do business?

_____
_____

INDUSTRY PROFILE CHECKLIST

Are the following taxes and costs of doing business a concern for this industry? If so, why?

☐ YES ☐ NO Employee, including worker's compensation insurance costs and unemployment taxes _____

☐ YES ☐ NO Property taxes _____

☐ YES ☐ NO Personal taxes _____

☐ YES ☐ NO Corporate taxes _____

☐ YES ☐ NO Sales/use taxes _____

☐ YES ☐ NO Business license _____

☐ YES ☐ NO Local taxes, including utility and impact fees _____

Are areas within the United States which offer attractive corporate tax structures, such as no business taxes, enticing companies within this industry to relocate and expand outside of the state?   ☐ YES   ☐ NO

Or is this state still considered to be an appealing place to do business?   ☐ YES   ☐ NO

WORKFORCE:

What is the breakdown, by percentage, of the workforce needs for this industry as a whole?

___% unskilled   ___% semiskilled   ___% skilled   ___% technicians   ___% professional/managerial

On average, what is the prevailing wage rate paid by this industry and its companies for these skill levels?

_____ unskilled   _____ semiskilled   _____ skilled
_____ technicians   _____ professional/managerial

Are areas with lower wage costs for the aforementioned skill levels being considered as possible site locations more now that ever before?   ☐ YES   ☐ NO

If so, which areas are competing for this type of business?

☐ Midwest   ☐ South   ☐ East   ☐ Overseas (specify: _____)

If the industry utilizes an unskilled workforce, is there a need for basic training, e.g., literacy?
                    ☐ YES   ☐ NO

Can this industry's work force be trained?   ☐ YES   ☐ NO

If the industry is technical, what vocational training or type(s) of skill is (are) primarily needed? _____
_____

Is there a need for customized training, such as welding or computer literacy?
                    ☐ YES   ☐ NO

INDUSTRY PROFILE CHECKLIST

How does this industry recruit employees?

☐ Through a personnel agency   ☐ Through in-house advertising
☐ Through job training programs   ☐ Other: _____

Do a majority of companies within this industry utilize job training programs (e.g., JTPA, PIC)?   ☐ YES   ☐ NO

On average and listed by percentage, how many people does this industry employ?

___% MANAGERS   ___% SUPERVISORS   ___% PRODUCTION WORKERS   ___% CLERICAL WORKERS

What strengths and characteristics would a typical company employee possess?

_____

What are the percentages of women and men in the industry's typical workforce?

_____% WOMEN   _____% MEN

How important are the demographics of the labor pool for this industry?

☐ VERY   ☐ SOMEWHAT   ☐ NOT IMPORTANT

Which figures, and why?_____

Is employee transportation a concern? ☐ YES   ☐ NO

Does the industry and its companies tend to locate within close proximity of each other and share a common labor pool?   ☐ YES   ☐ NO

EDUCATIONAL INSTITUTIONS AND THE WORKFORCE:

How important is the educational system: *VERY SOMEWHAT NOT*

– elementary   ___   ___   ___
– secondary   ___   ___   ___
– community college   ___   ___   ___
– university   ___   ___   ___

Does this industry as a whole use job placement programs offered by colleges or universities?   ☐ YES   ☐ NO

Is there a need for a vocational school to be located in close proximity to the companies within this industry?   ☐ YES   ☐ NO

INCENTIVES:

Does this industry know about enterprise zones?   ☐ YES   ☐ NO

If so, are these zones and their state and local incentives (primarily tax breaks) attractive?
☐ YES   ☐ NO

How attractive are the following incentives?   **VERY SOMEWHAT NOT**

- low-interest loans   —   —   —
- lower electrical rates   —   —   —
- readily developed industrial parks   —   —   —
- competitively priced land and land leases   —   —   —

What other incentives could be used to entice this industry to an area?

_____

Is a community which is poised to work closely with the relocating firm more attractive to one that is unresponsive?   ☐ YES   ☐ NO

If so, who is the best person/group for the community to work with:

☐ a person from the company   ☐ real estate manager
☐ a developer   ☐ other (specify: _____)

MISCELLANEOUS:

Does this industry primarily consist of: ☐ small business owners   _____%
                                           ☐ corporate facilities and subsidiaries?   _____%

What is the average facility size of companies within the industry? _____

When companies within this industry need to relocate or expand, how much time is allotted for a search?
            _____ days   _____ weeks   _____ months   _____ years

What is the geographic concentration (primary within this state and/or the United States) of this industry type? _____

Does this industry export?   ☐ YES   ☐ NO   If so, to which countries?

_____

Does the industry have a real estate division and managers associated with it?
☐ YES   ☐ NO

INDUSTRY PROFILE CHECKLIST

List the magazines and newspapers most widely read by the owners, executives, and plant managers of this industry.

_____   _____

_____   _____

_____   _____

List the trade associations most popular for this industry:

NAME _____   *NAME* _____

ADDRESS _____   *ADDRESS* _____

_____   _____

_____   _____

PHONE _____   *PHONE* _____

NAME _____   *NAME* _____

ADDRESS _____   *ADDRESS* _____

_____   _____

_____   _____

PHONE _____   *PHONE* _____

What are the critical and emerging issues facing this industry?

_____

_____

_____

_____

Could this industry and its companies offer telecommuting to its workforce?

☐ YES   ☐ NO

CHAPTER 6

SCORING WITH PARTNERS

Robert Cooper, CED
President, Spokane Area Economic Development Council

Robert Potter
President, Jobs Plus

A hiker stumbled while walking along a narrow path and fell into a deep ravine. Fortunately, he grabbed a shrub and was saved before plunging to the rocky floor 3,000 feet below. Another hiker saw him and threw him a rope.

"No thanks," he said. "God will save me."

An old prospector came along, saw the unfortunate fellow's plight, and reached over to try and pull the poor fellow out, at great risk to his own well-being.

"No thanks," said the hiker. "God will save me."

A rescue helicopter appeared and a rescue worker descended precariously by a cable. As the pilot struggled to save him and offered his hand down to him, the man said, "No thanks, God will save me."

Just then, the shrub gave way.

When the hiker appeared at the pearly gates, he asked, "Why didn't you save me?"

God replied, "I sent you the hiker, the prospector, and the rescue helicopter. What else do you want?"

—— o ——

If a community wants to be saved by attracting companies, it should not wait for divine intervention to intercede. From the very outset, practitioners need to identify and include necessary and appropriate partners. Successful recruitment of new businesses to your area is the result of numerous community partners acting in a sequence of events that meets, and hopefully exceeds, your prospects' needs.

Recruitment is definitely a team sport. If, as the community's economic development professional, you are the quarterback, coach, cheerleader, and manager in creating and playing the recruitment game, consider a time out. There's too much at stake for you to be a maverick and on the ball all by yourself.

In this chapter, you will learn how to identify and bring together your recruitment partners. No one partner will make or break a recruitment deal, but it is the synergy of partners acting together that can help you close deals and win recruiting contests.

If you are the quarterback, coach, cheerleader, and manager playing the recruitment game, consider a time out.

Who are your potential partners? Some will be obvious and, hopefully, others will generate new ideas for you to utilize. No recruitment deal will need all of these partners. But with experience you will learn how and when to put your best team in the field. Playing off David Letterman's Top 10 concept, here are ten types of recruitment partners separated into the private and public sectors:

PRIVATE SECTOR:

1. Financial/Legal
2. Utilities/Transportation
3. Labor/Education
4. Real Estate/Development
5. Associations
6. Hospitality
7. Quality of Life
8. Media

PUBLIC SECTOR:

9. State Government
10. Local Government

INVITE PRIVATE SECTOR PARTNERS TO PLAY

The eight private-sector partner categories all have something in common: they represent people who should be members of your economic development council or corporation. In other words, they should be investors in your recruitment process. For example, in Spokane, Washington, private sector members invest $600,000 annually to the community's local recruitment budget. The population of Spokane County is approximately 400,000. Just 19 miles across the state line in Coeur d'Alene, Idaho, the private sector contributes $200,000 annually toward recruitment activities. The population of Coeur d'Alene County is approximately 100,000.

The bottom line is, if you don't have private sector companies as members, start today to change that situation. This is an obvious indirect way the private sector can be a partner with you. The following pages will enumerate ways in which the private sector can be a direct partner in your recruitment process.

If you don't have private sector companies as members, start today to change that situation.

First and foremost, remember that a business relocation or expansion is based upon the economic viability of the move. Is it going to help the company be more profitable? Is it going to be more profitable to move to your state versus your competition? Quality of life is only the icing on the cake in their decision-making process.

Based upon the assumption that a prospect's move is being made through a sound business and planning process, your primary partners need to be:

- Financial/Legal professionals
- Utilities/Transportation sales staff
- Labor/Education providers
- Real estate/Development sales staff

FINANCIAL/LEGAL PARTNERS

Accountants

Have a local CPA firm complete a brief report or study comparing your state taxes against the competition. Have them do it for a variety of your target industries, company size and net profits. Make these reports available to prospects. Use accountants during the time when prospects are first visiting the community. They are very helpful in explaining your state tax system to out-of-state prospects. Usually this takes no more than 30 minutes. They also ask very good questions regarding a prospect's financial stability. This may help you cull out weak prospects. Arrange for the time accountants spend with your prospects to be on a pro-bono basis (i.e., gratis)—it is great public relations for them to see potential new clients.

Attorneys

Attorneys are not used nearly as much as accountants, but they can contribute sound advice regarding international trade laws, immigration, visas, etc.; procedures for establishing a new corporation in your state and the rules involved; land use rules and regulations regarding zoning, permitting, development; industrial revenue bonds and tax increment financing. Request that they provide counsel on a pro-bono basis, pointing out that your prospects are their potential clients. Market the pro-bono time provided by these professionals as community incentives to prospects.

Institutional Lenders:
Banks, Savings and Loans and Thrifts

Engage the help of bankers as an asset to your recruitment process by:

▶ Discussing financing for the prospect's capital equipment, building loans, operating capital, inventory, lines of credit, etc.
▶ Orienting them to both public and private sector financing (revolving loan funds, SBA 7A, SBA 504, HUD, block grants, etc.).

▶ Conducting credit checks on your prospects.
▶ Analyzing business plans, which helps you prioritize your time between real prospects and risky ventures. Use bankers' knowledge about the area's economy and include them as hosts when you are conducting prospect visitations.

Involve bankers in creating unique incentive packages for your prospects, such as pre-approved mortgage loans for your prospect's key staff when they move to your area.

UTILITIES/ TRANSPORTATION PARTNERS

Electrical/Gas Companies

Most large electrical/gas companies have key staff designated to an economic development strategy. Recruitment is usually a component of their strategies. Typical ways they can help you include:

▶ Preparing cost comparisons between your city and the prospect's current operations. (Get copies of their current utility bill, and your partner will interpret the rest.)
▶ Sharing advertising costs in certain publications.
▶ Sharing costs of participating in trade shows and sales missions.
▶ Helping you and your prospect review the capabilities of any industrial/commercial building to see if it fits their power needs.

Most utilities will also help your prospect in the designing of a new building. Use this pre-engineering study as an incentive for your prospect and have the utility donate their time. Many utilities have special energy-saving programs, so have your utility representative explain these programs. The staff of a region's utility company could be "loaned executives" to major prospects during the site development process. This is an excellent incentive, but use it only for your largest prospects.

Telecommunications

Telecommunications is more than just your local dial tone or long-distance telephone companies. Telecommunications is truly the infrastructure of the future. Both manufacturing and back office operations demand the best in digital switching stations, fiber optics, dual back-up capabilities, etc. From fax lines to sophisticated CNC machine computer systems, the telecommunications operators can assist you and your prospects in designing a program to meet their needs. Most telecommunication companies will help your prospect in reviewing the capabilities it needs with respect to specific industrial/commercial buildings.

Telecommunications is truly the infrastructure of the future.

Most telecommunication companies will also help in the designing of a new or existing building. Use this pre-engineering study as an incentive for your prospect and have the telecommunications company donate its time. Use your telecommunications staff early in the recruitment process. Have the prospect meet them during their initial visits. Ask your largest telecommunication provider to complete a brief study or report which discusses all of the telecommunications capabilities within their service area. Make this report handy for general inquiries from major telecommunications users, such as insurance offices, credit card centers, data centers, telemarketing operations, reservations centers, etc.

Water/Sanitary Sewer Companies

Many areas in your community or county will be served by private water and sanitary sewer companies. Introduce yourself to the key district staff for the relevant water and/or sanitary companies (relevant meaning those districts that serve your commercial/industrial prospects). Larger districts typically have professional engineering and marketing staffs to assist you and your prospects in water/waste-water capacity and design issues.

Transportation Companies: Trucking, Railroads, Ports, Air Cargo

Your prospects will need to ship their products out somehow, and you need to bring the right partners to the table to help them through this process. The availability and costs will be the prime issues to discuss. Have your transportation partners complete detailed surveys regarding their services and capabilities. These reports should be organized by the EDC for distribution to your prospects. Introduce your transportation partners to the prospect only when appropriate. Don't bring them in too early, as it would be information overload during the initial visit for your prospect. Your prospect may have an interest in property owned by railroads and ports. Know your key contact, and discuss the availability and incentives for their respective properties. Some of your transportation partners may also be interested in helping you promote the area by sharing costs of advertisements, direct mail campaigns, and trade shows.

Introduce your transportation partners to the prospect only when appropriate. Don't bring them in too early, as it would be information overload for your prospect.

LABOR/EDUCATION PARTNERS

Employment Resources

When you survey most corporate site location consultants and ask them what the primary needs of their clients are, they will usually respond, **"labor force."** Knowing that labor availability, productivity, and costs are paramount to your prospects, you need to respond accordingly with the partners you assemble. Key labor force partners include:

- **Human resource managers from local companies**—These individuals will be frank in telling your prospects the truth about your labor force. However, most of the time they close the deal by sharing availability and productivity data with prospects.
- **Private placement/employment agencies**—Your recruitment staff can use them for pay scale knowledge and availability of certain occupational titles that may be missing from the local state employment office.
- **Private technical/vocational colleges or institutes**—Good partners when your prospect has specific interest in their graduates and the quality of their programs. These institutions are often overlooked, but you need to have a working relationship with them. If your prospect is going to be hiring a significant number of employees, they may be quicker to respond with custom training programs than your public academic partners.

Education Resources: Colleges, Universities, and K-12 Education

Many communities are fortunate to have both public and private educational institutions. Your private partners are an extra bonus for your recruitment efforts. In the Spokane region are two private universities: Gonzaga and Whitworth. Gonzaga has a national reputation for its engineering, business, and law schools. Whitworth is also recognized for its academic excellence and international trade experience. From a recruitment perspective you can:

- ▶ Utilize the presidents of these institutions when hosting prospects.
- ▶ Utilize faculties to discuss the unique aspects of their students, departments, and research capabilities.

- ▶ Utilize institutions to promote educational options for the prospect's key staff and their families who would move to your area.

Private K-12 institutions have become a preferred option in many large metropolitan communities. Most prospects will naturally inquire about your community's private schools. You need key contacts with these partners to whom you can introduce your prospects. You should always have an inventory of your private K-12 schools, the number of students, and enrollment fees. All of these schools will have printed materials for you to mail to prospects. Take the time to tour their schools and understand their mission statements.

REAL ESTATE AND DEVELOPMENT PARTNERS

Architects/Engineers

These professionals will certainly add to the quality of your presentations. Architects are usually willing partners in giving free estimates for new construction or the remodel of existing buildings. Prospects will need this information for business loans or just to compare your city's business costs with those of your competition. Engineers are very helpful in cost estimates too. The determination of environmental impacts is occurring more frequently than others in the recruitment process. Most real estate transactions require a minimum of Level I environmental reviews. Environmental engineering firms can help you create unique incentives by providing this service for free or at reduced costs.

Architects are usually willing partners in giving free estimates for new construction or the remodel of existing buildings.

Real Estate:
Commercial and Residential

All of your prospects will eventually have to locate in a commercial facility, be it an industrial plant or office environment. Your partnership with the commercial real estate community is mandatory. How you work with them will be the tricky part. If you are a membership organization, the issue of equity or fairness in sharing your leads with them becomes important to both partners. Always remember: the needs of your prospects come first. Commercial brokers can help you by:

▶ Professionally showing or representing their commercial listings. As an EDC employee, never try to go around your broker or act on his or her behalf.
▶ Giving you knowledge as to the vacancy of certain buildings and the market rents for Class A and B buildings and industrial facilities.
▶ Cost-sharing in advertisements promoting your community and their buildings.
▶ Cost-sharing in the hosting of prospects to your community.
▶ Providing referrals to your organization when you work as a team on their prospect.
▶ Never sharing their leads with other brokers.

Residential brokers can be equally supportive in your recruitment efforts. Small companies that plan to relocate will evaluate your community from both a profitability and quality-of-life viewpoint. Housing will be very important to them and their key employees. Large corporations will be heavily oriented to the profitability and market penetration issues. However, they will eventually be concerned with the ability to relocate and recruit key employees. Residential brokers can help you by:

▶ Professionally showing the different housing areas and representing the community assets in general.
▶ Providing colorful brochures depicting the community with pictures of existing homes and their prices.

▶ Acting as ambassadors and hosts to your prospects during their visitation process.
▶ Joining your staff on sales missions to the prospect's facilities.
▶ Creating customized programs to the employees of the relocating company.

Once a company announces their relocation or expansion to your community, it is helpful to arrange for a residential broker to fly to the company's hometown to make a special presentation to the company's key employees and their spouses.

Contractors and Developers

These professionals are very helpful in giving you and the prospect free estimates on the cost of developing a new facility. Try to bring several builders and/or developers to the table for your prospect to work with. Make sure you have adequate information from the prospect prior to having your development partners spend their time on any proposed projects. Some of the larger developers may co-sponsor advertising programs and participate in hosting of prospects.

Business and Industrial Parks

Business and industrial park owners or managers have a direct interest in your success and the needs of your prospects. Most owners will be extremely helpful by: co-sponsoring special advertisements to promote your community and their parks, paying to host prospects or site consultants, producing quality brochures which you could use to promote your community, or participating in trade shows with your staff.

ASSOCIATION PARTNERS

In every community are associations or organizations that can be helpful to your recruitment efforts. The most obvious ones are:

• **Chambers of Commerce**—Good resources for passing on leads to your EDC. They should be financial investors in your program, have quality brochures or videos available, and serve as a great source for finding volunteers to use for hosting.

- **Manufacturing associations and networks**—Good sources of information for your prospects in their needs for industrial suppliers or sub-suppliers.
- **Port and redevelopment districts**—Unique legislative units of government that have financing or development opportunities for your prospects and should be financial investors in your recruitment program.
- **Associations of realtors and general contractors**—They should be financial investors in your recruitment program and usually have professional staffs and unique information/statistics to help with your presentations. They can also be helpful with sharing advertising costs and hosting.
- **Associated industries**—Membership organizations that help employers with personnel laws, hiring and firing practices, personnel handbooks, training seminars, wage surveys, etc. These types of organizations can provide you with prevailing wage information for your prospects.
- **Convention and Visitors Bureaus**—Sources for business leads/referrals. They also produce high-quality brochures and videos which you can use for promoting the community and tracking community events in calendars to use for prospect visitations.
- **Regional partnerships with other EDCs**—To share costs of hosting site selection consultants, conduct joint sales missions, exchange information, and present joint proposals to prospects you are mutually recruiting to the region. (See "Case Study: The Relocation of Harper's Furniture," page 95.)

HOSPITALITY PARTNERS

There are two primary hospitality partners to consider for your recruitment efforts: hotels and airlines.

Hotels can be valuable in-kind members of an EDC. Instead of them paying membership dues, use their hotel rooms for your prospects. This is a win-win-win partnership: the prospects stay in their hotels for free, the EDC saves its precious budget dollars for other recruitment uses, and the hotels provide a valuable public service while showcasing their properties. Each of your prospects is a potential future customer of theirs.

Airlines can serve a similar role as the hotels in your community. In securing your regional airlines to be in-kind members of your organization, you can receive a limited number of free airline tickets to use for sales missions or hosting prospects.

QUALITY-OF-LIFE PARTNERS

The two primary quality-of-life partners to include in your recruitment efforts are arts and culture, and sports and recreational partners.

Arts and culture partners may include a symphony, Broadway play series, civic theater plays, art galleries, and art museums. The Spokane Symphony, for example, is an in-kind member of the Spokane Area EDC and issues free season tickets to host prospects. Members of the boards of directors from the various organizations are often helpful in hosting prospects to their respective events. Their hope is that the company will relocate and be interested in supporting their activities.

Sports and recreation partners in your community may include a professional baseball team, professional hockey team, private golf courses, boating clubs, hunters, and fishing enthusiasts. Depending on the prospect's interest, try to match them with respective community partners. Once prospects are serious about your community, their representatives will visit several times with their families and key employees. You will need partners to help make their visits enjoyable and memorable. The professional sporting teams, as in-kind members of your EDC, may provide free tickets to their events. Use members of private golf and country clubs to host your prospects.

MEDIA PARTNERS

While the media is not a partner in the traditional sense of others cited in previous pages, they do play a very important role in any community. You need to establish some guidelines and develop a working relationship with both print and broadcast media.

*Establish guidelines and develop a working relationship
with both print and broadcast media.
Their management understands that an EDC's business success
will pay them direct dividends.*

The media should definitely become financial investors in your recruitment efforts. All television and radio stations, daily newspapers, and business publications should be dues-paying members. Their management often understands that an EDC's business success will pay them direct dividends.

Partnerships with their respective news departments should also be developed. Meet with local business reporters on a regular basis to establish your credibility as a business information source. Encourage them to promote good news. Use these positive stories as testimonials of the competitive advantages offered by your community, and distribute copies to your prospects.

Never leak a story about a prospect looking at your area. Your client's confidentiality is paramount, and your ethics as a professional economic developer is bound to this code of confidentiality.

If the media does get wind of a prospect looking at your community, do not confirm or deny it. Simply tell them you cannot respond to their inquiry and you will do your best to personally give them a story when you have one. Remind them again of the importance of this kind of confidentiality and how your community could lose a prospect if you don't maintain their confidence in your organization.

GET PUBLIC SECTOR PARTNERS IN THE GAME

Your public sector partners are equally as important as your private sector partners. You just have fewer options to choose from to help you on a regular basis, as compared to your private sector partners. There are two levels of public sector involvement which are critical to the success of productive partnerships for economic development organizations—state and local governments.

While the federal government can and does periodically play an important role in your recruitment efforts, especially in rural areas, your criteria may be oriented more to regular or frequent contacts between you and your partners. With changes in federal government, it appears the block grant concept is taking hold. Consequently, more programs and authority will be given to the state and local government levels.

When building partnerships with the public sector—regardless of which level, state or local—the common denominators are educational institutions, elected officials, and departments that impact the development process.

*When building partnerships with the public sector,
the common denominators are educational institutions,
elected officials, and departments that
impact the development process.*

STATE GOVERNMENT PARTNERS

Educational Institutions

Establish close working relationships with the administration and training providers at your community college. Don't hesitate to include them in your hosting itineraries or sales missions to the prospect's facilities. Community college systems are likely to be the primary providers of employment training programs for most of your recruitment prospects. Tap the resources of your state university systems. They not only create an ongoing pool of workers for your prospects, but they provide research and development opportunities for prospects to cooperate and collaborate with. Encourage community colleges and universities to be financial contributors and members of your EDC. They should also be represented on your board of trustees.

Elected Officials

Your state senators and representatives can be important partners in your recruitment efforts. Their role is to set policy for the state's economic future. They need your positive input. Some prospects like to know the state's attitude toward business. Use your legislators, when appropriate, to help answer this question. For example, the State of Washington passed legislation in 1995 to exempt sales tax on equipment purchases by manufacturers. This was extremely good news to local manufacturers and the companies we were working to recruit. The most obvious state-elected official who can help you is your governor. You may not always be able to use the governor, especially if there is another community in the state competing for the same prospect, because he or she cannot show favoritism. However, when you are the only community in your state being considered, the governor can write, call, or visit your prospect. Use this resource wisely and save the governor's time for the most important prospects.

State Departments

Every state has a Department of Commerce or Trade and Economic Development division. It is important to know recruitment staff and ensure that they know your recruitment strategy, including your industry targets, unique buildings and properties, sales mission, and trade show dates. Inquire as to their advertising schedule, and see if there are any opportunities for collaborating.

In rural areas, the state Department of Commerce is truly your partner, since you have a limited budget. Its staff can help you with your strategy development, business cost comparisons with other states, and hosting prospects. Seek to understand your Department of Commerce's target industries and any unique incentives they have to offer. Request that you receive any responses they get from their national advertising campaigns. Most states advertise in economic development and business journals.

Know your state's recruitment staff, and make sure they know your recruitment strategy, industry targets, unique buildings and properties, sales mission, and trade show dates.

Also be aware of other state departments that can help in your recruitment efforts. If you don't pave the way for your prospects, they will have to interface with those departments at some point on their own. Get to know the people who handle issues in your state's:

▶ Department of Revenue, for tax and license issues
▶ Department of Ecology, for environmental compliance issues
▶ Department of Employment, for programs to help screen, train, and place employees

LOCAL GOVERNMENT PARTNERS

Local government partners will probably be more familiar to you than state government partners. They should be—and usually are— very important to your recruitment success.

Local government partners can be categorized into educational institutions, elected officials, and city/county departments dealing with development issues.

Educational Institutions

The primary educational institutions at the local level are your K-12 school districts. You should have a directory of your county's school districts with names of key contacts. Your prospects will appreciate your assistance in organizing this information. Once your prospect is truly interested in your community, he or she will definitely want information on your public schools. Develop personal relationships with your area's school superintendents. They are great salespeople, and your ability to arrange for them to meet personally with the prospect is always impressive. Research and become knowledgeable about any K-12 skills center program or vocational/technical education programs in your district. This is a great source of labor for your prospects.

Elected Officials

The elected officials you should have as partners include city council members, the mayor, and county commissioners. These partners should know and have copies of your recruitment strategy. Your elected officials should receive quarterly progress reports on your recruitment activities. Don't just see them at budget time if they are funders of your program. Your city and county should be member-investors in your EDC. Many EDCs will have representatives from the city and county on their boards of trustees. Use elected officials for appropriate prospect visitations, as not all prospects are interested in meeting politicians. Know your prospect's viewpoints on this topic before you set up an ill-fated meeting. Be sure to invite your elected officials to all press conferences or open houses in which you celebrate a recruitment success.

Local Departments

Just as you have involved elected officials in your recruitment strategy, quarterly progress reports, hosting opportunities, and press conferences, apply the same efforts in working with your city manager and county executive officer. These two officials will drive your public budget requests and pave the way through the various bureaucratic departments for the benefit of your prospects. In addition to the senior executives for your city and county, you need to develop personal relationships with the planning director, public works director, and community development director. Close communication is a must.

Finding just the right partner is a possibility in just about any community. Through your own resourcefulness you can build a project team that will make an excellent impression with your leads and prospects. Sometimes, the right partner is in the surrounding states. The Harper's Furniture case study that follows is an excellent example of what can be accomplished when a team of economic developers in two states works together to make a project happen.

About the Authors ..... **Robert Cooper and Robert Potter**

Robert Cooper is President of the Spokane Area Economic Development Council, a private nonprofit corporation comprised of more than 250 member businesses. Mr. Cooper has more than 22 years of economic development experience and a broad knowledge of economic development issues. Bob Cooper can be reached at 509.624.9285.

Robert Potter is President of Jobs Plus Inc., a nonprofit corporation formed to diversify and broaden the economic base of Kootenai County, Idaho. The mission of Jobs Plus is to recruit quality companies that offer citizens top-quality career employment opportunities. Bob Potter can be reached at 206.667.4753.

CASE STUDY:

THE RELOCATION OF HARPER'S FURNITURE*

Depend on it: partnerships can breed greater productivity. Just look at the 1992 success in recruiting Harper's Furniture and its 500 jobs to north Idaho from southern California. People working together in public and private sector partnerships across state lines succeeded in landing one of the largest corporate relocations in this region's history.

TWO ORGANIZATIONS, ONE GOAL

In an effort to diversify the region's economy and generate economic growth, economic development organizations were established in north Idaho's Kootenai County and Washington's Spokane County in the late 1980s. Coeur d'Alene-based Jobs Plus, with a three-person staff and a $200,000 budget, and the Spokane Area Economic Development Council, with a 15-person staff and $1.2 million budget, represent a population base of nearly 500,000 residents within a 35-mile radius.

While the recruitment strategy of Jobs Plus primarily focused on small- to medium-sized companies, the organization sparked the interest of Harper's Furniture, an office furniture manufacturer with more than 500 employees and sales of $48 million in a 600,000-square-foot facility in Torrance, California. Its relocation to north Idaho could create a significant

---

*EDITORS' NOTE: We've included the Harper's case study because it gives an excellent example of what can be accomplished when the right partners join a project. It also shows that economic development projects are typically multi-year efforts. Finally, it illustrates how much follow-up work is involved after the day a project is announced.

number of jobs, import new capital to the region and help diversify its economy.

Idaho Leads the Way

Jobs Plus immediately began to establish a relationship with Harper's president and spent a great deal of time researching the company and visiting its operations to determine what Idaho could offer and what would be offered by competing areas.

While proposals submitted to Harper's by other localities included financial incentives far beyond what Idaho's could offer, Jobs Plus established its competitive advantage by building a solid relationship with company leadership early on. It positioned itself as critical to Harper's evaluation team and earned management's trust through hard work and proactive gestures.

The entire process took four years and involved a chain of stop-and-go events. When Jobs Plus initiated contact with Harper's, the company was family-owned. Later, Kimball International—a Fortune 500 company with operations in 13 states, three international subsidiaries, and 7,000 employees worldwide—purchased the company. New leadership took over, and the determination was made to relocate. Competition among communities increased to 15 states, and Idaho, Oregon, New Mexico, Utah, and Washington were ultimately announced as finalists.

Idaho was a serious contender despite its lack of financial incentives. The state offers low premiums and annual dividends for worker's compensation, grants $500 state income tax credits each time a job is created, and charges no tax on equipment purchased for production. Incentives involving labor costs and the tax increment financing were offered, which strengthened the region's position.

To land Harper's, the final proposal needed to include land to accommodate a 450,000-square-foot building, parking for at least 600 employees, and approximately $750,000 in pre-employment training funding. Other states still in the race were offering free land and up to $1 million in pre-employment training funds.

Leveraging Resources to Make Partnerships Work

Restricted by state laws and limited training resources, Jobs Plus developed innovative partnerships to boost the region's competitive advantage. It collaborated with the Spokane Area Economic Development Council to explore opportunities, and together the organizations tapped the combined resources of North Idaho College and the Community Colleges of Spokane to provide training equipment, resources, leadership support, and funding.

Since Washington State was no longer being considered by Harper's, the challenge for Community Colleges of Spokane President Dr. Terrance Brown was to demonstrate the value in spending Washington state vocational training funds in Idaho.

The Harper's proposed site was situated off Interstate 90 near the Washington/Idaho state line. Dr. Brown led the campaign to secure funding from Washington State based on the large number of Harper's employees who would live in Spokane. Dr. Brown was convinced that Harper's would create jobs for Washington residents and impact the city's economy through payroll and retail sales.

The Spokane Area Economic Development Council secured an additional $50,000 from Momentum, a nonprofit organization with 550 private-sector member-investors created to enhance Spokane's regional economy. In Idaho, North Idaho College President Dr. Bob Bennett and Idaho Department of Commerce Director Jim Hawkins approached Governor Cecil Andrus, who endorsed the recruitment initiative and pledged $150,000 from his own budget for the two-state program. The Governor's support led to an additional $110,000

from Idaho's Vocational Education Department.

Additionally, a new partnership was formed when both the Idaho Department of Employment and Washington State Employment Security Department teamed up to recruit employees for pre-employment training programs.

Now Jobs Plus had secured $777,300 in pre-employment training for Harper's, but it still had to find land for the company's facility.

Land to Land the Deal

A 30-acre stretch of undeveloped farmland in Post Falls, Idaho, was eventually gifted to Harper's by the Schneidmiller family, another critical partner. In exchange for this grant, the City of Post Falls agreed to extend road, sewer, water, and other infrastructure improvements to the site.

Infrastructure improvements were funded by a $470,000 Idaho Community Development block grant, plus another $100,000 raised by the City of Post Falls through the creation of tax increment financing. For a one-time investment of $600,000, the City's return on investment is about $450,000 annually in property taxes.

The City also realized that it would not have a huge influx of new residents to the community to impact city services and school districts. While most employees would be hired locally, only about 50 would relocate from California and Indiana. At least half of the new employees and their families would live in Spokane.

Partnerships Paid Off

In May 1992, a comprehensive proposal—including nearly $800,000 in training funds, a detailed training program plan, and 30 acres of free, improved land—was submitted to Harper's. It was supported by letters of commitment from the governors of both states, two college presidents, two economic development organizations, and the mayor and city council members of Post Falls, Idaho. By the end of August, Harper's called to report that it had made a decision to relocate to the area.

The Harper's plant was constructed in 13 months, all recruitment and training programs were delivered on schedule, and a full complement of workers arrived by late July 1993. Spokane's newspaper, *Spokesman-Review*, later cited the Harper's relocation as the region's top business story that year.

One of the most rewarding aspects of the Harper's project was developing new relationships that crossed state lines. Laboring together for nearly two years, the Harper's planning team became a tightly knit group of problem-solvers who worked easily together and were schooled by the experience. It was a unique situation, and it yielded valued achievement.

— *Robert Cooper and Robert Potter*

Project Summary:
HARPER'S FURNITURE

Incentives Provided:

- ▸ Free Land
- ▸ Free Infrastructure
- ▸ Investment Tax Credit
- ▸ New Job Creation Tax Credit
- ▸ Lower Worker's Compensation Premiums
- ▸ No Sales Tax on Equipment Used in Production
- ▸ Pre-employment Training and Support Services

Contributions *(itemized and rounded to the nearest $100)*:

IDAHO

Special State Appropriation	$150,000
State Board for Vocational Education	70,000
Consortium of Post Secondary Area	40,000
Vocational Education Institutions:	
State Employment Security (Job Service)	38,000
North Idaho College	34,000
Jobs Plus, Inc.	10,000

WASHINGTON

State Job Skills Program	$272,300
Community Colleges of Spokane	93,000
MOMENTUM (Private Investment Group)	50,000
State Employment Security (Job Service)	20,000

Total Training and Support Services	**$777,300**

Chronology: HARPER'S' MOVE

1990

Feb. 2   Call to Harper's by a Jobs Plus telemarketing volunteer.

Feb. 5   Letter and generic cost-comparison study sent showing how the company would save 31 percent combined in labor, worker's compensation and unemployment insurance by moving to North Idaho.

Spring   Potter begins frequent visits to Harper's plant in Torrance, California.

1991

Feb. 27   Idaho's first formal presentation to Harper's in Torrance, California by Potter, Tom Richards, President of Idaho Forest Industries, and a Jobs Plus board member; Randy Shroll, Idaho Department of Commerce; and Pete Kerwien, Washington Water Power. Governor Cecil Andrus addresses group in a conference call.

Summer   Following the death of its founder, Harper's is put up for sale by the family and subsequently enters negotiations with Kimball International. Joe Wisniewski, Vice President and General Manager of Harper's, becomes Harper's representative.

1992

Jan. 22   Kimball International announces its purchase of Harper's Inc.

Feb. 4   Wisniewski briefs Potter on Kimball and asks for update on cost comparison studies. At this point, five states are in the running: Coeur d'Alene, Idaho; Salt Lake City, Utah; Hobbs, New Mexico; Medford, Oregon; and Walla Walla, Washington.

April 8-10   Harper's executives visit North Idaho and tour proposed plant sites in Post Falls, Coeur d'Alene and Rathdrum. A working dinner focuses on pre-employment training.

Late April   Post Falls, Coeur d'Alene, and Rathdrum outline proposals to Harper's for free land and infrastructure.

May 29   North Idaho College and Community Colleges of Spokane submit a formal proposal for a two-state pre-employment training program, including flow chart, training tracks, and class hours.

May-June   All key players in Idaho and Washington write letters affirming their commitment to the Harper's incentive package, including the governors of both states, the two college presidents, and Idaho/Washington commerce and vocational education officials.

June 4   Potter learns that Harper's has narrowed the field of possible relocation sites to Idaho, Oregon, New Mexico and Utah.

July 9-10   Kimball/Harper's executives visit Idaho. In less than 24 hours, they visit all three sites and meet with 30 officials involved with the project. Governor Cecil Andrus attends a key breakfast session where the program focuses on pre-employment training and employee relocation.

July 27-29   Wisniewski visits Idaho to discuss relocation issues and lay the groundwork for formal announcement of Harper's move to Post Falls.

Aug. 3-24   North Idaho College consultant conducts a needs assessment on Harper's shop floor as a prelude to writing the first curriculum proposal to provide training for the company's workforce in Idaho and Washington.

Aug. 25   ANNOUNCEMENT — Harper's announces its move to North Idaho at news conferences in Torrance, California, and Post Falls, Idaho.

Sept. 10   The first curriculum proposal developed by the consultant is approved by Joe Wisniewski. It lists 58 manufacturing courses with population matrix. There is reference to "process cells," but no clear definition of training tracks. She calls it "a working document to begin dialogue."

Sept. 22   A similar curriculum proposal covering office skills is prepared and submitted to NIC. It lists 45 course descriptions, including 11 MAC/PAC courses and five APICS courses.

September   Training consultant prepares first draft proposal for establishment of Harper's Consortium Committee. The proposal is played out intact, although the finance subcommittee was not established until much later.

October   Presidents Terry Brown of CCS and Bob Bennett of NIC visit the Harper's plant in Torrance, California, while in the area to attended a national meeting of community college trustees.

Oct. 5   NIC/CCS hold news conference announcing Harper's curriculum, suggesting that 1) Harper's will select trainees with no guarantee of employment, and 2) there will be English/math prerequisites, and trainees might have to pay up to $1,500 for classes.

Oct. 15   The Harper's Consortium Committee (HCC) holds its first meeting, and NIC's Bob Ketchum is elected chair. Discussion centers on recruitment of trainees and possible assessment instruments.

TO NORTHERN IDAHO

Nov. 5 HCC splits up curriculum development duties as follows: NIC—welding, assembly and paint; CCS—APEX, PMA, CNC, break press and shear. Harper's assigns one technical advisor to each program.

Nov. 19 First training implementation schedule is distributed. It calls for workforce prep courses by NIC to begin in mid-February, 1993. A flow chart is distributed, breaking out manufacturing and office tracks.

December HCC recruitment subcommittee establishes flow chart for referral and assessment subcommittee.

1993

Jan. 5 Preliminary "complete" draft of curriculum developed by the consultant is released. This is similar to October 15 proposal and guides curriculum development for the next four months.

Jan. 12 A key air quality permit is granted to Harper's by the Idaho Division of Environmental Quality, clearing the way for the start of plant construction in Post Falls.

Jan. 19 CCS submits JSP Phase I grant proposal to State of Washington, seeking $72,400 for planning and curriculum development, as well as preliminary recruitment, screening and assessment of trainees. It funds a period from February 1 to June 30, 1993. Harper's' match is $78,884.

Jan. The city of Post Falls receives a $470,000 Idaho Community Development Block grant to pay for infrastructure improvements at the Harper's site.

Jan.-Feb. Curriculum developers and Job Service representatives visit Torrance, California, to observe factory production and define job duties.

Feb. Kimball International attorneys consult with consortium planners.

March 1 Greg Davis is appointed vice president and general manager of Harper's, replacing Joe Wisniewski, who joins another company.

March Construction begins on Harper's $50 million plant in Post Falls.

April 15 Greg Davis and other representatives from Kimball International attend day-long meeting of Harper's Consortium Committee. The company signals major changes in training curriculum and trainee recruitment.

April 23 CCS submits JSP Phase II grant proposal to Washington, seeking $253,372 in-state funds to deliver training, during a period from July 1, 1993, to June 30, 1994. Harper's' match is $651,297.

June 16 Harper's consortium abandons a plan to seek a single centralized training site for Harper's workforce. Idaho and Washington subsequently establish separate training centers in Post Falls and Spokane.

June Harper's consortium sets new guidelines for Harper's recruitment package. Testing by NIC and CCS will be used only as a tool for assessment of trainees, not selection.

July/August Harper's prepares recruitment package, including video and fliers to be distributed by Job Services in Coeur d'Alene and Spokane.

Aug. 9-16 Members of the Job Services staff and Harper's consortium undergo structured panel interviews with teams from Harper's and Kimball.

Aug. 18 Job Service offices begin to distribute 2,400 job application packets to men and women seeking to enter training in the first production track. About 60 percent are completed and returned.

Sept. 7-24 Job Service offices pre-screen about 1,500 applicants for about 430 openings in the first production track.

Sept. 20-30 About 700 applicants undergo structured panel interviews conducted by teams from Harper's and Kimball International.

Oct. 1-22 About 435 applicants selected by Harper's for training undergo testing and assessment by staff at North Idaho College and the Community Colleges of Spokane.

Oct. 25 Just under 430 students begin training in the first production track at NIC and CCS.

1994

Jan. 16-25 Job Service offices distribute 600 applications for 45 openings in the administrative/office training track. These students begin training March 7, for a total of 12 weeks.

Feb. 22-24 Job Service offices distribute 450 applications for 65 openings in the second production training track. These students begin training April 4, for a total of 13 weeks.

June 30 Training for the Harper's project ends, and the Harper's Consortium Committee is dissolved.

PARTNER IDENTIFICATION CHECKLIST ✓

PROJECT TITLE _____   PROJECT NUMBER _____

	NAME	PHONE / FAX NO.

PRIVATE SECTOR PARTNERS

Financial/Legal
Accountants _____ _____
Attorneys _____ _____
Institutional lenders _____ _____

Utilities/Transportation
Electrical/gas _____ _____
Telecommunications _____ _____
Transportation _____ _____

Labor/Education
Employment resources _____ _____
Education resources _____ _____

Real Estate/Development
Architects/engineers _____ _____
Real estate
— Commercial _____ _____
— Residential _____ _____

Associations _____ _____

Hospitality
Hotels _____ _____
Airlines _____ _____

Quality of Life
Arts/culture _____ _____
Sports/recreation _____ _____

Media
Print _____ _____
Television _____ _____

PUBLIC SECTOR PARTNERS

State Government
Educational institutions _____ _____
Elected officials _____ _____
Department contacts _____ _____

Local Government
Educational institutions _____ _____
Elected officials _____ _____
Departments _____ _____

CHAPTER 7

THE MARKETING PLAN

Leland F. Smith
President, Elesco, Ltd.

There is a great encounter in Lewis Carroll's Alice in Wonderland *when Alice meets the Cheshire Cat at a place where the road splits into several different directions. Loosely paraphrased, it goes something like this:*

"Excuse me, please," Alice said to the Cheshire Cat.

"Will you kindly tell me which road I should take?"

"That depends a great deal on where you want to go," the Cat answered.

"But I have no idea where I am going," Alice said.

"Then," the cat replied, "It doesn't really matter which road you take, does it?"

———o———

Like Alice, our ability to close sales is directly related to our ability to determine where we are going and how we are going to get there. Nothing happens in our economic system without a sale. Nothing gets manufactured, nothing gets warehoused, nothing gets distributed. The sales transaction is the locomotive that drives the whole train. Yet most people turn pale and dizzy at the thought of actually having to *sell* something. They will do almost anything to avoid the one-on-one encounter that pits their "Yes, I will" against someone else's "No, you won't." That's because selling is absolute. It is yes or no, pass or fail. We get our egos wrapped up in it and become driven by our fear of rejection.

So we do "marketing" instead. Marketing is *planning* to sell, instead of actually doing the selling. There is an assumption that if we do good marketing, then the sales will happen by themselves. That's nonsense. The purpose of marketing is to make sales happen. A marketing plan that doesn't produce sales is garbage. This chapter describes how to make sales happen by preparing a marketing plan that works.

GOALS AND OBJECTIVES:
Deciding on your Destination

One of Stephen Covey's *Seven Habits of Highly Effective People* (required reading) is to "Begin with the end in mind." That means focusing your efforts toward achieving the goals you want to reach. The product drives the process, not the other way around.

The marketing plan begins with setting goals and objectives that are realistic and achievable. This means setting annual program goals that reflect the needs and economic capabilities of the community. It also means targeting companies that are suitable for the size and resources of the community and have an economic rationale for locating there.

Marketing is planning *to sell*, instead of actually doing the selling.

A recent well-publicized site search by a large electronics company had communities of fewer than 10,000 people competing for a plant that would employ up to 4,500 workers, with about half of them degreed engineers. A lot of time, money, and effort was wasted chasing a facility that could not possibly locate in those communities.

Some general rules can be used to set annual recruitment goals. Here is a process that should work in most communities:

Assumptions —

Population size:	*30,000*
Labor Force (47%):	*14,100*
Employed:	*12,600*
Unemployed (10.6% of labor force):	*1,500*

If the goal is to reduce unemployment to 6.0 percent of the labor force, then the need is to generate an additional 654 jobs. An aggressive five-year goal to reach that figure would mean that about 130 new jobs need to be created each year.

However, not all of those jobs need to be produced by new industries. Primary industries generate incomes which, when they are spent locally, induce secondary employment. Employment multipliers usually range from 1.5x to 2.5x depending on the economic structure of the community. Using an average

multiplier of 2x, only 65 new jobs need to be created by recruiting new industries each year. In a community of 30,000 people, attracting 65 new primary jobs each year for five years should be a realistic and achievable goal.

Looking at the numbers this way helps the economic development practitioner to define rational program objectives and avoids the common pitfall of setting goals that have no basis in reality. If you land a Fortune 500 megaplant, that's great! But you should not set that as your goal if the chances of success are only 0.1 percent.

Of course, quantifying goals this way means that the success of the program can be measured in terms of current results instead of future prospects. There is no greater incentive to develop and work an effective marketing plan than to be held accountable for measurable results.

ELEMENTS OF A MARKETING PLAN

Okay, so we've decided where we want to go. Hopefully, we have done this in a way that is specific and measurable. Now we need a map that shows us how to get there. In business recruiting, the marketing plan is that map. In all marketing activities, there are three basic elements that need to be defined:

The product: What are you selling?
The market: Who are you selling it to?
The delivery system: How do you bring the product and market together to make a sale?

Too often the marketing plan jumps to the delivery system without adequately defining the product and the market. "Let's put an ad in a national business magazine, tell everyone how great our town is, then wait for the phone to ring." Those kinds of ads show up in every site selection magazine, promoting some town few people have ever heard of as the "ideal" location for every industry, regardless of that industry's needs. That's not only absurd, but it also shows a gross misunderstanding of what companies look for and the processes they use when looking for a location to site a new facility.

The Product:

What are you selling? An early decision needs to be made as to what product you are going to market. It may be a locational advantage in a geographic area. Perhaps your community is the product, or you may be marketing specific sites or vacant industrial buildings. The marketing plan obviously has to be oriented toward the product(s) you are trying to sell.

For most economic development programs, the product in a business recruiting effort is the community's ability to deliver the resources needed to support the location and operation of industry in its competitive markets. This product can be measured, both quantitatively and qualitatively, through the community evaluation process that was described in Chapter 3. The community assessment examines those factors that affect the location and operation of business enterprises, evaluating those factors in terms of industry's ability to produce its products at reasonable costs, effectively compete in its markets, and earn profits.

This exercise gives a different perspective on the community than one that focuses primarily on family lifestyles and community amenities. A community that is a great place to live and raise a family may lack the economic resources necessary to be competitive in attracting new businesses or to cause existing businesses to operate profitably and expand. Conversely, communities may have strong business resources even if they are not the greatest places to live.

The Market:

Who are you selling it to? Perhaps the most fundamental requirement of a successful marketing plan is the decision on what market you are going to sell to, i.e., to which industries and in what geographical locations. A common mistake in economic development marketing is to broadcast the message to the nation but to miss the opportunities that are right next door.

Identify your economic region. This can be done by examining the primary (export) sectors of the local economy and finding out where companies in those sectors sell their products and from where they obtain their supplies and services. If 99 percent of product sales are within a radius of 100 miles, that probably defines your market region. On the other hand, if the bulk of products are shipped to national or international markets, then your economic region may encompass a national or even global area. The market area is usually defined by the economic linkages that exist (or can be created) with other communities, states, provinces, or multi-state regions. The composition of that market is defined by the industry sets that are linked to your community through the flow of commerce.

There is no greater incentive to develop and work an effective marketing plan than to be held accountable for measurable results.

Identify your competitive market position. In that analysis, it is important to understand your community's role in its regional competition. For example, the major West Coast ports may compete with other ports on the Pacific Rim, with Gulf Coast ports, or even with all ports in North America. By accommodating flows of commerce, their primary product is to link domestic and international distribution channels in a market area that may encompass the entire world.

By comparison, a dry land port in central Washington may have a primary market that encompasses one or two counties, serving as a conduit for storage and distribution of agricultural commodities between the farm and the railroad. In that case, its principal competition is with nearby communities that offer similar services. The suburban community near a large metropolitan city probably doesn't need to look any farther than its next-door neighbor to define its market area, and to other nearby communities to define its competition.

CHOOSING YOUR MARKET APPROACH

Once the market area has been defined, there are three primary approaches to tapping into the market to develop sources for new industries:

- The "share-of-the-market" approach, which means garnering a share of the normal business activity within the local economic region. This is the standard real estate brokerage approach to marketing industrial sites and buildings. It involves recruitment, but only among firms that are expanding or relocating within the region plus firms that are moving into the region on their own initiative.

- Recruitment of firms from outside the local economic region. These are firms that are motivated to relocate or expand their facilities and will consider locations that meet their requirements. These firms can either be linked to the region's resources, or they can be "footloose" industries that have the option of locating almost anywhere they choose.

- Development of new business opportunities from scratch. The use of incubators to "grow" new businesses is an obvious form of this strategy. Another form is to identify opportunities based on resource linkages or gaps in the existing economic base and bring together the necessary requirements to create new businesses. This may mean recruiting selected companies, forming networks of existing firms, or starting a new enterprise. The end result is community-driven business formation, rather than simply marketing to established firms.

All three of these strategies include some form of marketing, although the last one is based more on creative resource utilization. Which strategy is appropriate for any particular community depends largely on what opportunities are available in the market. Obviously, the share-of-the-market approach is more appropriate to a major metropolitan center or a nearby suburban community than it is to a small, isolated, rural community: No market, no market share. Business recruitment is accomplished more easily in communities that have the infrastructure and support capabilities to be competitive with other communities in their economic region.

TARGET MARKET ANALYSIS FOR IDENTIFYING PROSPECTIVE INDUSTRIES

At this point, decisions have been made regarding the product to be marketed, the market area to be covered, and the type of market approach to be used. If the result of these decisions is a business recruitment program, then the next step is to decide which industry segments you are going to recruit. This assumes a targeted, "rifle shot" approach to business recruitment rather than the "shotgun" approach that opens the door to whatever industry is willing to walk in.

One of the most effective methods of identifying industries (and companies) for a business recruitment program is a target market analysis. The objective of the analysis is to identify industries that are likely candidates to locate or expand within the economic region, and whose locational and operating requirements match the resources and capabilities of the community that were identified in the community assessment. When filtered through the criteria of community goals, the resulting set of target industries becomes a wish list for the kinds of business activities you would like

The market area is usually defined by the economic linkages that exist (or can be created) with other communities, states, provinces, or multi-state regions.

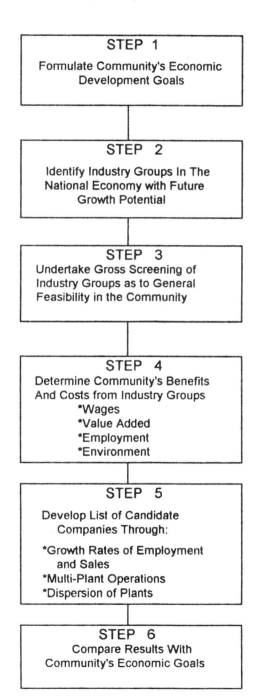

**BUSINESS RESEARCH DIVISION
UNIVERSITY OF COLORADO**

**Steps in Identifying and Evaluating Components
for Identifying Prospective Industries**

STEP 1

Formulate Community's Economic
Development Goals

STEP 2

Identify Industry Groups In The
National Economy with Future
Growth Potential

STEP 3

Undertake Gross Screening of
Industry Groups as to General
Feasibility in the Community

STEP 4

Determine Community's Benefits
And Costs from Industry Groups
*Wages
*Value Added
*Employment
*Environment

STEP 5

Develop List of Candidate
Companies Through:

*Growth Rates of Employment
and Sales
*Multi-Plant Operations
*Dispersion of Plants

STEP 6

Compare Results With
Community's Economic Goals

to recruit to your community and that have a practical reason for locating there.

The six-step chart shown here was developed by the University of Colorado for a target industry analysis performed for the industry recruitment programs at Colorado Springs. It was aimed at the national market and formed the basis for a national recruiting program. Industries were screened by four-digit SIC codes to identify those with forecast growth potential. The growth industries were examined for factors that influence their locational characteristics to find matches with the resources offered by Colorado Springs.

They were further qualified in terms of their operating characteristics in relation to the specific, measurable economic development goals of the community. Growth trends and locational patterns of individual companies within those industries were evaluated to identify prospects with the highest probability of expanding and/or relocating to a Colorado location. The resulting list of companies was then screened for their match with the goals of the program, and a final set of target companies was selected for the marketing program.

STEPS IN A
TARGET INDUSTRY ANALYSIS

Target industry analyses have been used successfully by many communities to select candidate companies for their industry recruiting campaigns. The Colorado Springs study targeted about 800 companies and 200 associations nationwide, resulting in the recruitment of several electronics companies along with the headquarters of the U.S. Olympic Committee and numerous sports-related organizations. In Boise, Idaho, a target industry study produced a list of 1,100 companies in the national market and launched a successful recruiting effort that was the catalyst for that city's recent industrial expansion.

EXAMPLE: In Porterville, California, a community assessment determined that the city's primary linkages were with the Los Angeles Basin area. A target industry study that was focused narrowly on the southern California market resulted in the recruitment of the southwestern regional distribution center for the WalMart Company.

An important recommendation for a target industry study: If you use an outside consultant, always make sure you end up with a list of specific companies that includes the names, titles, addresses and phone numbers, plus fax numbers and e-mail addresses if available, of the key decision makers. There is nothing more useless than a list of target SIC codes without the list of specific companies.

OTHER TECHNIQUES

Not everyone is sold on the community/industry match technique produced by a target industry study as the best way to identify potential industries. For more academic types, there are also variations of regional input-output studies, industry shift-share analyses, and regional location quotients. The major problem with these kinds of studies is that they rely on current and comprehensive data which are often unavailable at the regional or local level. The models break down when the data sources publish a big (D) to indicate that the data are not available because of nondisclosure requirements. Anyone who wants to explore these alternative kinds of analyses can find them described in most economic development manuals and textbooks.

SOURCES OF INDUSTRY AND COMPANY DATA

Whether or not an outside consultant is used to perform the market and industry analysis, every community economic development organization needs to be able to do its own in-house research, even if only to update the original target industry study. Following is a very short list of some of the standard data sources that are available in most libraries or can be obtained on CD-ROM or by on-line services. Some of these sources overlap, but by cross-referencing and comparing them it is possible to obtain an excellent composite analysis.

OVERALL INDUSTRY ANALYSIS —

U.S. Industrial Outlook, U.S. Department of Commerce, International Trade Division. Published annually. This is probably the first source for analyzing current and forecast trends for U.S. industries by four-digit SIC code. In addition to statistical data on value of shipments and employment, there are excellent narratives on industry trends and competitive factors.

Business Magazines:

Fortune, Forbes, Business Week, Inc., etc. These magazines publish annual performance charts of changes in sales, profits, employment, and other indicators for various sectors of the economy. *Fortune*, for example, ranks the top 25 industries in order of their sales growth from the previous year, using medians for all companies in each industry (not industry averages). While these are short-term changes, the list offers insights into which industries are likely to be looking at capital expansion budgets.

Trade Magazines:

If you want to research specific industries, then the magazines written for those industries usually have annual statistical reports and forecasts.

Value Line Data Base Service:

This source also offers information on industry changes, primarily as a means to support financial outlooks for individual companies.

EMERGING INDUSTRIES —

A good source for predictions of emerging industries is *Standard & Poors Compustat Services, Inc.*, which offers both hard copy and electronic forms of its analyses. A recent report identified wireless communications, multimedia systems, recycling, biotechnology, and flat-panel display electronics as emerging industries with high growth potential. Similar kinds of reports, especially for smaller businesses, can be found in *Inc.*, *Money*, *Entrepreneur*, and various investor publications.

ANALYSIS OF TARGET COMPANIES

The references below are to hard copy directories available in libraries or by purchase. Most of them are also available on CD-ROM, or by on-line database services. One of the most comprehensive on-line services is Dialogue Information Services, Inc. (developed by Lockheed) which offers access to most business information databases.

Moody's Industrial Manual

This is one of the true gems in the business. In addition to providing extensive information about public companies listed on the major stock exchanges, it also describes their facilities by location, size, type, and how much space is leased vs. owned. The biweekly updates have a special listing in the index for new company expansions. It is an excellent source of information on geographical patterns of company locations which often provide clues on future locational patterns as well.

Dun & Bradstreet Million Dollar Directory

There are several kinds of D&B directories, but the Million Dollar Directory serves most company research requirements. In addition to basic information, it also gives company performance data and describes market coverage. It includes both public and private companies, but the information on private firms should be viewed with caution as it is provided by the firms themselves and may not be entirely accurate.

Standard & Poors Corporations

This directory is similar to the D&B in providing basic information about major companies.

State Directories of Manufacturers

If the market area is within one state, or a region comprised of a few states, then the various state directories of manufacturers can be an excellent source of company data. In western U.S., the Database Publishing Company produces manufacturers registers for Arizona, California, Nevada, Oregon, Utah and Washington. For California, they also provide information on service companies, technology companies, wholesalers, and firms engaged in international trade. Their information is available in hard copy, floppy disks, and CD-ROM. They also provide a compilation of database services to assist in transferring the data to a marketing program. These directories are published with the support and cooperation of the respective state economic development agencies.

Other Sources

Several of the magazines listed above publish annual rankings of company performance, as well as by industry. Good results can often be obtained by looking at which companies are performing at the top of the charts, identifying their industries by SIC codes, then examining the overall industry characteristics to find other outstanding performers.

There are many other sources that can be used to analyze markets and select companies for a target marketing program. The ones listed above are only a small sample, but they offer a place to start. By relating the target selection back to the community analysis, it is important to identify the *reasons* why those companies should consider locating in your community.

EXAMPLE: When Jerome, Idaho, made a proposal to Micron Technology, it knew it couldn't meet the published requirements so it changed the specifications of the project. It proposed that Micron develop a satellite facility in Jerome instead of building an independent, self-supporting plant. The proposal showed how Micron could save several hundred million dollars on the construction of the plant, plus tens of millions of dollars in annual operating costs. Although the plant finally went to Utah, the Jerome proposal put it on the list of 13 semifinalists.

The Delivery System:

Bringing the Product and the Market Together

At this point you have analyzed your community and identified its strengths and weaknesses. You have also identified the locational and operating characteristics of industries by SIC codes and matched them to the community's resources to determine which kinds of industries you can and cannot support. You have further assessed the industry groups in terms of their growth patterns and your community's goals. With the target industries selected, you have performed research on specific companies and selected the ones you want for your marketing program. The only thing you need now is a way to contact them, i.e., a delivery system.

The key underlying assumptions that must be considered no matter what mechanisms are used for the delivery system are:

- ▸ Companies don't make decisions; people do.
- ▸ People don't make decisions for *your* reasons. They make them for *their* reasons.
- ▸ Given alternatives that are approximately equal, people will make the choices that best facilitate their jobs.

The objective of the delivery system is: (1) to contact the people who make decisions about company locations and facilities; (2) let them know that your community has the resources they need to meet their locational and operating requirements and that you will facilitate their evaluation of your community and the eventual location of their company there; and (3) have them respond to you with a positive interest. That's about all you can hope to accomplish in the initial marketing program. Other techniques are used, of course, after the contact has been made and the decision maker has expressed an interest in your community.

In the simplest terms, what you want from your marketing plan is qualified "prospects." There are essentially two forms of delivery systems. One is the "passive" approach where you do not identify specific contacts in advance. Instead, you place ads in magazines or put up a booth in a trade show and wait for people who see your message to come to you. You promote your product through your ad or display, and somewhat qualify your market through your selections of the magazines or trade shows you use.

In the simplest terms, what you want from your marketing plan is qualified "prospects."

While the passive approach may produce a lot of exposure, it doesn't necessarily assure that you will be exposed to the right people.

EXAMPLE: The development agency in Tucson used to place ads in Business Week *in January, aimed at the northeast market, showing a golfer and emphasizing the delightful desert climate at that time of the year. The ads typically generated up to 1,500 responses, largely from workers who wanted to know if there were jobs available in the warmer climate. There were occasional responses from business owners, but when April or May came around, many of them would no longer return phone calls.*

The more effective approach, especially when a target industry analysis is used, is the direct contact approach. This usually requires a combination of direct mail backed up with telephone calls. If appropriate, contacts can also be made by fax and/or by e-mail. These techniques are assessed in more detail in the next section which describes the factors involved in preparing the marketing plan.

PREPARING THE MARKETING PLAN

Develop a Marketing Budget:

The scope of the business recruitment effort, and therefore the marketing plan, will necessarily be limited by the size of the budget and the staff to support it. A common mistake that many communities make, especially boards of directors that want to sell the program to funding agencies, is to maximize the expenditures in "program" items and minimize the expenditures in staff and overhead costs. They forget that industrial recruitment is selling, not just marketing, and that selling is a labor-intensive, service-oriented enterprise. They blow the budget with ads in the *Wall Street Journal* then don't have adequate trained, dedicated staff to follow up on leads.

It has been estimated that there are 15,000 communities and economic development agencies working to attract fewer than 1,500 new facilities that are established in the United States each year. Some of these agencies are very large and have budgets in excess of $1 million per year to spend on development and marketing. At the other end of the scale are communities that put a sign on a piece of dirt and call that their marketing program. Obviously, the well-organized and well-funded program is more likely to be successful.

An adequate budget is a fundamental key to success in any marketing program. The budget needs to include sufficient staff to devote time to working the program, resources to get the message out in ways that will be most effective, and the ability to follow up on leads and prospects. Some communities use shared public and private resources to support their industrial recruitment programs, reducing the requirement for dedicated funds.

In part, the budget depends on the type of marketing that is done, the markets it aims at, and the volume of activity that is generated. It is gener-

> *Industrial recruitment is selling, not just marketing, and that selling is a labor-intensive, service-oriented enterprise.*

ally better to have a high-quality program aimed at a smaller market area than to spread the resources too thin by going after a broader market.

Following are sample budgets for three different levels of business marketing and recruitment.

In **Sample Budget A**, the marketing program expenses are $34,800, which represents about 34 percent of the total. Personnel expenses are $55,200, which is 54 percent of the total, and overhead costs are $12,600, or 12 percent of the total budget.

This budget might be representative of a business recruitment program that is housed in another agency, such as a chamber of commerce or a city department. There are only two

SAMPLE BUDGET A
Smaller office, 2-person staff: Budget total = $102,600

Personnel		**$ 45,200**
Salaries, direct costs:		
Manager	$ 30,000	
Clerical/research support	18,000	
Taxes, benefits (15%)	7,200	
Overhead		12,600
Rent ($500/month)	6,000	
Utilities ($100/month)	1,200	
Telephone ($100/month)	1,200	
Supplies ($200/month)	2,400	
Equipment leases, repairs ($50/month)	600	
Other overhead ($100/month)	1,200	
Marketing		34,800
Brochures, sales materials	6,000	
Advertising, direct mail	10,000	
Telemarketing	5,000	
Travel, trade shows	9,000	
Hosting local visits	4,800	
	Total	**$102,600**

people on the staff, and overhead expenses are pretty low. Most of the costs are aimed at getting and servicing prospects.

A budget item for telemarketing is listed under the marketing expenses, separate from the general telephone costs. As personal contact is the key to successful marketing, this item is an essential part of the marketing plan.

In **Sample Budget B**, adding a professional person dedicated to marketing and client follow-up has increased personnel and overhead costs by about 90 percent, reflecting an independent agency or subsidiary, and the marketing budget has increased by about 30 percent. The additional person allows the agency to increase the volume of its direct mail, travel and telephone contacts, but does not necessarily require additional costs for creating new product literature.

A three-person staff is probably the minimum threshold for a competitive program. It allows one professional to work in the field with prospects while a second professional makes marketing contacts from the office, responds to inquiries, and deals with the problem-solving details of current clients. This is especially true if the program director is re

quired to spend any significant amount of time doing fund raising chores and dealing with internal public relations.

A three-person staff is the minimum threshold for a competitive program. There is no point in having qualified professionals on staff without the resources that enable them to do their jobs effectively.

In this budget, the personnel costs are about 60 percent of the total, while marketing costs are about 26 percent. The remaining 14 percent represents overhead costs. Again, a major portion of the personnel costs are dedicated to working the program and providing the one-on-one services required to translate marketing into sales.

In **Sample Budget C** (next page), personnel costs have increased to about 65 percent of the total by adding a staff professional dedicated to research and analysis to support the marketing programs. This allows for continuous updating of new marketing opportunities, as well as meeting the problem-solving research needs required to convert marketing into successful sales. Again, a key assumption in this budget is that marketing is a labor-intensive activity and that there is no point in spending more money on program costs without having the people to follow-up on leads and to work with prospects.

The marketing budget is reduced to about 22 percent of the total, with the major new item being the addition of a video. The $6,000 allocated to this item in the annual budget could mean that the video costs $12,000 and is updated every two years, or it costs $24,000 and is updated every four years.

SAMPLE BUDGET B
Medium office, 3-person staff: Total budget = $174,600

Personnel		$105,800
Salaries, direct costs:		
Executive Director	$ 42,000	
Marketing/Services Manager	30,000	
Clerical/research support	20,000	
Taxes, benefits (15%)	13,800	
Overhead		24,000
Rent ($800/month)	9,600	
Utilities ($150/month)	1,800	
Telephone ($200/month)	2,400	
Supplies ($400/month)	4,800	
Equipment leases, repairs ($150/month)	1,800	
Other overhead ($300/month)	3,600	
Marketing		45,200
Brochures, sales materials	9,000	
Advertising, direct mail	11,200	
Telemarketing	9,000	
Travel, trade shows	10,000	
Hosting local visits	6,000	
	Total:	**$174,600**

SAMPLE BUDGET C

Larger-office, 4-person staff: **Total budget = $250,000**

Personnel		$162,150
Salaries, direct costs:		
Executive Director	$ 55,000	
Marketing/Services Manager	40,000	
Research support	26,000	
Clerical support	20,000	
Taxes, benefits (15%)	21,150	
Overhead		34,200
Rent ($1,200/month)	14,400	
Utilities ($200/month)	2,400	
Telephone ($300/month)	3,600	
Supplies ($500/month)	6,000	
Equipment leases, repairs ($250/month)	3,000	
Other overhead ($400/month)	4,800	
Marketing		53,650
Brochures, sales materials	10,000	
Video	6,000	
Advertising, direct mail	12,000	
Telemarketing	9,650	
Travel, trade shows	11,000	
Hosting local visits	6,000	
Total:		**$250,000**

Overhead costs remain about 14 percent of the total. No expenses are shown for capital equipment, such as computers, in any of the three budgets. This is a highly variable expense and could either be funded in an initial organization campaign or through annual line items in the budget. In either case, provisions need to be made to update and modernize the equipment. There is no point in having qualified professionals on the staff without the resources that enable them to do their jobs effectively.

It is generally better to have a high-quality program aimed at a smaller market area than to spread the resources too thin by going after a broader market.

Package the Product—
Develop a Marketing Brochure

Companies that are looking for locations to construct new facilities have specific requirements that they need to meet. Their initial review of communities is primarily an information search. They use the data gathered at this stage to narrow down their choices to those communities that appear to be able to offer what they need. They are not concerned about how wonderful the community is, or how nice it is to raise kids there. While these are certainly factors in the final decision, they first need to know that they can obtain the necessary labor force with the skills to do the job, the utilities required for their operation, appropriate transportation services, and the full range of other support capabilities that they have defined when they established the specifications for the facility.

The community's marketing materials, then, need to include enough factual information about the community to answer these questions. Some communities call their primary marketing piece a "fact book" or some other name that clearly identifies it as an informational document rather than a promotional piece. Of course, the information can be presented in ways that also highlight the favorable aspects of the community and promote its advantages.

There are several guidelines that can be used to develop a successful marketing brochure:

1. Begin with a detailed index, or use tabs to indicate where the various sections can be found. In a survey by the American Economic Development Council, several corporate real estate executives said they will not even look at a brochure that requires wading through many pages of irrelevant

information to find the specific data they want.

2. Include a community location map in the introductory material. The location map should show where the community is in relation to major cities in the region, along with distances and the main highway routes that connect them.

3. Include a community and site location map, showing the main features within the community such as an airport, rail lines, schools and universities, shopping areas, the general road network, etc.

4. Use graphics as much as possible to illustrate such information as overnight delivery schedules and cities connected by direct air routes. Graphics are also useful in showing trend data, such as population and employment growth.

5. Use *current* statistics and cite the sources. Companies want to know the date of the information and its credibility.

6. Indicate what special research services can be provided to update the data, obtain additional information, or adapt it to the specific needs of the prospect.

7. Indicate what technical support services are available, including any special incentives or financing assistance.

In general, the content of the marketing brochure will reflect the information obtained in the community assessment. The purpose of this document is not to sell the community, but rather to pass the first hurdle of getting the prospect to agree to consider the community as a potential site for its new facility. The selling is done when the prospect visits the community and makes an on-site inspection. When that occurs, it will usually be necessary to update the information that was presented in the marketing brochure. A computer-based data storage and retrieval system can be one of the most useful tools that a community can have to support its industrial site marketing programs.

Develop a Technical Support Package:

While marketing tends to focus on the community, most facility location searches end up with real estate decisions. The community that facilitates the work of the people doing the site search is likely to win more of those decisions.

A technical support package includes all of the information that is specific to industrial sites and buildings being offered. For an industrial park, it includes a graphic of the overall layout showing the road system, individual lots, rail systems (if any), and other site features. It also includes a detailed description of the utilities available to the development, including the water and sanitary sewer dimensions, capacity, static pressure, and design flows. Fire protection services and requirements should be summarized. The availability of electrical capacity and any secondary services should be indicated.

The package also includes all the information about prices or rents and terms that are available. It should include a copy of the covenants, conditions, and restrictions (CC&Rs), a copy of the applicable zoning ordinances, and any other information pertaining to allowable uses and development constraints.

The technical support package should also include information about permitting requirements and processes, permit fees, system development charges, and any other costs that will be incurred during the development processes. Any offsets, special incentives, or cost-reducing programs should also be described.

The objective is to provide a resource which enables the facility planner to determine how the project will work in your community. Satisfying this real estate requirement allows the facility planner to focus on the other variables in making the final decision.

Select the Market Area:

The importance of selecting an appropriate market area has already been discussed. One of the key considerations in this decision is the ability to follow up on leads, which requires adequate budget and staff. We would like to believe that our communities are so wonderful that company officials will want to hop on a jet and visit us as soon as they receive the marketing brochure. In reality, the selling process will probably require you to visit them. A community on the West Coast will have a difficult time selling itself to East Coast companies if it doesn't have a budget large enough to afford the price of an airline ticket. It is much easier to make sales calls on companies that are within a four-hour radius and can be reached by car than on companies that require a flight to another part of the country.

Select the Industry Targets:

This topic was also covered earlier in this chapter. It is important to remember that the targeted industries provide focus for the marketing program, but they do not define its limits. An ongoing prospecting system will turn up continuous leads, as will indirect forms of marketing such as advertising and trade shows.

Select the Delivery System:

Deciding how to do the marketing is part of the budget-setting process, so several of these steps need to be taken simultaneously. With a target industry approach to recruiting, the marketing will probably consist of direct mail to the target companies, followed by some form of telemarketing. It is becoming increasingly difficult to reach company executives with cold telephone calls, as more of them are using voice mail to answer all incoming calls. Faxes and e-mail messages are often being used, along with voice mail, to send the marketing message. Unfortunately, this is only one-way communication. Some executives will return calls, but others will not. This method works on fairly small percentages, so the total volume needs to be relatively large.

One of the advantages of a target industry analysis is that the study itself can be used as a major selling tool. Companies are much more impressed with communities that have done their homework and know their locational requirements than with communities that advertise they are the ideal location for everyone.

EXAMPLE: *In the Colorado Springs program, letters were sent to the chief financial officers of the target companies telling them that a University of Colorado study had identified their firms as industry growth leaders. When they were offered the opportunity to obtain a copy of the study, more than 95 percent responded with a request. Of course, the only price they had to pay was to put the economic development officials in contact with the companies' site selection executives.*

WORKING THE PLAN

Marketing a community is similar to marketing any other kind of intangible product: You need to get leads, follow up on them, and convert them to prospects. Once you have done that, the process switches from marketing to sales.

The Marketing Team

An important consideration in community business recruitment programs is deciding who will contact the prospects. Many communities use teams of volunteers for this purpose, while others rely on professional staff or some combination of the two.

If a volunteer team is used, the members should be picked for their technical knowledge rather than for their promotional enthusiasm. Representatives of utilities, banks, railroads, local government, industrial real estate firms, local colleges, or others with specialized knowledge are usually more effective in the problem-solving aspects of selling the community. Even better are the people who are currently operating successful businesses in the community who can talk about their own experiences. Personnel managers can discuss the labor aspects of operating there, while purchasing managers can talk about the availability and costs of supplies.

There is a great deal of organizational work required to put together a trade mission where the team can call on several prospects in one city. If there are enough leads or prospects, however, this can be a good way to develop personal relationships that will strengthen the staff's position in future contacts with these firms.

If a volunteer team is used, the members should be picked for their technical knowledge rather than for their promotional enthusiasm.

Another type of team involves the collaboration of people with jobs in economic development or industrial real estate marketing. For example, state organizations will often invite local economic development officials to join them on prospecting trade missions, sometimes hosted by the governor. Community economic developers can often enlist the aid of their professional counterparts with utility companies, railroads, port districts, or other firms and agencies that cover large regional territories.

The Work Plan

The marketing plan provides an overall approach to developing prospects, but it needs to be translated into a work plan to carry it out. This is also part of the budget process, with the funds allocated by month for the various major events.

The medium-sized office described above had a marketing program budget of $45,200 broken down into the following components:

Brochures, sales materials	*$ 9,000*
Advertising, direct mail	*11,200*
Telemarketing	*9,000*
Travel, trade shows	*10,000*
Hosting local visits	*6,000*

One approach to the work program might be to divide the year into three parts, combining the various marketing elements to achieve maximum effect.

The pattern in this budget is to advertise and go to trade shows three times during the year, succeeded by intensive follow-up with direct mail, telemarketing, and travel for prospect visits. This cycle provides an ongoing process of generating new leads, followed by personal contacts to turn those leads into prospects. While hosting prospect visits in the

	ADVERTISE	DIRECT MAIL	TELEMARKET	TRAVEL/SHOWS	LOCAL VISITS
January		200	500	750	200
February		250	500	500	1,000
March	2,500		500	1,500	300
April		750	1,500	500	500
May		250	500	1,000	200
June		250	500	500	1,000
July	2,500		500	1,500	300
August		750	1,500	500	500
September		250	500	1,000	200
October		250	500	500	1,000
November	2,500		500	1,500	300
December		750	1,500	250	500

community goes on all year, there is a program emphasis on hosting visits three months after the major campaigns are initiated and just prior to the start of the next cycle.

Of course, any number of variations are possible. A community that is marketing to a more distant area may want to have only two major campaigns each year, followed by personal contacts and hosting of prospect visits. The key is to have a work plan that continuously balances the marketing program with the follow-up contacts.

Follow-up Plan

Once the initial visit has been made and a lead is turned into a prospect, there is usually a period of further consideration and evaluation before the prospect decides whether the community is a candidate for a new facility. Regular contacts need to be maintained to keep the community's interest in front of the prospect and to keep the prospect's interest in the community alive. Additional questions may be asked that require specific research to obtain the answers. If potential problems or barriers are identified, then solutions need to be found.

This kind of contact is usually best handled by the professional staff, usually the person who is responsible for marketing. The process can be facilitated by using a tracking system that schedules contacts and provides reminders of when to call. Some offices use color-coded systems that signal daily review and contact, or weekly, monthly, or semi-annual reviews and contacts.

Closing the Sale

The sale is actually made when a company representative visits the community and evaluates it on-site, followed by the decision to locate the facility there. Regardless of how effective the marketing program is for generating leads and prospects, the visit to the community can make or break the recruiting effort.

A decision needs to be made as to who will meet with the client. The marketing team can be called upon to assist in this activity, or a team can be assembled for this purpose. Some companies prefer to work only with the professional staff because of their desire for confidentiality, but others are willing to be more open. When the team approach is used, it is important to provide sufficient training to enable the team players to understand their roles and to represent the interests of the community rather than their own firms.

There is no substitute for finding out what the prospect wants to see and learn, and then doing the homework to make certain that the visit is successful. Some communities try to make the prospect visit into an entertainment event, leaving little time for meetings and analysis to make sure that all the location criteria are being satisfied. A checklist, or even a model of the prospect's requirements, along with a carefully planned itinerary can be valuable tools to assure effective use of the time. Meals should be working sessions, providing good opportunities to bring resource people into the discussions to answer specific questions.

Companies will not locate in your community to solve your problems, so you will have to find out what you can offer them that makes your community a better location than anywhere else.

CONCLUDING COMMENTS

The ideas and suggestions given above are very generalized and only introduce the various elements involved in marketing a community. A community marketing plan needs to include all of these elements, but with much more detail that reflects the specific needs and capabilities of the community, including the budget and staff available for the program.

It all begins with setting realistic and achievable goals. Without a clear focus on what you are trying to accomplish, then any program is simply thrashing in the wind. Understanding the community's competitive strengths and weaknesses is fundamental to setting those goals. Companies will not locate in your community to solve *your* problems, so you will have to find out what you can offer them that makes your community a better location than anywhere else.

Selecting an appropriate market area is crucial to the success of the program. Placing ads in national publications when you don't have the staff or budget to respond is simply a waste of money and effort. Perhaps the best opportunities are right next door.

Selecting target industries gives the program focus and enables you to concentrate on your strengths. When done right, the target industry study can be used as a powerful tool to tell companies why they ought to consider locating facilities in your community.

With the product and the market identified, the marketing plan determines the delivery system. This is largely a function of the decisions already made, along with the resources available to support the program. It needs to be carefully crafted to assure a balance between marketing (generating prospects) and sales (closing the deals).

Business recruiting is highly competitive and there are no guarantees of success. A community can use whatever method works best for it, but it is important to remember that marketing is not something that can be turned on and off. It requires a long-term effort, there has to be continuity, and the program has to have sufficient resources to keep going until it finally pays off.

About the Author..... ## Leland F. Smith

Leland F. Smith is President of Elesco, Ltd., an Oregon Corporation that provides land use consulting and development services to public and private clients throughout the Pacific Northwest and western Canada. Elesco specializes in identifying revenue enhancement opportunities for underutilized or surplus real property assets and develops strategies for their implementation. Mr. Smith can be reached at 541.593.3963.

MARKETING PLAN CHECKLIST ✓

PROJECT TITLE: _____   **PROJECT NUMBER** _____

1. SET MARKETING GOALS

What results will make your program successful?

_____

_____

_____

2. DEVELOP A MARKETING BUDGET

Brochures, sales materials	$ _____
Video	_____
Advertising, direct mail	_____
Telemarketing	_____
Travel, trade shows	_____
Hosting local visits	_____
Other: _____	_____

Total Budget: $ _____

3. SELECT THE MARKET AREA FOR RECRUITING

_____

_____

_____

4. SELECT THE INDUSTRY TARGETS

_____

_____

_____

MARKETING PROGRAM CHECKLIST ✓

PROJECT TITLE: _____ **PROJECT NUMBER** _____

Adding a sharply focused marketing campaign to your program can make an enormous difference in your success. Depending on your local situation, you may need to prepare and mail general information to help get the attention of business people. But the most effective marketing comes from identifying the specific industries and companies whose needs match your resources. The more you can target your information to the specific needs of these firms, the greater will be your success.

	YES	NO
Does your area have an effective marketing program?	___	___
Does it get results?	___	___
Does it present your area's attractions convincingly?	___	___
Is that marketing program focused on industries or companies clearly identified as fitting your area's resources?	___	___
Do you have quality marketing pieces:		
• basic data brochures?	___	___
• promotional pieces?	___	___
• videos?	___	___
Do you monitor the efforts of your sales program?	___	___
Do you have well-qualified people selling your area?	___	___
Are they aware of all your community's assets?	___	___
Do you have a yardstick to measure their efforts?	___	___
Do you support their efforts to sell your area?	___	___

How do you rate your area's marketing program:

☐ *Superior*   ☐ *Excellent*   ☐ *Average*   ☐ *Below average*   ☐ *Poor*

What can you do to improve it?

_____

_____

_____

CHAPTER 8

THE MASTERS SPEAK

Jack Wimer
Editor, *Expansion Management Magazine*

The U.S. Open golf tournament was being held in Tulsa, Oklahoma, a few years back and a Pro-Am tournament was put on as one of the ancillary events. During the Pro-Am a rainstorm blew up and threatened to end the tournament. One of the professional golfers turned to well-known evangelist Oral Roberts and said: "Oral, can't you intercede on our behalf and do something about this rain?"

Oral Roberts responded, "Sorry, that's in Management. I'm in Sales."

———o———

If you are in economic development, you indeed are in sales. The essence of sales, of course, is getting the attention of the buyer. Many people do this with advertising. If you don't think advertising works, just finish this phrase: "I'd walk a mile for a _____." If you said Camel, you are a good example of how advertising works. You see, it has been more than 25 years since that advertisement ran on TV. Most economic developers find that advertising is not enough. They must do more. They must create something special that doesn't just grab the attention of the buyer, it holds a memory. That's why special promotions and special events are so popular with economic development.

THE "BILLBOARD TOP 24"

Through my work at *Expansion Management Magazine*, I have the opportunity to meet many economic development professionals through-

out the United States. The following text identifies some of the best and most innovative programs I've encountered. Take a look at what's playing on the "Hit Parade." If you see a tactic you may be able to use in your marketing program, give the contact a call and discuss how well it is working for them.

THE AUDIBLE

Produce and distribute a prepaid telephone calling card. The Kansas City Area Economic Development Council published 1,000 telephone prepaid calling cards ($10 face value) with a picture of the Kansas City Skyline on one side of the card and the information on how to make the call on the other side. When the user dials the 1-800 number to use the calling card, they are greeted with a 30-second message singing the praises of the city's technology infrastructure. These 1,000 cards were mailed out to corporate decision makers

and had a powerful impact on many of them.
Contact: **Martin Mini, 816.221.2121.**

GO LONG

Market your airport. A number of cities have decided instead of marketing just a particular city that they should market an airport area inside the city. Two examples of this are the new marketing program surrounding the Baltimore–Washington International Airport and also the new Denver International Airport. While Denver, unlike Baltimore, has a huge amount of undeveloped land nearby, there are obviously possibilities for development near the site of the airport in Baltimore, too. This appears to be a good strategy as long as you concentrate the marketing on an airport-dependent or airport-related companies. High technology firms also enjoy airport proximity.
Contact: **Jay Hierholzer, 410.859.7029.**

WAIT A MINUTE, MR. POSTMAN

Do a postcard mailing campaign. While a lot of mail gets put in the trash can, first class mail postcards rarely do. That's what they learned in Miami, Oklahoma. In fact, if there is a picture on one side, studies show just about everyone will turn over and read the back. So, if you have some form of message to put on the back that can be a quick update of information, then this is a good way to get this information into the hands of corporate site location decision makers. It is important to not send out these postcards unless you have something to say. Use this method to communicate new and interesting things about your community. People have found an acceptance level of these to be high—up to about six per year—so do not send postcards more than once every two months.
Contact: **Mark Young, Miami, Oklahoma, 918.542.8405.**

BRING IN THE CLOWNS

Put on a familiarization tour. Many cities such as Charleston, South Carolina, Bullhead City, Arizona, and Research Triangle Park, North Carolina—make time to host journalists and site selectors. They usually invest in an airplane ticket and a couple of nights of hotel rooms to allow the journalists or site selectors to interview local business owners. While it is not guaranteed to produce a story, it often does. The best part about this method is that even if you don't end up with a story the reporter gets the background on your community, so next time they need a quick quotation from someone, the reporter will know who to call. Contact: **Ted Levine** at DCI, **212.725.0707.**

TALK TURKEY

Hold a special event and invite site locators. Every year the State of Oklahoma puts on the Lieutenant Governor's Annual Grand Slam Turkey Hunt. Site selectors pay their own way to get to Oklahoma City, but once they enter in the Capitol building they are treated with a presentation on the State of Oklahoma and flown in the state airplane to a good place to hunt for those elusive springtime birds. State employees such as game wardens are the guides, and they have an opportunity to talk about the people and the work ethic in their state of Oklahoma.

In a similar fashion, the State of Wyoming puts on a program where they invite celebrities and site selectors. Paul Newman and others have participated in the Lander, Wyoming, Singe Shot Antelope hunt. The Contestants are taken out to a place where hunting might be good, but they are given only one bullet. There are large ceremonies surrounding this event, such as a "blessing of the bullet" by an Indian medicine man. The pomp and circumstance involved give site selectors and site consultants an opportunity to get a feel for some of the interesting cultural aspects of those parts of the country.
Contact: **Vivian Watkins**, Director, Wyoming Department of Economic Development, **307. 777.7284.**

HOME (PAGE) RUN

Assemble a home page on the World Wide Web. A number of cities have assembled home pages to market their community for people who are surfing on the Internet. They do it because it works. Here are just a few cities that have done a web page:

http://www.state.ky.us/	Commonwealth of Kentucky Web Server
http://wvweb.com/	Welcome to the West Virginia Web!
http://www.infoanalytic.com/beatrice/	Beatrice, Nebraska USA
http://www.swcolo.org/	Welcome to Mesa Verde Country!
http://limestone.kosone.com/kingston/	Greater Kingston Community Gateway
http://mitc.org/MBINet/	The Maryland Business Information Network
http://www.ethom.com/roswell/	Roswell, Georgia USA
http://www.infoanalytic.com/cook/index.html	Welcome to Cook, Nebraska USA: The Best Small Town in America
http://montrose.frontier.net/City_of_Montrose_Info_Center.html	City of Montrose Info Center
http://www.bot.org/ragenda.html	The Greater Washington Board of Trade: Regional Affairs
http://www.chesterfield.mo.us/	Chesterfield
http://www.bjournal.com/	Blue Ridge/Smoky Mountains Interactive
http://www.gnofn.org/chamber/	The Chamber Business Network is Open For Business
http://www.okstate.edu/stillwater/introduction.html	Introduction to Stillwater, Oklahoma
http://amarillo-tx.arn.net/	Amarillo, Texas
http://www.embark.com/mcny/	Welcome to Monroe County, New York
http://rohan.sdsu.edu/dept/intlcomm/CityofFuture.html	City of the Future
http://simcoe.ois.on.ca/home.html	Ontario Investment Service (OIS) WWW Site
http://141.225.240.7/tsbdc.htm	Tennessee Small Business Development Center
http://ttdc.buffnet.net/htm/business.htm	Doing Business in the Town of Tonawanda
http://www.gov.ab.ca/dept/dept.html	Alberta Government Department Home Page
http://www.public.iastate.edu/~Iowa_SBDC/	The Iowa Small Business Development Center
http://www.haywood.cc.nc.us/wncedc/	WNC EDC
http://www.episet.com/nepean	The City of Nepean
http://howard.hbg.psu.edu/psdc/psdchome1.1.html	Pennsylvania State Data Center: Welcome!
http://borderbase.utep.edu/	Texas Centers for Border Economic Development
http://www.csi.nb.ca/econ-dev/	New Brunswick, Canada - Economic Opportunities
http://www.htdc.org/index.html	HTDC Web Server
http://www.saxony.de/index_e.html	WFS - Saxony Economic Development Corporation
http://www.tdoc.state.tx.us/commerce/	Welcome to the Texas Department of Commerce
http://www.nocdc.bc.ca/	Community Futures Development Corporation of the North Okanagan
http://www.co.utah.ut.us/uveda/uveda.htm	Utah Valley Economic Development Agency
http://megamach.portage.net/heartland/index.html	Heartland Community Futures Development Corp.
http://nanaimo.ark.com/~cfdc/	Community Futures Development Corporation - Central Island
http://leap.nlu.edu/	LEAP
http://www.medc.org/	McAllen Economic Development Corporation
http://www.accunet.com/leesum.htm	Lee's Summit Economic Development Council
http://www.hk.super.net/~ainacio/CN/ZH/main/zhuhai.html	Zhuhai Special Economic Zone
http://www.htdc.org/hsdc.html	Hawaii Strategic Development Corporation
http://www.swcolo.org/Business/MCEDC.html	Economic Development Services
http://www.c3.lanl.gov/ED/	Doing Business In New Mexico
http://www.southwind.net/ict/cedbr.html	CEDBR
http://www.cob.uwf.edu/~webpage/cbred.html	UWF: CBRED Home Page
http://www.asiandevbank.org/index.html	Asian Development Board
http://www.ded.state.ne.us/	Nebraska Department of Economic Development
http://www.ded.state.ne.us/crd/crd.html	Nebraska Community and Rural Development
http://www.rurdev.usda.gov/other_sites.html	WWW Economic Development Information Sites
http://ceedone.ceed.panam.edu/index.htm	Center for Entrepreneurship and Economic Development
http://arch.buffalo.edu/internet/h_economic_development.html	[UB PAIRC] Economic Development Agencies and Resources
http://www.ci.sat.tx.us/edd/eddindex.html	City of San Antonio, Economic Development Department

PIGGY BACK

Take advantage of existing sporting events. Arizona took advantage of a great opportunity to market their state and luring site selectors during a 30-day sports extravaganza. Because, these events were played in Arizona, the governor put aside $2 million to market the state during the 30 days. In late

1995 and early 1996, Arizona hosted the Copper Bowl, the Andersen Consulting World Championship of Golf, the Fiesta Bowl, the Tucson Open, the Phoenix Open, and of course Super Bowl XXX. During these events Arizona had TV commercial advertisements with all of the employees from the Arizona

Department of Commerce during these sporting events. In addition, they also did several direct mail campaigns. They sent out a black onyx paperweight that says "The Greatest 30 Days in Arizona's Sports History" to CEOs of large companies. They also posted the Arizona XXX extravaganza billboard in the Phoenix airport. Arizona also sent out a special VIP card that looked like credit cards that states the bearer is a VIP and it has a hotline number on it. They coordinated with restauranteurs, golf clubs, and theater owners to be a part of the service. Theoretically, the VIP would get the best seating, golf tee time slot, limousine service, or whatever. The last mailing piece will be in February, when they send out a questionnaire to see how they enjoyed Arizona and ask them if they have relocation or expansion plans in the near future.

Contact: **Jim Kurtzman**, Arizona State Department of Commerce, 602.280.1394.

This can also be done on a smaller scale, as they do in Redding, California, with their Discover Shasta County Days. They host an event where they bring prospective companies in for two days mixing fun and pleasure with a tour of industrial parks. At the end of the session they do a debriefing. The program is planned at the same time as the Redding Rodeo, one of the largest rodeos in California.

Contact: **Jim Zauher**, Economic Development Corporation of Shasta County, 800.207.4278.

An interesting variation on that theme is provided by the Omaha Nebraska Economic Development Council, in association with the Greater Omaha Chamber of Commerce. They do a Select Tour annual event timed to coincide with the College World Series. They take prospects to a game of the world series and have an Executive Briefing Week. The interesting twist is that they specifically invite owners of businesses who are women and minorities.

Contact: **Rod Moseman**, 800.852.2622.

MARCHING TO A DIFFERENT DRUM

Is your community trying to bounce back from a military base closing and the loss of hundreds of jobs? Williams Gateway Airport in Mesa, Arizona, marked the first anniversary of the closing of Williams Air Force Base with the addition of five aerospace companies and a flight training facility. Their goal was to create jobs and replace the 4,000 that were lost after the closing in 1993. A year later, more than 500 jobs had been created since the operation was turned over to the Williams Gateway Airport Authority.

Contact: **Mary Baldwin** at Williams Gateway Airport, 602.644.2398.

HEAD FOR THE BORDER

Would you like a list of qualified prospects who have been seeking a site in your part of the country, but haven't yet put together a deal? Would you like that list for free? Of course you would. If your community is near the state line, here's the way to get it. Many states are offering some form of low-interest Community Development Block Grant loans to companies wishing to move jobs to their state. Most of the time, more companies apply than the state has money to fund. By going to the state capitol of your neighboring state and digging through the public records, you can find out which companies have applied for loans in areas near yours, but didn't do a deal because the money ran out. They may be just ready for a friendly call from your organization.

Contact: Who let us in on this one? We can't say. He's doing it successfully from an area close to several other states and doesn't want anyone to get wise!

CHEAP DATA

Get the information you need to make a good lifestyle choice with Smart Moves, a new computer software program developed by PHH Fantus. With Smart Moves, you have access to vital information—housing market conditions, school system quality, crime statistics, local taxes, facts about the people who live in each neighborhood, even phone numbers for local contacts that can provide you with even more information. Smart Moves gives you all this data for over 1,800 communities in 154 metro areas in the United States. Best of all, Smart Moves only costs about $40.

Contact: **Fantus, 800.526.4744.**

BOX THEIR EARS

Create a box score of your own. The Orange County Partnership in Goshen, New York, did. They created a county box score, giving a breakdown of information that would be useful to companies considering their area for expansion (see below). It's a winning idea. Check it out.

Contact: **Michael DiTullo, 914.294.2323.**

INFORMATION, PLEASE

Make an information/resource list. What major corporations have headquarters in San Antonio? What are the primary industries of the area? How are the schools? What is the percent of Hispanic leadership and who are the leaders?

For the answers to these questions, and just about anything else going on in San Antonio, Texas, expanding companies can turn to the San Antonio Resource List. It's a comprehensive record of government officials and movers-and-shakers, along with phone numbers. There's also brief background material on educational, military and scientific institutions, as well as tourists attractions. Best of all, you can do it, too.

A guide like the San Antonio Resource List is easy to compile and is a valuable tool for site-seekers who want to talk to people already established in the area and find out what your community has to offer. San Antonio's PR firm put this one together, but an economic development team easily could compile such information and have it ready to impress prospects.

For more information about San Antonio's Resource List, contact: **Tammy Valentine**, Dublin McCarter & Associates, Inc., **210.227.0221.**

AT YOUR FINGERTIPS

Say you're a corporate site selector for a major manufacturing company. And you need information about relevant issues affecting business and industry in an area where you are considering a move. Wouldn't it be nice to have that information at the flip of your rolodex? The Connecticut Economic Resource Center (CERC) already has filled the rolodexes

ORANGE COUNTY BOX SCORE					
	1984	**1988**	**1990**	**1992**	**1994**
Value of Construction	$120M	$428M	$314M	$314M	$176M
Amount of Retail Sales (billions)	1.1	2.0	2.3	2.5	2.6
Single Family Housing Units Sold	1,103	2,140	1,509	1,678	NA
Average Home Selling Price	$65,594	$134,034	$139,722	$140,858	$135,000
Number Employed (thousands)	106.0	127.7	123.8	129.5	140.7
New Corporate Move-Ins	0	12	18	13	9
Corporate Expansions	0	11	4	9	5
Number of Business Parks	3	15	20	22	23
Industrial Office Space in Parks	850 MSF	3.8 MSF	7.1 MSF	9.5 MSF	10.6 MSF
Index of Business Activity	120	161	170	176	NA

of hundreds of prospects around the country with a specialized rolodex card. They mailed the cards with a letter that basically says, "We're the ones to call when you need comprehensive information about business in Connecticut." The card is slick and eye-catching with the CERC logo, contact names and phone numbers. And this way, you're always on the desks of your favorite prospects. What better way to be in their faces?

For more information about how well this marketing strategy has worked for CERC, call 203.571.7136.

SHORT AND SWEET

Send out a quick info card. Well, you'd have known if you were on Fairfield County's mailing list of corporate executives and news media. The Fairfield County (Connecticut) Information Exchange sends out a monthly postcard (and we mean postcard-size, that's all) called *News Notes*. It is a quick look at interesting facts about the state and Fairfield County. Their postcard contains information such as: Did you know that Connecticut's cost of doing business is continuing to decline as ▷

legislators enact further corporate tax rate reductions? Or that Stamford is the third best city in the country in which to raise kids, according to Washington D.C.-based Zero Population Growth? If you were sending out fast-facts about your community, you'd probably be getting several more phone calls a day from prospects. It is an inexpensive, effective way to reach your target audience.

For more information about what type of information they use and what the response has been, contact: **Fairfield County Information Exchange, 203.359.3220.**

IN A NUTSHELL

What could be more useful to an expanding or relocating business than a list of all the companies that have done the same in your area in an entire year? Take a look at this well-organized list of all the companies that expanded or relocated in Jacksonville, Florida, in 1994. In a nutshell, it is a business prospect's dream. And the media likes it, too! For a copy or more information, contact **Cathy Disbrow Brown, Partners in Progress, 904.366.6652.**

Company	Contact/ Phone	Type of Business	Projected Jobs	Capital Investment	Facility Size	Date Announced
ADtec, Inc. Jacksonville	Keven Ancelin 904.720.2003	Mfg. Cable	15	600,000	12,000	2/01/96
Ainsley Warehousing	Ron Schuster 315.478.7904	Warehousing	70	12,000,000	315,000	2/29/96
American Energy	Bill Guiney 904.284.0552	Solar Thermal	20	1,200,000	13,0000	9/22/95

THIS PROGRAM'S NO LEMON

The city of Lemon Grove has created the New Business Assistance Package—which contains everything from a flow chart of the business permitting process to relevant application forms (indexed and color-coded, we hasten to add)—to aid new companies trying to set up shop in this southern California town. The packet's emphasis, reports Robert Richardson, a city management analyst, is on simplicity.

Contact: **Robert Richardson, 619.464.6934.**

FOOD FOR THOUGHT

Sixteen million acres and 65,000 farms contribute to Indiana's agricultural productivity, making it one of the top states for food processing activity in the nation. The Indiana Department of Commerce thought it was noteworthy information for expanding and relocating food processing companies, so they made a book out of it. In conjunction with the Office of the Commissioner of Agriculture, the Indiana DOC published an eight-page brochure for food processors. It highlights state statistics and information, and lists several of the more than 500 food processing companies that call Indiana home.

If you want to see how they put it together, call the **Indiana Department of Commerce, 800.463.8081.**

PUTTING YOURSELF ON THE MAP

Make a map of international investment in your county, state or metro. PSI Energy in Plainfield, Indiana, assembled a state-wide map with pictures of the flags of foreign nations represented in foreign-owned businesses around the state. You, like PSI, may find yourself surprised as just how much foreign investment you already have. This map is a great device for showing your board how the global economy has effected your state, and it is also an excellent recruitment map when foreign visitors come looking for buildings and sites.

Contact: **Robin Sadler at PSI Energy, 317.831.1949.**

RETIREMENT? AS AN INDUSTRY?

Thinking of new ways to market your community? Think senior, as in...senior citizen. Did you know that there are organizations like the American Association of Retirement Communities (AARC) that actually specialize in the economic enhancement of communities through the promotion of retiree attraction as an economic development strategy? In other words, they can help you market your community as a retirement haven. Take Hendersonville, North Carolina. The migration of retirees caused Hendersonville to experience an increase in the demand for homes and other related goods and services. This increased demand has stimulated the economy and expanded the tax base. Migrating retirees bring with them most of their financial assets, in particular pensions and Social Security checks. A staggering $12 million in Social Security payments are received by residents of the community each month. Marketing your area as a retirement community can bring about many economic, cultural and social opportunities.

Contact: **AARC, 800.517.3847.**

THE MIGHTY PEN

The written word is a powerful thing, especially when it is the first impression you make on a prospect. *Inside E.D.* has received some state and community newsletters we think are top notch. Here's a just a small sampling of how you can make community news work for you. The Oklahoma Department of Commerce recently launched a zippy news bulletin called *Oklahoma News Update*. Each update provides information on two or three new Oklahoma programs or topics—subjects like telecommunications or aerospace, economic development, worker's compensation reform, hot new industries, and major companies relocating or expanding in Oklahoma. *Oklahoma News Update* is designed to be helpful for prospects and the media alike.

Contact: **Tina Majors, 405.521.2161.**

EVERYONE'S A STAR

The Tennessee Chamber of Commerce does a good job of showing off the stuff they do best. They do twice a year annual events where they bring in prospects site consultants and their wives during the Sarah Lee PGA and they stay at the Opryland Hotel. They meet with the Governor and Mayor and visit the Nissan Motor plant. The best part is that these people also get to go to songwriter sessions. They do this with the same site consultants year after year to establish a close relationships with them.

Contact: **Janet Miller, Tennessee Chamber of Commerce, 615.259.4742.**

WAKE THEM UP

Put up a billboard. The High Desert Regional EDA has a billboard that is located between Los Angeles and Las Vegas on I-15 that reads: "Reward: $1,000 for relocating your business to the high desert." There are 48,000 commuters on this highway each day. They get a larger response from this billboard than from anything else. They have gone so far as to set up site tours because of this billboard.

Contact: **Robin Orman, 619.245.0433.**

HAVE IT YOUR WAY

Take a site selector where he or she wants to go. The Economic Development Council of Utah takes site selectors and consultants on tours...but they do it more personally. They take them where they want to go as opposed to where the EDC thinks it should take them. Since the State of Utah doesn't offer incentives to companies, they do a Comparative Operating Cost Analysis where they compare other areas that perhaps the company has also selected and compare the savings that the company will save in the next 10 to 20 years.

They have these cost analyses ready for CEOs when they arrive. (Pay attention, because these guys landed the Micron semiconductor plant.)
Contact: **Tammy Kikuchi, 801.328.8824.**

These are just a few of the promotions and events that people have found to be successful. Keep in mind that the key to success is not always in the quality of the plan or in the uniqueness of the event. In most cases, a mediocre event, executed superbly, is far better than a superb event executed in a mediocre fashion.

About the Author..... Jack Wimer

Jack Wimer is currently the editor of *Expansion Management Magazine.* His background includes serving as Vice President of PHH Fantus and an economic development consultant with Midwest Research Institute. Mr. Wimer is a seasoned journalist and was nominated for the Pulitzer Prize. He also helped the economic development industry pierce the veil of the information age by conceiving and developing Forté, a target industry analysis and economic development marketing program that won the 1992 Microsoft Windows World Open Competition. Jack Wimer can be reached at 913.381.4800.

CHAPTER 9

EVALUATING MARKETING EFFECTIVENESS

James Mooney
Principal of Business Development
Northern Indiana Public Service Company (NIPSCO)

Maury Forman
Program Manager for Education and Training
Washington State Department of Community, Trade and Economic Development

There once was an economic developer who had the opportunity to pass a mental hospital each day on the way to the office. One day he noticed a certain patient, and not long after that he made it a habit to stop each day and observe this patient in action.

The patient was pitching an imaginary ball game. He stood there, got his sign from the imaginary catcher, went into his wind-up, and then pitched the imaginary ball.

Finally, one day the mayor caught the economic developer staring at the patient and asked, "Why do you stop every day and look at the poor fellow?"

He replied, "Because the way things are going with my marketing program, I'll be there soon and I'll probably be catching for him, so I want to see how his curve breaks."

———— o ————

No matter how successful you are at the other aspects of economic development, executing a cost-effective attraction campaign will sometimes drive you crazy. This chapter will provide some ideas that may assist in recognizing that you do not have to reinvent the world to make your community noticeable. In fact, as a practitioner you will soon realize that certain things work and certain things work considerably less well. In this section you will:

- Gain an understanding of the most commonly used marketing techniques,

- Learn ways to maximize your effectiveness at these techniques,

- Learn how to evaluate the effectiveness of economic development marketing.

THE MOST COMMON TECHNIQUES

The overwhelming desire to attract new investment to a community places virtually every organization in the marketing arena in some way, shape, or form. This is both a good and bad situation. On the plus side, this means that a plethora of information is available for evaluating marketing results and effectiveness. The negative side means that the prospect will be inundated with information regarding the next perfect place to locate their ▷

business. The challenge to the economic developer, then, is to create a marketing program that renders the greatest return on the marketing dollar.

One of the best sources of information for economic development marketing (among other things) comes from M. Ross Boyle. Ross is the editor and publisher of *GSO Research Report for Economic Development Professionals*. If it is not on your list of periodicals, it should be. The following survey results are reprinted with permission from his *Economic Development Organizations Survey Report*, January 1995.

PROSPECTING TECHNIQUE	% USING OFTEN	% RATING EFFECTIVENESS AS:	
		High	Poor
Direct Mail	33	10	22
Staff Marketing Trips	26	26	8
Trade Shows	21	13	14
Advertising	15	5	25
Hosting Special Events	9	11	10
Telemarketing	7	4	12
Volunteer Marketing Trips	5	6	14
Foreign Marketing Missions	4	5	12
Public Relations	4	3	12
Computer Internet and Web	3	1	12

The table above describes the frequency of use and the effectiveness of ten marketing techniques designed to identify and qualify business attraction prospects. Direct mail is the most frequently used technique to make contact with potential attraction prospects but staff trips to meet with these prospects on their home ground are, by far, the most effective prospecting technique. The other two techniques often used by at least one in six survey respondents are booths in target industry trade shows and media advertising. Trade shows get an average effectiveness rating. One in 20 economic development organizations call

advertising highly effective while one in four consider it a poor technique. Almost one in 10 organizations frequently host special events for key executives of prospect companies, a technique that gets a slightly above average efficiency grade. The other five techniques listed in this table are often used by few organizations and all get low effectiveness ratings.

Media advertising is the most controversial economic development prospecting technique. On the plus side, it enables organizations to bring their message to very large numbers of potential prospects at a low per-viewer cost. On the minus side, most of these viewers are not realistic prospects. Further, if an E.D. organization is to effectively compete with all other advertisers, it must invest in size and repetition. This makes an effective advertising program a costly undertaking. You have already seen that most E.D. entities have very small budgets, limiting their capacity to mount effective campaigns. When they spend modest amounts on this technique, it is not surprising that they view the results as being poor. Nationally, 80 percent of those organizations that spend anything on advertising allocate less than $25,000 a year on this activity. Just 2 percent can afford to spend more than $100,000 on advertising. The more an organization spends on advertising, the more positive it is about the effectiveness of the tool.

Economic developers use several media to deliver their advertising message to business ▷

attraction prospects. The table below presents their frequency of use, nationally, and the perceived effectiveness of each medium. Economic development trade magazines (e.g., *Area Development; Business Facilities; Expansion Management Magazine; Plants Sites, and Parks; Site Selection*) are often used by one in six organizations. One in eight frequently use either trade publications for industries they have targeted, or business magazines serving geographic markets they have targeted. One in 10 advertise in local newspapers in target market areas. The other four media are frequently used by less than one in 12 organizations. All of these media get more "poor" than "high" grades, but target industry trade magazines get better ratings than other forms of advertising, followed by economic development trade magazines.

ADVERTISING MEDIUM	% USING OFTEN	% RATING EFFECTIVENESS AS:	
		High	Poor
Economic Development Trade Magazines	16	5	13
Target Industry Trade Magazines	12	6	11
Local and Regional Business Magazines	12	4	16
Airline Inflight Magazines	6	0	11
National Business Magazines	5	1	13
Radio and Television	2	2	10
National Newspapers	1	0	13

Economic development and target industry trade magazines are the most frequently used advertising media in four regions—South Atlantic, Mid-South, Great Lakes, and California. Regional business magazines are used as much as target industry magazines in the South Atlantic and Great Lakes regions. Organizations in New England and the Mid-Atlantic are most likely to advertise in local and regional newspapers and magazines. Southwestern communities outside California favor regional business and economic development trade magazines. Fewer than one in 10 Plains and Northwestern organizations use any of these

media. Among the lesser used media, national business magazines get the most business from organizations in California and the South Atlantic; national news papers (Southwest and South Atlantic, inflight magazines (South Atlantic), and radio and television (New England). The South Atlantic reports the best results for both economic development and target industry trade publications; Great Lakes and California communities give the highest rating to regional business magazines; those in New England and the Northwest give local newspapers the best marks.

There are many forms of direct mail used in economic development marketing. The following table identifies the most often used and the most effective materials. ▷

The first column identifies various types of direct mail advertising. The next two columns present user evaluation of their effectiveness.

MARKETING MATERIAL	% RATING EFFECTIVENESS AS:	
	High	Poor
Tailored responses	55	1
Fact sheets	41	1
General brochures	26	6
Target industry brochures	20	5
Comparative computer reports	20	6
Videos	10	16
Computer Disks	3	9
Gimmicks	1	10

TOWARDS A MORE PRODUCTIVE IMPACT

Now that you have learned about the most commonly used marketing techniques, it would be valuable to discuss ways in which you can make each method more productive for your program. If you haven't discovered it by now, you will soon learn that large sums of money are spent in economic development marketing efforts. Your goal is to learn how to spend them efficiently.

Direct Mail

This is the most commonly used method of economic development marketing. To get the most out of your direct mail campaign:

- Look at your mailing offering as your reader would:
  — Does the number one benefit hit you between the eyes?
  — Does the number two benefit follow closely behind?
  — Does the outside envelope encourage you to open it—now?
  — Does the letter discuss the reader's needs, product benefits, features, and endorsements and how to respond?
  — Do graphics support the copy?
  — Does the reply card tell the whole offer?
  — Is there a reason to act now?
  — Do you make it easy to reply?
- Be sure to use a toll-free telephone number for the prospect to respond.
- Make your offer clear and repeat it several times. BE SURE TO ASK FOR THE ORDER!
- Make the mail-back coupon a direct miniature of your ad.
- Always include information as where to get in touch with you: company/ organizational name, address, telephone number, Internet address, etc.
- Have several bold sentences stating clearly your community's main advantages.

Staff Marketing Trips

Staff marketing trips are the second most utilized marketing tool for economic developers. While the most effective, this type of marketing can often generate the highest per-visit marketing costs. The following tips will increase your effectiveness:

- Use a travel agent to find you the most appropriate hotels for meeting rooms and support services.
- Call the hotel and verify the information provided by your travel agent.
- Fax your prospect a meeting confirmation two days in advance of your meeting. Since those days are commonly used for traveling to the site, have your secretary send the fax while you are on the road.
- Open the meeting with small talk about noncontroversial issues. Sports and weather are common grounds (however, for discussions about the weather, you will want to be sure to put à positive spin on the subject). You may want to obtain a local paper and discuss local issues that may apply to the prospect. You can do so by arriving a couple hours early and looking up information at the local library.
- Bring appropriate reports and marketing material for the prospect. In most instances, the reason for the meeting and subject matter to be discussed will have been addressed prior to the meeting. Bring information supporting these topics with you.
- Plan for the next steps necessary to meet your prospect's needs. If warranted, bring this information to the meeting as well to show how you understand what they need to do next.
- Send a follow-up fax thanking the client for the meeting as soon as possible. For extended trips, use a fax modem and sent these thank-you faxes from your hotel room.
- Stay in regular contact with your prospect after the meeting.

Trade Shows

Trade shows offer some of the most cost-effective methods of getting in front of prospective customers. The challenge is to attend each trade show with a focused approach to maximizing the potential it offers. In order to accomplish this success, the following ideas may prove beneficial to your program:

- To save money, consider striking up a deal with another community to share the cost of the booth. Remember, businesses choose regions before they choose communities. Partnering in this manner may increase your exposure earlier in the decision-making process.
- Have your staff focus on meeting your objectives by getting names, addresses, and telephone numbers of potential customers. Pretrain them in how to elicit this information so they can adequately handle traffic flow.
- Use professional-looking displays, and make sure your people are completely knowledgeable about the community you represent and the services you can provide.
- Develop a brochure for the event.
- Staff your booth with enough people. Make sure they are personable, extroverted, and friendly.
- Your booth staff should have good social graces, as these shows invariably mean parties where many of your most important contacts are made.
- If you have a community video, have it running in your booth with free copies available for prospects.
- Never smoke, eat, groom, or sit down in a trade show booth.

Media advertising is the most controversial economic development prospecting technique.

Classified Advertisements

The number of specialized publications allows your community to select narrowly targeted audiences. Magazines provide long life for your ads and offer a prestigious, quality environment. Deadlines, however, occur long before publication, making it difficult or react to fast-changing market conditions. To get the most from your advertising program, consider these tips:

- Pay for a good design of the first ad, then update the writing at a lower cost.
- An ad will be cheaper (per exposure) and more effective if you run it several times.
- Design an ad based on what attracts you to other community's ads.
- Try not to use abbreviations.
- Do not use esoteric or trade-specific terms.
- Word your ad so that it contrasts with your competitors.
- Use facts to stress your advantages; avoid economic development clichés.
- Find a catchy headline, and use it in your advertising and direct mail efforts.
- Withhold certain information that may, in itself, generate phone calls.

Public Relations Events

Marketing through public relations events is sometimes a controversial component to the economic development profession. Often, people do not understand how this marketing technique works for the community. Critics will sometimes refer to this as the "party circuit." However, public relations events are simply another form of call trips. Toward that end, they should be viewed as one of your more productive marketing tools. Here are some ideas for making public relations events more productive for your program:

- Communicate the news you wish to have disseminated by writing a news release to the local media.
  — Address your release to a particular department (business, entertain-

ment, civic affairs, etc.), and use the specific name of the editor of that department.
  — If your news is really hot, send it to the news or city editor.
  — Tie in your information with the news of the day. Issue statements that pertain to the news stories about your community.

- Give an award or scholarship each year to students, practitioners, or businesses who demonstrate excellence in job creation, architectural achievements, setting new records in exports, etc.
- Sponsor local events. This serves as a way of developing favorable name recognition for your program. Co-sponsoring can involve little or no money.
- Provide complete, newsworthy stories to get a free publicity story or interview. This is the bottom line in public relations.
- Stage an event that shows the public how a product or service works.
- Join civic clubs and community organizations.
- Join local boards. This helps to sell your program and your credibility. (Warning: joining too many boards will dilute your effectiveness and ability to make substantial changes in your community.)

Telemarketing

It is interesting to see the widely varied perceptions of telemarketing in economic development. For those who view it as cold call marketing, the perception is very poor. For those who see it as an integral component to a multisensory, sustained marketing effort, the support is very strong. If used effectively, telemarketing can be a successful transition between your advertising or direct mail programs and your personal calls on prospects. Here are some ideas for making the best of your telemarketing campaigns:

- Never read from a script or even try to memorize one.

- Talk clearly. Use short sentences.
- Use an outline to structure your telephone presentation.
- Relate to the prospect first as a human being, not just a sale.
- Make the presentation concise, but loaded with benefits.
- Be sure to answer all questions. Have the answers to objections ahead of time.
- The greater the number of people you call, the more sales you will close. Remember: volume, volume, and more volume.
- Use people who know enough about your community to address issues immediately. If they cannot do so, have them promise to get back to the prospect within 48 hours—then do so!
- The purpose of the call is either to:
  — close the sale
  — schedule a meeting
  — report information and findings

As you consider various marketing techniques, you may find reasons to choose one which is not listed as one of the most popular or productive methods in this chapter. Your responsibility is to find a technique that works best for your community and your situation. Regardless of your selection, these tips will help you to get the most output from your program. Use these guidelines to make your program as productive as possible.

EVALUATING MARKETING EFFECTIVENESS

Regardless of the type of program an economic development agency selects, the next most important activity to undertake is to evaluate the effectiveness of the marketing program. This effectiveness can determined through either a conversion rate, a cost per lead or a combination of both. The conversion rate is a percentage of leads that ultimately invest in the service territory of the economic development organization. If a direct mail campaign were to generate 100 responses and 10 of those responses were to invest in the service territory of the organization, the conversion rate would be 10/100 or 10 percent.

The cost per lead is simply the number of leads generated through the marketing tool divided by the cost to execute the marketing campaign. For example, if a direct mail program costs $457,333 and generates 892 leads, the cost per lead is 457,333 ÷ 892, or $513. The following information will show you how to evaluate a lead generation program and make decisions regarding whether to maintain a certain program or to try other methods.

In an international survey of economic development organizations, data was collected regarding; the amount of money spent on various marketing methods, the number of genuine inquiries resulting from each method, and the number of actual investments resulting from that method. The data presented was verified for accuracy and tabulated to produce

Regardless of the type of program an economic development agency selects, the next most important activity to undertake is to evaluate the effectiveness of the marketing program. This effectiveness can determined through either a conversion rate, a cost per lead or a combination of both.

the following results. The first table shows the various promotion methods, the total amount spent, the number of inquiries (leads) generated by each method and the cost per lead (in descending order of effectiveness).

METHOD	COST	LEADS	COST/LEAD
Conferences/Seminars	388,200	1,235	314
Direct Mail	457,333	892	513
Trade Shows	976,000	1,186	823
Directory Listings	83,000	93	892
Adds in General Magazines	384,650	400	962
Sales Representatives	573,000	508	1,128
PR Campaigns	616,000	291	2,117
Trade Press Adds	1,045,000	464	2,254
Newspaper Adds	742,000	158	4,696

As you can see, when evaluated in terms of cost per lead generated, conferences/seminars outpace direct mail. This form of evaluation is particularly useful for organizations that are challenged with justifying their existence on the basis of how much each lead costs. However, this evaluation does not show the whole picture. The next table shows the various promotion methods, the number of inquiries generated by each method, and the actual investment generated by each method. From this information, the conversion rate is generated.

METHOD	INQUIRIES	INVESTMENTS	CONVERSION RATE
Sales Representatives	508	104	20%
Newspaper Adds	158	12	8
Adds in General Magazines	400	14	4
Direct Mail	892	23	3
Trade Press Adds	464	10	2
Conferences/Seminars	1,235	22	2
Directory Listings	93	1	1
Trade Shows	1,186	12	1
PR Campaigns	291	1	Negligible

The astonishing conversion rate of person-to-person marketing is identified in this table. It is no wonder that economic development organizations are telling M. Ross Boyle that they would prefer to increase the number of staff sales trips. It is obvious from this data that this type of marketing is the most effective when evaluated in terms of conversion rate. ▷

This point is even more irrefutable when one combines information from both tables. A combination of both tables shows the various promotion methods, the total amount spent on each method, the number of actual investment projects acquired and the cost per investment project acquired (in descending order):

METHOD	COST	INVESTMENTS	COST/INVESTMENT
Sales Representatives	573,000	104	5,509
Conferences/Seminars	388,200	22	17,645
Direct Mail	457,333	23	19,884
Adds in General Magazines	384,650	14	27,475
Newspaper Adds	742,000	12	61,833
Trade Shows	976,000	12	81,333
Trade Press Adds	1,045,000	10	104,500
Directory Listings	*	*	*
PR Campaigns	*	*	*
* Not Meaningful			

Keeping your program on track is one of the key elements to success in economic development marketing. This success can be achieved when you stop on occasion and evaluate your program's progress and challenges.

In one of Sherlock Holmes' cases, learning that a dog didn't bark was a vital clue in solving a mystery. Sherlock's brilliance allowed him to observe what *wasn't* there when everyone else was looking at what *was*. You need to be as observant about your program, so you can maximize its effectiveness and impact. Take a critical look at how your program is being executed, what works best, and how you might "tweak" it to make it more effective.

Use techniques like those identified in this chapter, either in this manner or customized to fit your own program. Stay focused and sane—the profession has a way of throwing you a curve ball when you least expect it.

(NOTE: See page 209 for information about the authors.)

CHAPTER 10

THE SITE TOUR

Cindy Brown
Industrial Development Consultant, PacifiCorp

Once upon a time there was a small community nestled in a valley not far from a major freeway interchange. A booming resource-based economy provided family-wage jobs for anyone willing to put in a hard day's work. You didn't even need a high school diploma or any special training—you could learn that on the job. Then one day things began to change. The mills in town started laying people off and two shut down altogether. Unemployment was up and the economy was so depressed even the downtown diner began to feel the negative affects. Things were not the way they used to be, on that the townsfolk could agree. But what could they do to make it better?

The city leaders talked the grave situation over. After much discussion and reflection they came to the conclusion they needed an economic development wizard who could turn things around. After all, they had a great town and several nice industrial sites perfect for a new plant on the edge of town. They just needed someone who knew what they were doing—someone who could send the message out and bring some new jobs to their town.

——— o ———

This chapter will discuss the site tour. You will learn what is necessary to put together a competitive, professional tour of your community. The site tour that may appear as a flawless, low-key event takes a great deal of planning and preparation. Many economic development programs have collapsed at this stage. Use these tips to ensure that your program not only exceeds at this point, but that it does so by eliminating your competition.

After an extensive search, an economic development wizard was found who could perform the miracles the townsfolk needed. He was given a small budget, an office with an outdated computer, and one phone line. The town people breathed a collective sigh of relief and waited for the miracle to occur.

Over the next six months, the wizard diligently worked on the miracle, but the harder he worked the more discouraged he became. He learned the lesson anyone who has spent much time in the economic development field of dreams has learned: economic development takes time. It takes planning and preparation. It takes a community with a bias for action. It takes working together to make it happen. A community needs to be ready—so the miracle can occur.

Communities that wait until a prospect is on their doorstep to attempt to get their information together and their community organized have little or no chance for success. Look at it like going on a blind date: You've dressed in your best clothes, combed your hair, brushed your teeth, and now you're ready to meet. If you need to rush out and get a haircut or buy a new outfit and you only have two hours, you will not have enough time to get ready. Site visits are the blind dates of economic development. They do not come along every day, but when they do you and your community need to be ready to make a great first impression.

Anyone who has spent time in the economic development field of dreams has learned: economic development takes time.

Site visits occur for a variety of reasons. A community may have received a lead because of their advertising and recruitment efforts, or from their state economic development department, or they may be contacted directly by a business who thinks your community may fit their needs. It is wise to remember that a site visit is first a process of elimination before it becomes a process of selection. There are usually many sites to choose from, and the site selector's first job is to decide as quickly as possible which sites should be eliminated so they can evaluate the sites that best meet their needs. This process can be complicated by the fact that you may not be working directly with the prospect but through a site consultant, a state agency, or another economic develop-

ment ally. What this means to you as an economic developer is: you need to do your best to understand the company's siting needs and motivations, even if you have to work through others to gather and provide the information. Here are some helpful suggestions for building your team:

- ▶ **Get to know the people in your state who can help recruit new business.** Make sure they know what advantages your community has to offer. Provide them with updated photos and information on available buildings and market ready sites.

- ▶ **Find out if there are other economic development organizations doing good work in your region.** Meet with them and find out what they are doing that is working.

- ▶ **Get acquainted with your development community.** Industrial/commercial brokers and developers want growth to happen too. They can be a good source of leads and contacts. You may also succeed in linking with out-of-town developers who are willing to build industrial parks in your area but would not have considered doing so if you had made the effort to build relationships with them.

- ▶ **Work in partnership with your fellow "wizards."** Prospects do not see us as compartmentalized communities with clearly drawn boundaries, but more like regions. Site selection tends to be very competitive, but remember that companies are going to make the decision on the area that best meets their business needs. If it is clear to you that your community does not fit those needs, but you are aware of a community or site that does, providing support to that community can foster positive relationships and build bridges of cooperation for your organization in the future.

Then it happens . . . A few months back you received a call from a company that wanted information on your community. You, as the wizard, responded with some basic community and site information and invited them to come for a visit. Now they are ready—what do you do?

DO YOUR HOMEWORK

The first thing you need to do is find out more about the company. A site questionnaire similar to the Site Selection Checklist at the end of this chapter will be an effective tool. (Another example is provided in Chapter 2.) The questionnaire should cover many different issues and may not apply to all projects; but if you can answer all of the pertinent questions while working on a project, you will know a lot about your prospect and their needs. Find out where they are based, their financial condition, and what has been happening in their organization. Dun & Bradstreet, your local library, or a research consultant can help you in completing this step. You might check with your local utility provider, as they may have resources to help you in gathering this data. This step is important, because you need to know that you are expending your time and energy on courting a company who is legitimate, financially capable of making a decision, and not running from a problem they created in another community. Once you've completed the due diligence step, you need to start preparing for the site visit itself.

PLAN THE SITE VISIT TO MEET THE PROSPECT'S NEEDS

To be effective, site visits must be well planned, flexible, and arranged around the prospect's needs. If you don't know what those are, find out. Many horror stories have resulted because the host community did not understand the client's needs. You don't want to learn when the client gets to town, for example, that your community doesn't have sufficient water capacity and won't until after some date way into the future.

In the case of clients who use a consultant as the conduit for site selection, you still need to make sure that the site visit is planned around what the site selector wants to accomplish. Your town may have a fantastic presentation on what makes it a great place to live, but if your prospect wants to be low-key and come into town and only meet certain players, work with that request.

SET THE STAGE

Have a preliminary meeting with individuals who will be involved in the site visit. This is a step many people want to skip because of time constraints. If you can't meet face to face have a conference call to discuss what you are anticipating will happen when the prospect is in town. Much like a director of a play, the person in charge of the site visit needs to make sure everything is in order and your community is reading from the same page. The preplanning meeting will give the economic development practitioner the chance to bring all the players up to speed on the project and lay out expectations for the visit. Regardless of how you accomplish this task, it needs to be done *before* the prospect arrives in town.

> **Regardless of how you set the stage, it needs to be done before the prospect arrives.**

HOLD A TRIAL RUN

A common practice in economic development is to hold a trial run. You can do this with everyone informed; however, you will never get the quality of testing that you would if you can find someone to act as a prospect and visit your community. This prospect should be willing to play the role seriously. Request that they ask pointed and direct questions to the key individuals who are visiting your community. Ask them to challenge the information.

This process will aid you in flushing out your great community representatives from the not-so-great. It will tell you (and them) what topics need further preparation and give you some time to bring the information and the players up to speed as you prepare for the day when the real site tour occurs.

Confidentiality—More than one project has disappeared because someone on the team forgot they were privy to confidential information. You may need to remind those involved that the site visit is a confidential affair. Not long ago a local newspaper printed a detailed article on the potential siting of a new plant. Most of the people on the team only knew the project by a code name, yet somehow the press found out about the project and printed this informative and speculative article. Needless to say, the client was furious and threatened to look elsewhere.

Credibility—It is very important that your community demonstrates its ability to be honest and open about its situation. If a potential company or its consultant is doing his or her homework, he or she will know a lot about you. Be truthful with your responses, and if you don't know the answer to something, write it down and find out. It is difficult, if not impossible, to have the answer to every single question they might ask. If you want a prospect to trust you, you need to be truthful, you need to be helpful, and you need to follow up when you say you will. After all, they are making a decision that will have a significant impact on their company's financial future.

---

*Try to plan your
business assistance team
around strong team players
with a bias for action.*

Role Clarification — Everyone involved should know what role they need to play to have the site visit be a success. If a city official doesn't seem very interested in a prospect siting in his or her community, the prospect may pick up on this and mention it after the visit. Make sure that a member of your team who is supposed to cover a specific topic is prepared to do that. If you are concerned about what they need to say or do, consider talking to them privately about it. Loose can-

nons are the ones that cause the most concern. Oftentimes they aren't aware of the negative impact their off-the-cuff remarks can make. My advice is: try to plan your business assistance team around strong team players with a bias for action. If you have a problem, don't ignore it or it could backfire at the most inappropriate time.

Managing Expectations—It is important that anyone involved in the site visit realizes that a site visit does not automatically mean a siting will occur. As stated earlier, site selection is often a process of elimination before it becomes a process of selection. The site visit gives the company the chance to see for itself if your community has the qualities it is looking for. Site selection often takes a lot of time. It is highly unusual for a site visit and an announcement to occur within a short span of time. Even if a community makes it onto the prospect's short list, it is not unusual to work on a project for six to twelve months before hearing a final decision. If you are the poor wizard working the miracle, it is important that the townsfolk understand that miracles take time. Communicating and educating those involved in what you are doing and what's going on with various project can go a long way towards managing local expectations.

DEVELOP A DETAILED SCHEDULE FOR THE SITE VISIT

Develop an agenda for the site visit that includes as much detail as possible: times, places, who you will be meeting with, and the topic of the meeting. If you have done your homework, you will know when your prospect is arriving and when they are planning to leave. Time has a way or moving too fast when you have a lot to accomplish. Be sure and include travel time and time for meals if that is relevant. Planning the visit out will help you determine if you can get everything done in the time allotted. Leave some time in the schedule so your prospect can make phone calls or attend to things back home if they need to.

THE PROSPECT'S VISIT

The prospect's visit is very important in the decision-making process, as it provides the opportunity to display what your community has to offer in terms of land, labor, and lifestyle. The site visit is an opportunity to really "see" the dirt, talk with peers (other facility operators), and evaluate the quality of the labor force.

Make every attempt to schedule a visit of your community for the prospect. Depending on the company, number of jobs, and capital investment, a prospect's visit could be hosted (including plane flights, hotel room, dinner, etc.). If the prospect wishes to bring his or her spouse, special accommodations will need to be made.

Itineraries for community tours and meetings vary depending on the prospect and facility needs. Your community should be prepared to handle one-day confidential tours as well as full presentations that include a slide show and reception.

SAMPLE ITINERARY:

1 **Meet with your prospect** to review the day's agenda and answer any questions or special needs of the prospect.

2 **Tour sites and/or existing buildings.**

3 **Meet with local area officials and staff**—city manager, public works director, planning director, environmental health and air pollution control officers, etc.—to discuss projects.

4 **Lunch**, if appropriate, with a local plant manager.

5 **Meet with representatives** from labor and training agencies, utility companies, railroad, etc.

6 **Tour community** (downtown, housing, schools).

7 **If your prospect stays overnight, return him or her to the hotel room** early enough to make phone calls and freshen up before dinner. Leave a small gift in the room that represents your community.

8 **Dinner**, if appropriate, with city official(s) and a local business leader.

HELPFUL HINTS:

▶ **Start meetings as early in the day as the prospect wishes.**

▶ **Conduct tours in vans.**

▶ **Provide either hot coffee or cold drinks.**

▶ **Bring a mounted map** to show where the site is in relation to the community, transportation systems, etc.

▶ **Prepare a binder or booklet** that includes a map, the specific plot plans of each site with all data regarding infrastructure at site, plus any proposal from the community to provide services.

▶ **Include the day's agenda** and a detailed list of the representatives your prospect will be meeting. All representatives' names, addresses, and telephone numbers should be included, as well as information and brochures on local companies with whom the prospect is meeting.

▶ **Provide an 8½ x 11 business card holder** in the binder for the prospect to insert business cards received throughout the day.

▶ **"Coach" all representatives** so that they do not ask leading questions or refer to the company by name.

▶ **Bring a cellular telephone.** Depending on the company, you may want to bring a portable phone for the prospect to make calls back to their office. Otherwise, schedule breaks and make an office room available so your prospect can make calls privately.

▶ **Bring a video camera.** Lend prospects a video camera to use during the site tour. This allows them the opportunity to bring back a visual record of the site and is especially helpful if they need to share information with others who were not on the trip.

▶ **Dress appropriately.** If you are going to be getting in and out of vehicles walking around sites, dress appropriately. Suits, heels, and other professional attire are typically not the best choice.

▶ **Send a thank-you note.** On the day after the prospect leaves, send a personal note on your community's stationery thanking the prospect for his or her visit.

STICK TO
YOUR SCHEDULE

On the day of the site visit, do your best to start on time and stick as close to your agenda as possible. Provide everyone involved a copy of the agenda so they know how much time is allotted for their portion of the visit. If you get too far behind, it will throw everything off schedule. That could be important if you have meetings set up with individuals who have time constraints. Use your time wisely: Start early, have working lunches, and have the fewest people involved who can answer the questions and provide assistance. Try to refrain from running your prospect so ragged they can hardly wait for it to be over.

ARRANGE APPROPRIATE
TRANSPORTATION

It is important that you keep key members of the site visit team together on the visit. Borrow or rent a vehicle large enough to take all members in the same vehicle if possible. It's much better for everyone involved to hear and see the same things.

SHOW YOUR
BEST SITES

It is better to show prospects only the sites that meet their needs rather than every potential site which might work. You not only demonstrate your professionalism by doing your homework up front, but you save your prospect time and frustration looking at numerous sites that did not fit the siting criteria they specified. Showing sites that do not have a firm price or a commitment by the owner to sell is a risky move. As part of your up-front preparation, you should know which sites your community has available, what existing infrastructure is in place, and the potential development hurdles which will need to be overcome to make the site "market ready." Ideally, you will have market-ready sites that are competitively priced and ready for development.

PLAN THE ROUTE
FOR THE SITE VISIT

You often have several routes to get to a particular site. Plan to go in a route that makes sense so you don't have to backtrack. Remember, you only have one chance to make a good impression, so taking your prospect through the run-down part of town on the way to the site may not be the best idea. Don't hide the facts, but think about how you present them. Plan where to park on the site to give your prospect the chance to walk the ground if they are so inclined. Make sure you know where water, sewer, gas, and power connections are that would serve the site. If you haven't personally walked the site, plan to do so before the site visit occurs. The owner of the land or a knowledgeable real estate person can help prepare you for the visit. Knowing of any planned improvements or infrastructure upgrades to the site is also useful.

The pre-visit exercise can be very important, and here's just one example of why. A large manufacturer from the East Coast was looking for a site in the Northwest. They had specified that access to the site and proximity to rail were critical factors. Our information indicated the site had good access and a rail spur was located at the north end of the site. During a walk-through the week before the visit, we learned the rail spur had been removed. The locals were unaware that this had been done. Had the pre-visit not been made, it could have been a very embarrassing situation.

GET ORGANIZED

Provide prospects with a three-ring binder that includes the agenda, community description, site maps and descriptions and other pertinent information. This not only helps your prospect stay organized, it can also help keep everyone on schedule. Ask team members who will be providing information to three-hole punch it so it can easily be incorporated into the binder. For a finished look, consider having the binders printed with your community name, organization, and your community's key marketing message.

PREPARE A WRITTEN PROPOSAL

The prospect may be visiting various locations before narrowing his or her search to several states or communities. You want to ensure that he or she remembers your community and has all of the information needed to put your community on the short list for serious site consideration. One thing that can be very helpful is to prepare a written proposal. Here are a few suggestions:

- Write it specifically for the prospect.
- Answer all of the questions they asked.
- Include a map of your community.
- Have color photographs and complete descriptions of the property and/or buildings you intend to show the prospect.
- Have a letter from an important local official welcoming the prospect to your community and pledging support.
- Organize it so it is easy to follow.
- Have at least two other people read it for accuracy.

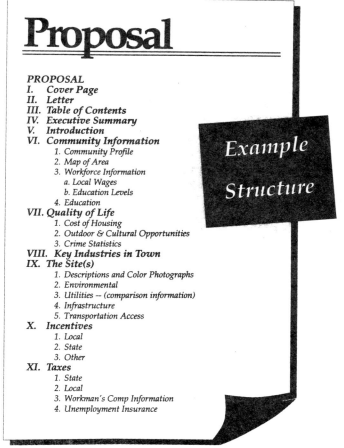

Proposal

PROPOSAL
I.   Cover Page
II. Letter
III. Table of Contents
IV. Executive Summary
V.   Introduction
VI. Community Information
    1. Community Profile
    2. Map of Area
    3. Workforce Information
      a. Local Wages
      b. Education Levels
    4. Education
VII. Quality of Life
    1. Cost of Housing
    2. Outdoor & Cultural Opportunities
    3. Crime Statistics
VIII. Key Industries in Town
IX. The Site(s)
    1. Descriptions and Color Photographs
    2. Environmental
    3. Utilities — (comparison information)
    4. Infrastructure
    5. Transportation Access
X.   Incentives
    1. Local
    2. State
    3. Other
XI. Taxes
    1. State
    2. Local
    3. Workman's Comp Information
    4. Unemployment Insurance

Example Structure

- Spend the time and money to make it look professional.

(EDITORS' NOTE: See Chapter 13 for excellent examples of different types of proposals that detail each stage of the process.)

PLAN THE ENDING

Just like a concert, each site visit comes to an end. Consider beforehand how you want to orchestrate that. Your prospects may be leaving to catch a plane or getting in their car to drive to the next community, or you may have the opportunity to have dinner with them. Don't leave this part of the visit to chance. At this point, there are a number of things you want to determine:

— Does your prospect have more questions or concerns about anything they saw or heard?

— Is your community a place where they would consider doing business?

— What would it take to get them to site in your town?

When you part company, be sure to determine what happens next. The person responsible for coordinating the visit should take the lead on this. Clarify and reiterate the things on which you will be following up. Clarify timing and other key considerations at this time, if appropriate. Make sure the prospect knows who will be working with them during the follow-up phase. If additional information is needed, get to work on that immediately. If your community made a favorable impression, failing to follow up in a timely manner could change everything.

DEBRIEF

Get the hosting team together as soon as possible for a site visit debrief. It is important for the key players to talk about what happened during the visit. What worked well? What didn't? How can we improve in the future? Obviously, some things are beyond your control, but others aren't. This isn't a time to point fingers and hand out blame, but rather a way to evaluate as a group what was learned and how to put that learning to work for your continued success.

The opportunity to host international prospects may happen, but for many of us it is not an everyday occurrence. Colleagues with substantial international recruitment experience, however, suggest:

▶ **DO YOUR HOMEWORK**—Take some time to find out about the company and the country in which it is located. Just a few minutes on the Internet or at your local library is time well spent. Also check with your state's economic development department, the *World Almanac*, the *Japan Company Handbook*, and global business data sources.

▶ **RESPECT THE NEED FOR CONFIDENTIALITY**—Once again, it is important to stress issue of confidentiality. Communities need to be especially sensitive about a company's corporate objectives. There is a widely held belief that if you can't keep a company's visit confidential, they won't trust you with other sensitive information.

▶ **RESPECT CULTURAL DIFFERENCES**—If there are several members of an international company visiting and there is a senior member, be aware that person may likely be a decision maker. Body language of the group may be a good indicator of who is in charge. You may notice members of a delegation waiting for a certain person to be introduced first. Begin with small talk first to make your prospects comfortable. There should be a noticeable transition from the introductions into the main part of the business discussion. Often a formal welcome by the host can set the tone for the transition.

▶ **EXCHANGE BUSINESS CARDS**—The business card exchange is viewed very differently in, for instance, the Japanese culture. The card itself is viewed as a representation of the person and should be treated with respect. If you handle the card carelessly, barely glance at it, and put it in your back pocket, you could unintentionally send a message that you are not interested in your guest and their business. An effective way to handle this part of the greeting is to take the card with both hands, bow slightly, and pronounce the last name out loud preceded by "Mr." or "Ms." After the cards are exchanged, place them face up in the order that the prospects seat themselves at the table. This way, you can put names and faces together. These hints may seem like common courtesy, but here's one horror story: a city official first cleaned his fingernails with the visiting dignitary's business card and then proceeded to pick his teeth with it while the community briefing was taking place! You do not want this to happen to you.

▶ **BE MINDFUL OF LANGUAGE DIFFERENCES**—Remember, English is a difficult language to learn. Common mistakes made in interacting with non-native English-speaking prospects are:

• *Talking too fast.* You need to make sure that the prospect is following what you are saying. Speak more slowly than you typically do, and enunciate clearly. Clarify to ensure that there are not more questions and that the prospect has understood what you said.

• *Using jargon or acronyms.* Foreigners often don't understand our jargon and extensive use of acronyms. Be aware of what you are saying, and avoid using words that may be confusing to the prospect.

• *Giving too much detail.* Answer the questions you are asked as succinctly and clearly as possible. Talking too much and providing a lot of unimportant details or "war stories" is a common mistake that host communities make.

• *Repetition.* Answer the question the same way even if you get asked it twice or more. A common occurrence during site visits is to be asked a question by one or two people regarding the same topic. Because a prospect may not have done many overseas projects, there is a predisposition towards wondering about the accuracy of the information they are getting. It is possible they may not have understood your response the first time, or they are simply trying to clarify their understanding of your answer. Be consistent and truthful. If you don't know the answer to a question, just say so, make a note of it, and get the answer as quickly as possible. Don't be surprised if you get some of the same questions in writing that you think you've already answered. It is not unusual for information to be sought by a number of different sources within a company to verify its accuracy.

▶ **ADVICE ON GIFTS**—Find out what the state or others involved in the site visit are doing for gifts, and coordinate accordingly. Since your prospect is likely traveling to various locations, be sensitive to the ease of transporting your gift. A locally grown product or small memento of your community is better than a bulky or heavy present. Presenting the gift when all of the conversation is nearly finished is a good way to wrap up the visit and lets you express your appreciation for the opportunity to meet and present your community.

▶ **MARKETING MATERIALS**—Reportedly, whenever you are given written materials in Asia, you are also given an envelope in which to put them. That's a nice touch. It can keep a brochure from getting wrinkled or torn, and it also makes it easy to mail. If you are going to hand your prospect materials, only give them things that are relevant and useful to them during the visit. Offer to mail the information to the prospect's office so it will be there when he or she arrives home.

FOLLOW UP

After the site visit ends, the real work begins. If the visit went well, you probably have a lot of loose ends to tie up. There are questions to get answered and details to verify. Getting the prospect to select your community as *the* place will keep you busy.

If you are doing your job, you will also be trying to determine what other communities are being considered. Find out what advantages or disadvantages you may have over the prospect's other choices. If you think you have a transportation or energy supply advantage, spend some time quantifying what that might mean to the prospect's bottom line. Knowing that information can be a real competitive advantage. On one project, for example, it was determined that electricity rates in a particular community were 53 percent less than another one being considered by the prospect. That translated into thousands of dollars per year to the prospect's bottom line. The more you can quantify the advantages of being in your community, the better chance you have of making it onto the short list and ultimately being chosen during the final siting decision.

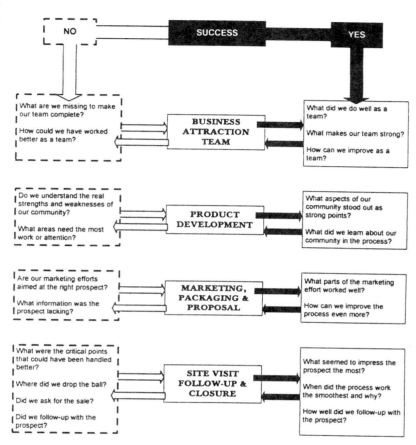

TRACK PROSPECTS

It is a good idea to track your prospects and their needs over time. Doing this will help answer simple questions, such as:

— What type of land requirements are you typically experiencing?
— How many of your prospects wanted to buy an existing building?
— How many wanted to lease a facility?

Tracking this information not only helps you be more effective, but it can be a persuasive tool in convincing developers to work with you in meeting your community's industrial space demands.

Here is a simple spreadsheet for keeping track of the site visits you participate in, what the needs were, and the current status:

COMPANY TYPE	NO. EMPL.	BLDG. SQ.FT.	N = New E = Existing	B = Buy L = Lease	NO. ACRES	DECISION: A = Announced U = Undecided O = Outside your area	CAPITAL INVESTMENT

As you can see, there are no "wizards" in economic development. There are simply professionals who know how to plan, coordinate, and execute a site visit to make it look simple. As with any other skill in life, the more site visits you orchestrate, the easier it becomes. The wizardry occurs when everyone knows their responsibilities, assumes them, and executes a successful site tour. Each prospect will dictate his or her own needs and requirements for the specific site tour. You will find, however, that there are many common themes between them.

It is really pretty basic. Once you have a strong organization in place with all of the elements needed to create the miracle, you can get to work creating it. It's true: successful site visits are a lot of work and require organization and preparation. While each one has its own nuances and surprises, site visits are a good way to look at your community through someone else's eyes. Take advantage of that opportunity and learn from it. Economic development alchemy is not for the faint of heart. (But you already knew that.) There is nothing like the sense of accomplishment that comes from seeing dirt moving and walls going up and people going to work, knowing that you were part of making the miracle happen.

About the Author.....Cindy Brown

Cindy Brown is an economic development practitioner who works for PacifiCorp, a large Northwest-based electric utility company. She has experience in recruitment of both national and international companies. PacifiCorp operates in seven western states, so Ms. Brown brings a unique multi-state perspective from working with communities of all sizes. She has a B.S. degree in business administration and marketing and is a member of CUED and AEDC. Ms. Brown can be reached at 503.464.6297.

SITE SELECTION CHECKLIST

PROJECT TITLE: _____   **PROJECT NUMBER:** _____

Please provide as much detail as possible. If you plan to phase in your operation, provide your initial requirements as well as your plans for expansion.

BUILDING: **Initially** *(sq. ft.)*   **Ultimately** *(sq. ft.)*   **Column Spacing** *(ft.)*

   Size —
      Production area: _____   _____   _____
      Office area: _____   _____   _____
      Warehouse: _____   _____   _____
      Other: _____   _____   _____   _____

   Approximate overall facility dimensions: _____

   Clear ceiling heights (ft.): _____
      Production area: _____   _____   _____
      Office area: _____   _____   _____
      Warehouse: _____   _____   _____
      Other: _____   _____   _____   _____

   Floor thickness —
      Production area: _____   _____   _____
      Other: _____   _____   _____   _____

   Which areas of the building require heating and/or cooling and/or ventilation?
      Production area: _____   _____   _____
      Office area: _____   _____   _____
      Warehouse: _____   _____   _____
      Other: _____   _____   _____   _____

   Truck dock requirements: _____

   Compressed air requirements: _____

   Lighting level requirements:
      Production area: _____
      Office area: _____
      Warehouse: _____
      Other: _____   _____

   Other building requirements: _____

LAND:

   Size and dimensions of property desired: _____
   Zoning requirements: _____
   Types of transportation access at site: _____
   Other needs: _____ _____ _____

SITE SELECTION CHECKLIST

WATER:

Average discharge per month: _____

Percent of total discharge for manufacturing process: _____

Composition of waste discharge (i.e., chemicals, heavy metals, solvents): _____

_____ _____

PROCESS EFFLUENT DISCHARGED INTO: _____

Air: _____

Water: _____

Solid waste (produced, both hazardous and nonhazardous): _____

Liquid waste (produced, both hazardous and nonhazardous): _____

ELECTRICITY:

Total installed kW:

Approximate load factor: _____

Approximate peak demand: _____

Average demand: _____

Service voltage needed: _____

Peak hour of operation during the day: _____

NATURAL GAS:

Estimated production process gas consumption/month: _____

Estimated total monthly gas consumption for all uses: _____

LABOR: Provide a breakdown of your labor needs by job skill type. If possible, include labor wage rates and worker's compensation codes.

Job Skill Category	Number of Employees	Current Wage Rate	Worker's Compensation Code
_____	_____	_____	_____
_____	_____	_____	_____
_____	_____	_____	_____
_____	_____	_____	_____
_____	_____	_____	_____

Training needs: _____

_____

OPERATION SCHEDULE:	**Initially**	**Projected Ultimate**
Days/week:	_____	_____
Hours/day:	_____	_____
Shifts/day:	_____	_____

SITE SELECTION CHECKLIST page 3 ✓

TELECOMMUNICATIONS (i.e., video conferencing, remote computer connections to mainframe):

_____

TRANSPORTATION:

Rail service: _____

_____

Air service: _____

_____

Motor freight: *Inbound*   *Outbound*

   FTL services number of trucks daily: _____   _____
   LTL services number of trucks daily: _____   _____

What major market areas would a new facility in your region serve, and how many FTL and LTL truck shipments would be made to each of those major market areas?

Market Destination	*FTL/Year*	*LTL/Year*	*Lbs./Year*
_____	_____	_____	_____
_____	_____	_____	_____
_____	_____	_____	_____
_____	_____	_____	_____
_____	_____	_____	_____

PROPOSED GEOGRAPHICAL REGION(S) UNDER CONSIDERATION: _____

ESTIMATED COSTS OF PROJECT:

   Building(s):   _____
   Land: _____
   Production equipment: _____
   Inventories: _____

SOURCES OF FINANCING FOR PROJECT: _____

_____

_____

TIMING OF PROJECT:

   Location selection: _____

   Projected date of occupancy for production/distribution purposes: _____

_____

CHAPTER 11

IS IT A DEAL OR A DOG?

James Hettinger
President, Battle Creek Unlimited

with assistance by
Janette A. Burland

Toronto Dominion Bank filed a lawsuit to recover $3.5 million from Edward Del Grande who had borrowed from the bank for his businesses. The bank had received a loan application from Del Grande and had approved the full amount. When they tried to claim their money, Del Grande countersued for $30 million, saying the problem was that the bank had loaned him too much money. Del Grande charged that if the bank had been more prudent, his company could have survived the down market in real estate and been able to make the debt payments on the loan.

———— o ————

As an economic development professional, you have every interest to make sure that Edward Del Grande does not become your next prospect. In order to prevent just the situation identified above, this chapter will assist you with separating the good deals from the bad ones and moving forward toward successful closure on new investment in your community.

It is clearly in your best interest to develop both a process and the instincts to determine a good deal from a bad deal. It is, at least, your professional responsibility to develop a vibrant and reliable employer base within the community. The ability to recognize, pursue, and realize a good economic development deal

serves the goal of building a sound employer base.

To some extent, you will be judged by the kinds of prospects and deals your community receives or generates. Board members and community stakeholders may come into contact with the kinds of prospects you generate and pursue. If those prospects are not of sufficient quality or the deals of sufficient quality, your perspective and judgement may be called into question.

Finally, the pursuit of prospects and transactions exacts a toll on organization resources and staff time. You cannot afford to waste increasingly precious resources on deals that are bad (dogs).

Consequently, the reduction of bad deals or bad transactions and the simultaneous pursuit of good deals or good transactions constitutes good offensive strategy for the pursuit of sound economic development. You are well-advised to proactively search out good potential deals. This means identifying business organizations that are manifesting the signs that a new physical deployment of resources is imminent. More than anything else, it means building relationships with quality business organizations that might be showing signs of placing new facilities or new production capability.

It is good defensive strategy, too. Your credibility, and that of the development organization and the community, is enhanced by the ability to provide good as opposed to bad transactions. When community leaders lament that all they are getting are giant waste-to-energy incinerators as economic development transactions, it is likely that outsiders see the community as desperate enough that it will accept any kind of project. Thus, everything from incinerators to casinos may be on the drawing board for a community perceived as desperate. Even if the perception of desperation is accurate, incinerators or casinos may not be the fastest route to re-establishing a certain credibility or to building wealth in a community.

Thus, for many reasons, it is vitally important that you develop mechanisms for the screening of deals or transactions. A natural screen with which all practitioners are endowed is the ability to listen to what the suspect/prospect is saying. Do not just listen; listen very carefully. Many times, local practitioners get so caught up in selling their communities that they don't allow suspects/prospects to clearly state their concerns about the possible project or to articulate what it is they need to pursue the project.

Before attempting to define a good transaction or a bad transaction and before attempting to assign characteristics to either situation, it is useful to take a look at the process of business development, and to reach an understanding of how the process itself contributes to the distinctions.

TO THINE OWN COMMUNITY BE TRUE

Every competent practitioner understands that the bread and butter of economic development is the proactive retention and enhancement of the existing business base. Justifications for this approach abound. The existing business base employs people, pays taxes, and most likely contributes to various community charitable causes.

Retention and enhancement of the existing business base is cost-effective economic development. There are not the demands for travel or the preparation of expensive promotional literature. Helping a local business stay in town or creating the conditions whereby a local business can expand in town is good for the credibility of the local developer. It shows the development organization "takes care of its own," and that the community cares. Later on, when a community is being considered by an outside company as a possible site for the location of business facilities, that company, in its own due diligence, will make inquiries among selected parts of the local business base. If you have paid necessary and sufficient attention to retention and enhancement of the existing base, the reports are likely to be good.

Such a sequence illustrates the importance of retention and enhancement to the strategy of attracting businesses from the outside. There is a real opportunity, in these circumstances, for success to beget success. The quality and quantity of the success may be directly related to how extensive the local practitioner's efforts have been with regard to retention and enhancement.

The bread and butter of economic development is the proactive retention and enhancement of the existing business base.

Many times, local practitioners get so caught up in selling their communities that they really don't allow suspects/prospects to clearly state their concerns about the possible project or to articulate what it is they need to pursue the project.

The other obvious advantage which is useful to this analysis is that you, the local practitioner in retention or enhancement projects, are for the most part dealing with known commodities. In most American communities, any practitioner—if that practitioner is diligent —will know the business base or the business composition of the community.

All of this does not deny the real possibility that retention or enhancement may contain bad deals or the outcome of certain negotiations may result in an uneven transaction. These activities, nonetheless, arm you with knowledge about the company with which you are dealing. In most cases, the local company's history is known. If it is not known, the history of the firm can be learned much more efficiently than gathering research on an outsider company. Thus, in retention or enhancement projects, you have a real advantage in knowing the target or the quarry. Knowing the prospective counterpart in a transaction is always a strong advantage and a hedge against a bad transaction.

DEFINING YOUR TARGETS

Speaking of "targets," you will greatly reduce the chances for a bad transaction by finely targeting the outside marketing strategy and by approaching suspects or prospects about which you are able to generate information. Use of information and advice from the existing business base can assist with identifying quality suspects or prospects. In addition, the plethora of on-line computer databases can help identify quality companies. You can routinely order corporate registrations, annual reports, and news articles via computers.

For example, articles from news wire sources help identify suppliers for companies seeking relocation or expansion sites. Often-times, the expansion or relocation is not the focus of a news article, but instead is incidental to other factors in the story. Diligent searches on the wire services might identify silent international joint partners, lending institutions, or environmental histories of the product the firm produces. Quality awards, a past strife with lawsuits, or new research developments can all be found through on-line data bases.

Annual reports provide clues to executives you should contact, if you wish to follow through with a somewhat vague lead. From parent companies to product lines, annual reports bring valuable details to sorting the prospects from the suspects.

You can also reduce the chances for a bad deal by getting to know and continuing to work with consulting firms that specialize in finding new locations for business organizations. As in any other profession, site selection consultants range from the very good to the very bad. You need to find the good firms, develop relationships with them, and enhance the relationships over time. Top-notch consulting firms will demonstrate the professional capability to handle their clients. When you find such a group, keep in contact with them. Not only does information from you broaden their base of knowledge about your locale, it provides the specifics that, ultimately, might prove significant.

You should, similarly, cultivate other multipliers such as investment bankers, utility industrial developers, railroad industrial developers, and certain construction companies or architectural firms to find prospects about which information is readily available. Fine-tuning a marketing strategy, like retention, does not guarantee good transactions. It does increase your ability to screen out the dogs.

ESTABLISH GUIDELINES

Nonetheless, you will want to establish some guidelines to enable identification of a prospect and a project that will be successful and will be good for the community. Thorough review of a community's business base mix may give some clues as to what kinds of businesses have flourished in the community. The same analysis may reveal the so-called "import gaps," where local businesses may be sourcing goods and services from well outside the area.

Labor considerations become important in defining conditions. Does the community possess highly educated and/or high skilled people? Is the available labor skilled, semiskilled, or unskilled? How can the community meet the prospect's labor needs? Do the training structures of the community enable it to continuously supply qualified workers to a company with rapidly changing technology? Mismatches in labor supply can create some daunting problems. What about the position of the prospect with regard to unionization?

For example, an increasing interest on the parts of plastics manufacturers in your region is a good indicator that it is time the local community college or vocational training site began offering programs in plastics technology. Similarly, computer training, robotics courses, and team-building or quality program workshops ought to be available for businesses in that will need them.

In Battle Creek, Michigan, international manufacturers in the industrial park, the City of Battle Creek, Battle Creek Unlimited (BCU), and Kellogg Community College combined efforts to implement the Regional Manufacturing Technology Center—a skilled trades training center conveniently located in the heart of the industrial park. Approximately 90 percent of students attending the Regional Manufacturing Technology Center are sponsored by their employers or prospective employers.

You should closely monitor state-funded training programs, as well as newly developed apprenticeship, school-to-work, or other local workforce-preparedness options.

Taxes or the tax structure of a state and a community may also help to define what kind of prospect will lead to a good economic development transaction. Capital-intensive business organizations do not fit well into structures that do not disproportionately tax labor intensity. Similarly, a number of other factors come into play regarding the fitness of a community for a company, and vice versa. If the production process involves the utilization of large amounts of clean water, it would hardly fit for the company to be located in a water-starved area. These factors should be accounted for early in the process. Responsibility for these factors rests with you and the site selection team.

Closely monitor state-funded training programs, as well as newly developed apprenticeship, school-to-work, or other local workforce-preparedness options.

Thus, aggressive strategies you undertake to retain and enhance the local employer base, as well as a targeted attraction strategy backed by research, can go a considerable distance toward setting the stage for good transactions and reducing the likelihood of bad ones.

In fact, if you perform these functions well, the resulting success and momentum will bring forth prospects and potential deals that will challenge any evaluation system and judgement.

Potential transactions that come to the practitioner's doorstep may or may not be the result of a good local development program. As mentioned earlier, success begets success. However, in your case, success may also beget marginalism. In such circumstances, you have to rely not only on research capability, but on instincts, which must be progressively developed over time.

The process, to this point, should allow for an assembly of characteristics of what we might call a good deal. The characteristics are structural and procedural.

KEY ATTRIBUTES OF A GOOD DEAL

1. **The deal is made possible because a business organization adheres to the profit-making motive** and has specific corporate objectives, necessitating deployment of corporate resources.

2. **The business organization and the local practitioner have done their due diligence** and have concluded that the possibility exists for a good fit between company and community.

3. **The business organization provides the practitioner with a detailed questionnaire** which covers the essentials of the infrastructure, and continues well beyond, searching out subtle aspects about the community. The implication, here, is that the more exhaustive the transacting parties are in doing their homework, the better the chances for a good deal.

4. **The business organization provides timely and qualitative responses** to the local practitioner's questions and needs for information.

5. **Incentives should not be necessary for the transaction to ensue**, even though the business organization may demand them. Incentives must to be incidental to the project; they can never be the main reason for the transaction to take place. If the practitioner is aware of a nearby competitor with more or less the same deal, incentives can act as a tie-breaker.

6. **Information about the business is readily available** through database checks, research, state filings, annual reports, etc. Local practitioners can start with the *Directory of Corporate Affiliations, The Thomas Registers, U.S. Industrial Outlook,* and state manufacturers directories, to name a few.

7. **The business organization is interested in meeting key community leaders** and is interested in how things happen in the community. This tells the local practitioner that the business organization is concerned about how it will be perceived in the community. It also tells the local practitioner that the company intends to be around for a long time.

8. **The business organization settles in the community without a disproportionate impact on the infrastructure of the host community**. If the business is a bean processor and the community's sewage treatment system is barely capable of handling the discharge, future development opportunities may be compromised. A good transaction contains an appropriate fit between the company's use of the infrastructure and the community's ability to provide an infrastructure.

As indicated earlier, success builds momentum and, to an extent, the positive publicity will generate additional prospect activity. The significant difference for the local practitioner is that the prospects will be generated by other than the direct proactive efforts of the practitioner. In these cases, the ability to make good and accurate judgements will help you. As observed earlier, much of this ability can be developed over time as part of your professional maturation process.

KEY ATTRIBUTES OF A "DOG"

1. **The suspect/prospect comes from other than the practitioner's existing employer base** or from other than the practitioner's targeted outside marketing strategy. While this is not a strong indicator of a bad deal in the offing, remember that the suspect/prospect came from circumstances beyond the reach of the local practitioner, thereby not being immediately subject to verification.

2. **The suspect/prospect needs financing** or the project will not take place. Studies show that companies choosing location based upon a financing need are likely to be marginal companies from the beginning.

3. **The suspect/prospect needs incentives** or the project will not take place. Many of the same studies show that companies choosing a location based upon a need for incentives are likely, similarly, to be marginal companies.

4. **The suspect/prospect does not appear to know his or her business** and the circumstances in which it will grow.

5. **The suspect/prospect does not respond in a timely manner** with adequate information. In such cases, the suspect/prospect does not have the information; does not want to provide it for whatever reason; or does not consider it important. In any case, the local practitioner cannot forego the responsibility of assuring a good fit between community and company. This responsibility cannot be met if the practitioner does not have adequate information.

6. **The suspect/prospect is inconsistent.** Local practitioners should closely observe management styles of the suspect/prospect and, if at all possible, attempt to learn something from the venture about employee relations. Compare what you observe with what you see as prevailing practices within the community. An inconsistent management style or one that disrupts labor peace in the community is definitely undesirable. Due to the current low unemployment rates in many parts of the United States, labor pool considerations become much more important. Many relocations have this factor involved in decision making.

7. **The business organization has a disproportionate impact on community infrastructure.** In order to maximize community resources and the appropriate use of the infrastructure, local practitioners need to assess the "fit" between the prospect and the community. Certain food processors, for example, may require extensive use of water or sewage treatment. Capacity of the community system to meet current and future needs will impact not only the prospect's ability to grow and expand, but, more generally, the community's ability to accommodate future growth on the part of current and future employees.

INQUIRIES

The momentum causes inquiries to be made. Suspects/prospects will begin to appear at the door. While this may sound like paradise for you, these are the potential projects where the fit between company and community may not seem so clear. You are well advised to field as many of these inquiries as time and resources permit. Failure to do so may cause the community to miss out on the possibility of being on the ground floor of a good project.

The point is, you will have to do some sorting. Additionally, a well-documented failure to respond might wind up on the front page of the community newspaper during your annual fund drive. Interactions with the suspects/prospects are vitally important. Again, you need to be a good listener. You need to practice and possibly accomplish the following in such interactions:

1. **Study the person without being intense or obvious**. Make notes on the meeting afterwards. Making copious notes, during the conversation, can cause you to miss something; or worse, it may cause enough insecurity in the suspect/prospect that additional information is more difficult to generate. During these interfaces, consider the following:

   — Does the person seem to actually believe what they are telling you?
   — Is their language general and sweeping, or do they speak to specific objectives to be accomplished by the proposed project?
   — Does body language reflect what is being articulated?
   — Do they have a practice of dropping names and places?

2. Within the suspect/prospect's articulation of the project, you need to **learn how to separate genuine enthusiasm for the project from false hopes**.

3. **Listen for the suspect/prospect's grasp of their business**. Do they know their business? Do they know their competitors? Do they build planning and product adaptation into their project?

4. **Are the suspect/prospect and the proposed project facilitated and sustained by the profit motive?**

5. Create a division of labor after the suspect/prospect interface. **Delegate specific tasks to every party involved.** Failure on the part of the suspect/prospect to perform the task or to provide you with additional information is cause for concern.

6. **Attempt to create a process in which the suspect/prospect has to accomplish several specific tasks.** These tasks should be easy enough so as not to constitute an unreasonable or business-hostile process. Requesting a report on sewage discharge or air emissions from the proposed project is a reasonable request for you to make. After all, somebody must help determine the fit with available public infrastructure.

7. **Assess the timeliness and quality of the response by the suspect/prospect.** In fact, throughout the process, the practitioner should continue to assess and reassess the timeliness and quality of the response.

Three other considerations should enter into your analysis of the potential transaction. First, if the suspect/prospect places importance on the availability of incentives at the expense of other, more fundamental business location factors, you should begin to develop a healthy store of skepticism about the project.

Secondly and similarly, if the proposed financing of the project is given a priority at the expense of other, more fundamental business location factors, you should develop some skepticism. Understand, at the same time, that new projects may well be financially risky, or the project start-up genuinely needs an infusion of capital. In this case, you are well-advised to review those notes from the suspect/prospect interface and to consult with experts who can give you some element of risk evaluation.

Thirdly, if the suspect/prospect insists that the project is being done to "provide jobs for the community," gently recommend that the suspect/prospect find another community which may appreciate such a display of magnanimous behavior. The conscientious local practitioner is looking for companies that are in place to be competitive and to make a profit. Perhaps, after the company has become profitable, it can then begin to do charitable activities. Your first responsibility is to induce good companies which, first and foremost, seek to make a profit through the strategic placement of corporate assets.

WHAT IS A SUSPECT?

For our purposes, a suspect is a business organization which would have a reason to be doing business in our area. A prospect has given indication that it is definitely seeking a business location.

To operationalize the distinction, BCU has attracted seventeen Japanese-owned enterprises to the Battle Creek area. These businesses were first identified through their export activities to the United States. BCU was able to find out what Japanese companies were sending products to the United States. In the case of Battle Creek, BCU was interested in which companies were sending auto parts to customers in Detroit. These companies were classified as "suspects." It was known they had a reason to conduct business operations in the Midwest.

WHAT IS A PROSPECT?

As their business developed and world economic conditions changed, they began seeking locations. At that point, they crossed over the line and became "prospects." Through requests for site information, hiring site selection consultants, or physically visiting potential sites, the business organizations became bona fide prospects.

Another distinction here is helpful. Suspects may request information from communities or from development organizations, but they have not, through this action, actually commenced a site selection search. The suspect's request for information may be pursuant to the formulation of a business plan which has yet to be completed.

Prospects, however, have a business plan, and it is implemented through the site search.

You can verify prospect status through the qualitative search for community and site information. Prospects are likely to ask for very specific community and site information. Questions may range from the infant mortality rate for a community down to the water runoff of a particular site under consideration.

Suspects may ask for general and development program information. Suspects are very rarely at a stage where they need to be concerned about wetlands on a particular site. Thus, suspects are differentiated from prospects in the stage of development, in the information sought, and the requests made of the local practitioner.

The first responsibility of the developer is to induce good companies which, first and foremost, seek to make a profit through strategic placement of corporate assets.

Tracking suspects and prospects necessitates a systematic approach. You need to have general information about each suspect/prospect. Such information may include the business organization's structure, officers, board of directors, current sites, banks, products, patents, etc. As you cross over from suspect to prospect, your files will need to record specific requests made of the development organization, last contact, with what person, and an entry describing the status of the project at the point of last contact.

Suspects and prospect tracking files will differ substantially because the prospect file will become larger and more specific. The diligent practitioner will have recorded the specific informational requests made by the prospect and this information will be above and beyond the more general requests of a suspect.

In summary, you have a professional obligation to build a vibrant and resilient business base. This can better be done if you utilize a systematic approach to identifying and tracking suspects and prospects. Suspects are differentiated from prospects in that prospects are actually seeking a location for the deployment of business assets.

Optimize their opportunities for good deals by doing your retention and enhancement diligently while pursuing a targeted outside attraction strategy. In all three areas, you enhance the opportunities for a good transaction by knowing the companies—at home and outside the community.

You will receive inquiries from suspects and other sources who may be interested in doing a project. Listen carefully to suspects, and to look for certain signs. Independent verification through computers and other information outlets is of vital importance. Finally, through the process of business development, the attributes of good and bad transactions can be identified.

*About the Author.....*James **Hettinger**

Jim Hettinger is Executive Director of Battle Creek Unlimited, the lead economic development organization in Battle Creek, Michigan. Jim's program has been instrumental in creating new investment in the vacated Fort Custer Military Base. He has marketed Battle Creek on a global basis and has been instrumental in creating a diverse and stable economy for Battle Creek Michigan. Jim can be reached at 616.962.8096.

DUE DILIGENCE CHECKLIST ✓

PROJECT TITLE _____ **PROJECT NUMBER** _____

The following outline is a guide to business analysis. It is intended for professionals who review loan applications, recruit businesses, or have other direct contact with private companies. Sections I through IV constitute a minimum level of knowledge about a business. Not all of the topics will be relevant for a particular project analysis.

		TO	
	DONE	DO	N/A

I. REFERENCE CHECK

A. Call personal references, as well as industry contacts who may know the principals.

B. Call suppliers and customers, as well as former co-workers. — — —

C. Call educational institutions to verify degree claims. — — —

D. Investigate past relationships with banks and creditors. — — —

II. LITIGATION REVIEW

A. Assess the status and outcome of any legal action taken by, or against, the company or its principals. Specifically:
1. Litigation which may adversely affect the business. — — —
2. Any criminal records. — — —
3. Any "gray areas" such as divorce suits or personal liability actions which may affect the conduct of business. — — —

B. Request information on any bankruptcy proceedings, past or present, which affect the principals or the company. — — —

III. BUSINESS OVERVIEW

It is important to know the background of the company. If you are working with a business plan or an annual report, you will find the information there. At a minimum, the following items are ones which should be clearly stated and easily explainable.

A. **General Description**
1. Brief history of company, including sales and profits. — — —
2. Business objectives (e.g., expansion, capital improvement, new product line). — — —
3. Products or Service:
   a. Product description.
   b. Competitive advantage (e.g., weight, size, cost), including technology review. — — —
   c. Proprietary status (e.g., who holds patent rights). — — —
4. Current and projected market share. — — —
5. List of board members. — — —

B. **Industry Overview**
1. Current market trends
2. Status of competition — — —
3. Pricing — — —

C. **Other Issues.** _These are potential red flags which should be carefully screened._
1. Has the business changed names or location? ☐ YES ☐ NO
   If so, why? _____
2. Has there been recent turnover of principals? ☐ YES ☐ NO

	DONE	TO DO	N/A

3. Were there recent product changes? ☐ YES   ☐ NO
4. What is the status of suppliers? _____
5. What is the competition's view of this company and its products?
_____

D. Financial Background
1. Balance sheet — — —
2. Income statement — — —
3. Cash flow — — —
4. Has the business prepared a source/use statement? ☐ YES   ☐ NO

IV. PROJECT INFORMATION

A. What is the basis of the contact? Is the company's objective to, e.g., seek funding, relocate, restructure, or expand? _____
_____

B. If the company is seeking financing, what are the financial requirements of each of the following items (whether or not the company is seeking funds for them)?
1. Research — — —
2. Product development — — —
3. Working capital — — —
4. Machinery and equipment — — —
5. Real estate or leasehold improvements — — —
6. Marketing — — —
7. Other (specify: _____) — — —

C. What funding sources are involved in the project (whether or not the agency is being asked to participate)? — — —
1. Equity—evidence of which should be documented. — — —
2. Private Lenders.
   If from an institution, are there letters of commitment? ☐ YES   ☐ NO
   What are the rates and terms? _____
   Are there special terms? _____
3. Public Agencies. Who is participating—federal, state, or local government?
   Ports or nonprofit agency? _____
   What are the terms and conditions? _____
   Has a separate review been completed? ☐ YES   ☐ NO
4. What past investments have been made in the company, and by whom?
   _____
   _____

D. What are the requirements for second round financing?
1. Bank interest: _____
2. Venture funding: _____
3. Stock offering: _____

DUE DILIGENCE CHECKLIST

V. OPERATING PLAN

This component of the review is the one through which the public sector can usually interact best with the business. After the initial review, this is a logical place to begin the more thorough analysis.

		DONE	TO DO	N/A
A.	**Geographic Location.** *It is important that the following issues be understood by the economic development professional as well as by the business.*			
	1. Labor rate.	—	—	—
	2. Labor availability.	—	—	—
	3. Level of labor force training (and how additional needs can be met).	—	—	—
	4. Proximity to distributors and customers.	—	—	—
	5. Proximity to suppliers.	—	—	—
	6. Tax structure (from all sources).	—	—	—
	7. Utility rates and requirements.	—	—	—
	8. Zoning and applicable local laws.	—	—	—
	9. Local source of components (ease of supply).	—	—	—
B.	**Facilities and Improvements**			
	1. Current development plans.	—	—	—
	2. Expansion needs.	—	—	—
	3. Office and manufacturing floor space requirements.	—	—	—
	4. Machinery and other capital requirements.	—	—	—
	5. Lease vs. purchase requirements—should reveal costs; planning should be consistent with three- to five-year period.	—	—	—
	6. Review appraisals or rehab cost estimates where appropriate.	—	—	—
C.	**Manufacturing Plan**			
	1. Describe manufacturing process (include major subcontract decisions).	—	—	—
	2. Discuss "make or buy" decisions.	—	—	—
	3. Show details of expected overhead expenses.	—	—	—
	4. Discuss inventory required for various sales levels.	—	—	—
	5. Describe inventory control systems, as well as quality and production controls.	—	—	—
	6. Discuss flow of material and purchasing structure.	—	—	—
	7. Determine how quality can be ensured.	—	—	—
D.	**Employment**			
	1. Discuss the immediate job requirements and pay structure.	—	—	—
	2. Project mid-term and long-term job requirements.	—	—	—
E.	**Product.** *Frequently the first question asked of a business is, "What's the product?" As such, it is usually overemphasized. Understanding the product does not mean understanding the company.*			
	1. Describe current status of the technology and design. Indicate existence of engineering prototypes, field test items or pre-production units (as appropriate).			
	2. Discuss program for completing the development work, including major tasks, significant milestones, and overall "time to market."	—	—	—
	3. Identify key technical people who will participate in the development process.	—	—	—

	TO	
DONE	DO	N/A

4. Identify and discuss anticipated development problems and approaches to their solutions. Include discussion on the timing of product introduction and its effect on costs. — — —
5. Show details of product costs, including design, development, field testing, tooling and consulting. — — —
6. Discuss patent status and other technology protection. — — —

VII. FINANCIAL REVIEW

Not all of the information listed below will be needed. Failure to provide requested material, however, should be regarded as a red flag. Items such as tax returns should be requested (and treated) with sensitivity.

A. For existing companies: financial statements and tax returns for the last three years, including profit and loss (P&L) statement and balance sheet. — — —

B. Interim financial statements (less than 60 days old). — — —

C. Projections, including:
1. Pro forma balance sheet showing effect of financing. — — —
2. Two-year project P&L. — — —
3. If start-up (or below break-even), cash flow statement for 12 months, or three months beyond break-even point. — — —
4. Break-even analysis (itemization of fixed and variable costs), including cost-volume projections. — — —

D. Discussion of assumptions. *(Accountants' notes should accompany all statements and projections. This is a particularly important point, often overlooked. The notes frequently contain clues to the answers sought unsuccessfully in the pro formas.)* — — —

E. Current financial statement of affiliate or subsidiary company. — — —

F. Current financial statement from each principal with 10 percent or greater share of business. — — —

G. Consider requesting personal tax returns. *This is an optional step but is useful when where a greater level of certainty is sought. This is routinely required by banks making larger loans.* — — —

H. **Ratio Analysis.** *With existing companies, spreadsheets should be prepared to determine viability of the business—with and without a new debt structure. Although ratios can be misleading, the following provide important baseline data:*
1. **Debt to Equity**—*compares company financing through lender-investors against that provided by owner-investors.* — — —
2. **Quick Ratio**—*compares current assets (those which can be immediately converted to cash) with current liabilities.* — — —
3. **Percent of Sales Growth**—*change in sales over the last four quarters, as well as over the previous three years.* — — —

VIII. MARKET ANALYSIS.

There is frequent confusion between the market analysis and the marketing plan. The analysis is concerned primarily with assessment of the prevailing market conditions. It considers the environment in which new products must compete. The marketing plan (Section IX) deals primarily with how the new product will be marketed.

		TO	
	DONE	DO	N/A

A. **Market Potential.** Define markets and discuss history and future trends. ___ ___ ___

B. **Customers**
   1. Who are major purchasers? What are their characteristics?
   _____
   2. Significance of prices, quality, service, and environmental pressures. ___ ___ ___
   3. Buying and ordering patterns. ___ ___ ___
   4. Actual contacts—and results. ___ ___ ___

C. **Market Size and Trends**
   1. Quantification of total market of interest. ___ ___ ___
   2. Past growth rates and reasons for growth. ___ ___ ___
   3. Forecast of future trends (3 to 5 years). ___ ___ ___
   4. References and sources of data and estimates. ___ ___ ___

D. **Description of Market Niche.** Also determine that the target market will provide for a reasonable return on investment. ___ ___ ___

E. **Competition**
   1. Assess direct competition, including comparative matrix of products, showing price and performance. ___ ___ ___
   2. Assess competitor's capabilities. ___ ___ ___
   3. Describe successful competitors—consider how market share will be gained at their expense. ___ ___ ___
   4. Generic competition—describe other means of providing the same or similar customer benefits; discuss potential competition and customer alternatives. ___ ___ ___
   5. Describe how the competition can be expected to react to the introduction of your product, and how to counter that reaction. ___ ___ ___

F. **Market Share and Sales**
   1. Discuss the basis for sales projections; include customer commitment, reaction of competing and extraneous factors (such as social changes). ___ ___ ___
   2. Describe, in table form, estimate of total market (dollar volume), projected sales, and estimated market share that these sales represent. *Estimates should include both total number of units and total income by quarter for the first two years, and annually thereafter.* ___ ___ ___

IX. MARKETING PLAN

A. **Product Plan.** Describe approach to product family, including market targets, features and timetable for introduction—support the need for multiple products. ___ ___ ___

	DONE	TO DO	N/A

B. **Sales and Distribution Plan.** Describe sale and distribution of products. —— —— ——
   1. Discuss basis for choosing distribution channels (or direct sales), effectiveness of that channel, and ability to command attention. —— —— ——
   2. Address sales commissions and margins for retailers and wholesalers. —— —— ——

C. **Pricing.** Describe basis for current and future pricing—is it based on current competition? Discuss penetration strategy and value as perceived by the customer. —— —— ——

D. **Promotion.** Describe advertising plan and sales promotion—how do these support sales estimates? Are public relations a problem? Can they be used to the company's advantage? —— —— ——

E. **Service and Warranty.** Is this being used as a marketing tool? Describe approach and implementation plan—discuss effect on pricing and profits. —— —— ——

F. **Marketing Strategy.** Are the elements listed above combined into a single coherent market strategy? Is it understood by the whole team? To what extent is the company truly "market driven"? —— —— ——

X. **MANAGEMENT TEAM**

A. **Organization**
   1. Describe the roles of key managers, their primary duties and the proposed organizational structure. Determine whether managers have worked together previously. —— —— ——
   2. Indicate where key functions are not being met. —— —— ——
      a. Discuss proposed solutions. —— —— ——
      b. Determine whether contractual help is required (e.g., design, marketing, accounting). —— —— ——

B. **Management Personnel.** Include detailed resumes for each key member. —— —— ——
Stress past accomplishments in similar roles (include specific successes such as sales, productivity improvement or technical breakthroughs). —— —— ——

C. **Management Compensation and Ownership**
   1. State salary to be paid to each key person. —— —— ——
   2. Describe stock ownership plan. —— —— ——
   3. Discuss equity positions and performance—dependent stock options or bonus plans? —— —— ——

D. **Board of Directors.** Identify board members and include a background statement, as well as a summary of benefits each will bring to the company; include investments made into the company. —— —— ——

E. **Management Assistance and Training Needs.** Describe candidly the strengths and weaknesses of the management team and board of directors. Discuss the kind, extent, and timing of support needed to overcome any weakness. —— —— ——

F. **Supporting Professional Services.** Discuss professional services retained by the firm. Address plans to acquire future services. Review costs. —— —— ——

DUE DILIGENCE CHECKLIST

XI. **OVERALL SCHEDULE.**
This review ties together all major tasks and events on a common timeline. It shows the interrelationships of product development, production, marketing and sales. The schedule should recognize those activities which could cause slippage in the timeline. It should also identify milestones critical to the venture. ___ ___ ___

XII. **CRITICAL RISKS AND PROBLEMS**

    A. Identify and discuss the major problems and risks likely to be encountered in the venture. Indicate which business plan assumption or potential problems are most critical to the venture. Describe plans for minimizing the effect of unfavorable developments in each risk area. ___ ___ ___

    B. Prepare sensitivity analysis and include affects of sales reduction, increases in fixed cost, and monthly burn rate. ___ ___ ___

    C. Prepare report on site visits and meeting with principals. ___ ___ ___

    D. **Capitalization**
        1. Show the names of current stockholders (over 10 percent) and number of shares held. ___ ___ ___
        2. Indicate how many shares of common stock are reserved for future key personnel. ___ ___ ___

XIII. **APPENDICES**
Carefully review any exhibits that may be attached to the business plan. Examples include credit reports, product brochures, news articles, market research data, description of technology, and supporting exhibits to the financial statements. ___ ___ ___

DEAL OR DOG CHECKLIST ✓

PROJECT TITLE _____ PROJECT NUMBER _____

	YES	NO
Is the educational attainment and skill level of the local workforce a good match with labor needs of the suspect and its product?	—	—
Are local training programs in place which can overcome discrepancies in workforce skill levels and readily adapt to incorporating new manufacturing or management technologies, as required by the suspect?	—	—
Is local representation in organized labor within the range of acceptability for the suspect?	—	—
Are local natural resources (water, land, or air quality attainment) in adequate supply for the production process of the suspect?	—	—
Has the suspect historically remained amenable to complying with local environmental regulations?	—	—
Has the suspect the capital and resources for this relocation or expansion?	—	—
Will incentives not make or break the deal?	—	—
Has the suspect provided careful details regarding infrastructure, housing, educational, and workforce skill level, utility and natural resource needs, or other specific aspects which indicate a good match between the suspect and the community?	—	—
Has the suspect responded to your questions in a timely and thorough manner?	—	—
Have you been able to compile research, articles, and other data about the suspect?	—	—
Is the suspect enthusiastic about meeting key community leaders?	—	—
Is the suspect well-acquainted with such aspects of the business as competition and research and development status?	—	—
Does the suspect recognize the circumstances under which the business will thrive and grow?	—	—
Does the suspect have a business plan?	—	—
Will the suspect bring a presently imported good or service to the local business and industry mix?	—	—

EVALUATION: *If you checked more than 10 of the 14 boxes in the "yes" column, you may begin to consider your suspect a prospect. On the other hand, more than four check marks in the "no" column indicate the suspect is suspicious, indeed. When suspects are dogs, cull them out and spend your time more productively with truly good deals.*

CHAPTER 12

UTILIZING INCENTIVES

Kate McEnroe
President, Kate McEnroe Consulting

The Amarillo Economic Development Corporation gave new meaning to the overworked and doubtful phrase, "The check is in the mail." The agency sent out legal bank drafts of $8 million to each of the fastest growing U.S. companies. The checks were good only if an enterprise located in an new facility in the main city of the Texas panhandle. "It wasn't a gimmick—we're talking cold hard cash," said Michael Bourne, Executive Director of the Amarillo Economic Development Corporation. Nine months after the campaign was launched, Amarillo has gladly cashed three of those drafts.

———o———

There are few topics as frustrating and confusing in economic development as incentives. The good news is, you are not alone. The only economic development professionals who are not concerned with incentives are those who have no companies interested in expanding or relocating in their communities, and those people often have even bigger problems.

A recurring theme throughout this chapter will be the importance of deciding about your state or community's strategy regarding incentives *before* a project appears that requires an immediate response. Although it sometimes seems that it takes forever to get a company make a decision, when you are asked to make a response, feedback is required immediately, and there is little time to build consensus from the ground up.

WHY DO THEY KEEP ASKING?

Frustration is often tinged with the implication that companies seeking incentives are endlessly greedy with no concern for the finances and future of the communities. Whether it is "fair" to request or "right" to grant incentives is hotly debated, but thus far the debate seems to have had little influence on the realities of the economic development marketplace.

From the community's perspective, those who object to incentive programs often feel that:

- Businesses should not be receiving incentives paid for with dollars that could be going into education and other important programs.

- Businesses offer no guarantees that they will stay in the community or maintain employment even after incentives are granted.
- Granting incentives to selected companies provides an open invitation to an escalating cycle of demands.
- Companies are often bluffing, and communities can receive all of the economic benefits of new employment and investment without giving up any of those benefits in the form of incentives.
- Companies should display more loyalty to their communities and want to be good corporate citizens; they should not demand incentives as payment for coming into or staying in the community.
- States, cities, and counties should all agree not to given incentives and to compete on their merits.

On the other hand, those in favor of aggressive state and community policies believe that discussion of right or wrong is outweighed by competitive realities of the marketplace and the pressure to announce attractive expansions and relocations. They believe that if handled responsibly, granting incentives will result in economic benefits to the area far exceeding the value of "giveaways" and that no community is so attractive and so compelling as the only possible choice that competitive issues should be ignored.

From the perspective of the prospects and their advisors, requests for incentives are the logical result of tighter margins and a broader variety of good location choices. Their positions focus on the benefits that they bring to the community and a desire to share in those benefits themselves. Commonly expressed positions of prospects include:

- Communities should look upon incentives as investments, which carry some risk but also the potential for great reward.
- If businesses don't thrive, there will be fewer overall tax dollars for education; the community still gets the lion's share of the tax and employment benefits a new business generates.
- Communities can't "give away" what they don't have; when they say that they have "lost" revenue by giving incentives, they are assuming that companies would have chosen them anyway, even at a cost premium, which isn't true.
- A decision maker or consultant's primary responsibility is to make the best decision for the company's bottom line, and that responsibility is not fulfilled if negotiations are not pursued.
- Loyalty to community is an important company value, but not at the expense of competitiveness; a business is worth nothing to its community if it goes under. It is not the role of the new employer to solve problems that existed in the community before they arrived.

In much the same way that community politics affects an area's approach to incentive policy, corporate politics and culture affect the definition of a successful site location project and often create an environment which requires the prospect to be an aggressive negotiator. The business environment in the United States today encourages, demands, and rewards cost cutting and aggressive negotiating. In our personal lives we thrive on finding sales, factory outlets, and flea market bargains. Paying the sticker price for a car, for example, is generally regarded as naive, as is failing to take advantage of every legal means of reduc-

The most effective incentives for a project are those that target a key area of competitive advantage for the company or offset a disadvantage of the community.

ing income taxes. In the business world, even the smallest purchases are often subject to some form of competitive bidding. The same mind-set has come to characterize many facets of the site location process. To be successful, a site selector wants not only to find the best place to do business, but to make "the best deal." If the best deal means getting as much or more as anyone else has gotten in incentives, it is easy to wind up in a situation of escalating demands.

WHAT KINDS OF INCENTIVES ARE THE MOST DESIRED AND THE MOST EFFECTIVE?

The most desired incentives, some might say, are any and all of them. In reality, however, resources are not unlimited and communities must operate within the legal guidelines imposed by states and the political and economic realities of their own environment.

The most effective incentives for a project are those that target a key area of competitive advantage for the company or offset a disadvantage of the community. For that reason, it is important to have a sophisticated understanding of your area's targeted industries when designing an incentive strategy. For companies that are competing primarily in the area of product and service quality, training the workforce may be a critical area of assistance. This would apply to industries where there is little product differentiation, and successful companies are those that provide exceptional service. It also applies to companies that are implementing new manufacturing processing and technologies and must manufacture to high quality tolerances. Companies that are in industries competing on cost will be attracted to incentives that reduce their land or facility cost, or their tax liability. This will include industries that are producing commodity products. Some industries, particularly those filled with companies trying to beat a competitor to market with a new product, are very time sensitive; in these cases incentives which save time or guarantee delivery dates, such as infrastructure preparation or permitting assistance, are particularly appealing. Computer related businesses are often a classic example

of this type of industry, since the product life of hardware and software versions gets shorter and shorter every day. Since time is so often a critical location factor, incentives that delay a client's schedule will not be effective if alternatives are available. This situation often arises in the area of infrastructure. Commitments to clear and grade a site or build a road, for example, are only perceived as incentives if the project can wait for the work to be done, and if the competition offers no faster-track alternative. Communities and states should review their target industries, and make sure that the types of incentive programs they are prepared to support match the needs of the industries being targeted.

When resource constraints are prohibitive, or creativity is called for, providing effective linkages for existing and new businesses can be a high impact, low cost inducement strategy. Acting as a resource to bring together employers and employees has always been a role for economic development professionals, but it will become even more critical and complex in the future. In addition to the connections to traditional full time workers, companies are looking for ways to connect with older workers, students, temporary workers or agencies, small businesses and independent contractors, and multilingual workers.

There is also a role for economic developers to play in connecting prospects with suppliers and customers. Once companies are established, it is not uncommon for chambers of commerce and other business organizations to foster this type of networking. Engaging in this type of matchmaking *before* the decision is made can provide the prospect with one more reason to perceive an area as more attractive and better prepared.

For the future, the most valuable connection may be to users of a company's byproducts. By-product disposal (as distinguished from hazardous waste disposal) is projected to be one of the fastest growing operating costs for manufacturing and service businesses alike. At the same time, commercial uses are being developed for a wide range of by-products, including paper, oil, and rubber. The major stumbling block for many of these ventures is the inability to match producers of by-products with users. By playing a role in facilitating these matches, a community is also helping itself minimize its own waste disposal burden.

WHAT ARE OTHER STATES AND COMMUNITIES REALLY DOING?

The interest and excitement around incentive programs generally focuses around those programs that are offered in only a few areas. It is fanned by publicity surrounding incentive packages offered to large projects such as chip plants and auto plants, which are often offered one-of-a-kind programs. Industrial training programs are a good example of programs that are still highly valued, but have come to be expected since they are available in almost every state. While there are clear differences in the capabilities and funding of the programs, these differences are not always apparent in the early phases of a site selection.

The ability or inability, and willingness or unwillingness to *exempt projects from property taxes* remains of great interest, and seems to be expanding. Several communities have made a practice, however, of separating out the school portion of the property tax and not allowing that portion to be exempted.

Several states have *tax credit programs tied to job creation*; in many cases, these are available only in distressed areas, or the amount of the credit is dependent upon the economic conditions in the county. At times, however, the credits are designed in such a way that they are of little benefit, because they can only be taken in the earliest years of a project, when income levels may be very low.

Several states, particularly in the Mid-Atlantic and Southeast, have established *discretionary funds* under the control of their governors that can be applied to special projects in the form of infrastructure improvements, land

cost buydowns, cash grants, and other uses. In many cases, matching funds are required from the local community.

At the time of this writing, speculative building programs are returning in several parts of the country. In some communities, funds are raised for a speculative building with the expectation that the sale of that building will finance future buildings, however in many cases *the building is provided to attractive prospects free of charge* through a lease arrangement. When publicly funded, construction costs are raised either from general funds or from specially designated tax revenue accounts, such as the one-half cent sales tax for economic development that communities in Texas can pass. Often, private funding is sought from local individuals and businesses, including construction companies, and utilities.

Some of the most aggressive programs now available leverage the incremental personal income tax generated by new employees as the basis for providing *cash payments or credits* to a company. These programs are spreading, and now exist in some form in Oklahoma, Ohio, Kentucky, Arkansas, South Carolina, Nebraska, Indiana and others. Oklahoma's incentives, for example, can generate cash payments equivalent to 3 to 5 percent of the company's payroll. For a call center employing approximately 500 at an average center-wide salary of $17,000, the benefit would amount to approximately $3 million, paid out quarterly over time.

One of the most interesting developments in incentive programs is that they seem to be additive. In other words, states that implement an income tax based credit do not cancel property tax abatement programs or industrial training programs.

Another interesting development is the rising influence and impact of private funds in

If incentives are used prominently in marketing programs, it should come as no surprise that many prospects will be focused on incentives from the outset.

FREQUENTLY OFFERED INCENTIVES	
State Programs	**Local Programs**
Loan Programs	Property Tax Abatement
Grant Programs	Payment in Lieu of Property Taxes
Designated Road Building Funds	Discounted or Free Land
Designated Infrastructure Development Funds	Discounted or Free Building
Recruiting and Training Assistance	Temporary Space
Sales Tax Exemptions	Utility Extensions
Enterprise Zone Programs	Site Preparation Assistance
Job Tax Credits for Distressed Areas	Zoning Changes
Cash Grants for Job Creation	Relocation Grants or Assistance
Investment Tax Credits	
Cash Grants to Offset Lease Investment	

incentive packages. Several areas are beginning to change their balance of public versus private funding, and to free themselves from the restrictions and political repercussions of tax-based incentives by using private funds. Occasionally, a single contributor will surface with a contribution to land a specific project. In many other cases, these programs are being developed on a regional basis and are used to develop industrial parks serving multiple counties, speculative buildings, discretionary funds for cash grants, and other project-specific grants. This pattern typically emerges when local city or county councils and commissions decline to make proactive investments that others feel are critical to success. At that point, a fund-raising consultant is retained or a local committee is formed to solicit contributions from businesses that will benefit from new job creation and investment. Typical contributors include local, regional, and state banks, gas and electric utilities, telephone companies, construction companies, architects and engineers, and major corporate citizens. Usually, the contributors are asked to make a two- to five-year commitment in order to ensure some stability of programs that are developed with the funds.

A MARKETING TOOL OR A SALES TOOL?

It is important to understand exactly what can and cannot be established through the use of incentives. Incentives are typically used to increase prospect traffic to an area and avoid open competitions (a marketing tool) and/or to close a deal that has come down to a short list (a sales tool). If incentives are used prominently in marketing programs, it should come as no surprise that many prospects will be focused on incentives from the outset. Promoting incentives to increase prospect traffic and short-circuit competition can be very effective, however, if program elements are communicated clearly and accompanied by realistic portrayals of an area's other assets and liabilities. Many states and communities have chosen at different points in time to feature incentives in their advertisements and direct mail programs. On a state level, Oklahoma is one of the most recent examples of this strategy, with full-page advertisements in national newspapers and publications featuring its Quality Jobs Program which provides cash payments to companies who create new jobs in the state. Kentucky's statewide incentive programs gained great exposure in a short time through a highly effective "road show" built around a simple one-page worksheet showing the variables and calculations that determine incentive levels. At the community level, Amarillo, Texas, has offered "million-dollar checks" in its targeted direct mail programs to companies willing to relocate to the community, and has advertised its positive results in the *Wall Street Journal*. Pueblo, Colorado, continues to be an oft-cited example of a community that used an incentive-based marketing approach several years ago to draw prospects into a community funded industrial park. For a community experiencing significant unemployment and in need of a method of quickly increasing employment opportunities, marketing incentives proved to be the right strategy at the right time.

For this strategy to be appropriate, three conditions should be met:

▶ **Have the general agreement of your leadership, your business community, and the population that business recruitment is necessary to the future economic health of the area.** If existing businesses in your area are already having trouble recruiting employees, or if you have more leads than your real estate market, labor market, or energy can handle, then this lead-producing strategy may not be appropriate.

▶ **Have something different and attractive to say.** While most states are rightfully proud of their industrial training programs, for example, this type of incentive program is very widespread and will not be compelling enough to generate incremental inquiries.

▶ **Be specific in your offer.** Vague references to incentives will have little impact. The best approaches are those that have found a way to simplify calculations and enable a company to quickly determine the impact on its bottom line.

It is also important to remember that a marketing program that focuses on an incentive will attract prospects that are somewhat preoccupied with incentives.

For many areas, lead generation is not the primary issue. Desirable companies are interested — and are looking — but something is missing that would successfully close a deal. When used as a sales tool, if properly designed and implemented, incentives can help to swing decisions on expansions and relocations to a community by:

— Satisfying the need for negotiation.
— Differentiating among areas that are very similar.
— Meeting competitive standards for infrastructure readiness.
— Satisfying corporate financial benchmarks
— Offsetting one-time relocation costs.
— Providing assurances in an unfamiliar environment.

Incentives also have their limitations, which should be considered before a great deal of hope is invested in these programs as a means to turn around an economic situation. In competition for projects that have short time frames, incentives will not be effective as a substitute for timely delivery of a site, building, or labor force. Incentives are also generally ineffective as a means of overcoming long term fatal flaws; for example, if the project *requires* access to an international airport, incentives may cause the decision maker to relax the requirement from one-hour distance to one and one-half-hour distance, but they are not likely to eliminate that requirement entirely.

In competition for projects that have short time frames, incentives will not be effective as a substitute for timely delivery of a site, building, or labor force.

WHO ARE THOSE CONSULTANTS ANYWAY?

Although a large number of projects are managed by the principals of the companies, an increasingly broad variety of consultants are now playing a part, not only in site selection but in incentive negotiation as well. Consultants fall into several categories, and while they are generally capable of evaluating the full range of location issues, they may have a special area of expertise that is particularly stressed in their evaluation. Construction firms, accounting firms, real estate brokers, and stand-alone site selection firms are all involved, although the approaches they take and their compensation arrangements differ. Consultants market their incentive negotiation services by offering to maintain the client's anonymity as long as possible, by acting as extra staff resources, and by providing access to information regarding what incentives are possible nationally, and what other companies with similar projects have been given. In some cases these services are provided on a flat fee basis, in other cases incentive negotiations are "thrown in free" with commissions earned through real estate transactions, and in a limited number of cases, the consultant charges a commission or sliding performance fee based on the value of incentives that are negotiated. In each case, however, a consultant tries to provide value above and beyond what a client believes that they could achieve for themselves. For this reason, when a consultant is involved, it is often the case that they will try to "push the envelope" beyond programs, such as Industrial Training, that they define as "as of right." An "as of right" incentive is one, like industrial training or statutory tax exemptions, that is almost automatically available to any company meeting the criteria, as is often viewed only as a starting point for negotiations. It is critical to understand this perspective in order to understand why there is often a lukewarm reception to an incentive program that the community fought long and hard to be able to offer. If a given incentive such as training assistance or sales tax exemption is available in every location under consideration, and if there is no real or perceived difference be-

tween the offers, then the incentive has little value as a competitive advantage. A competitive advantage is perceived only when an incentive offered in one area with quantifiable financial benefits is not matched in every other area.

Another thing to keep in mind is that the consultant's time frame for getting responses often differs from the client's time frame for making an announcement. In many cases, a company must have a complete business case for a project—with all projected costs and incentives documented, ready to present for approval—and the consultant is committed to meeting that deadline, which often corresponds to a board meeting. What happens at that internal meeting can then raise further internal issues that have nothing to do with the choice of community or the incentive offer but may delay a decision. Often, the company takes time to review alternatives such as outsourcing, mergers, purchases, or divestitures at this point, and the project appears to go "on hold," but this does not mean that the earlier deadlines were unimportant or merely a "fire drill."

One word of advice regarding working with consultants: in most cases, avoid the temptation to circumvent the process. If there is a consultant involved, the company has invested money in managing the process in that manner and will have their reasons for not appreciating someone else trying to change the rules of the game. There have been cases where a community consciously or unconsciously finds out the identity of an anonymous prospect and bypasses the consultant; I have never heard of an instance where this worked out to the advantage of the community, but there are cases where it hurt the community badly.

WHAT ABOUT THOSE QUESTIONNAIRES?

Many consultants and companies now make a practice of sending out long, detailed questionnaires at the outset of a project. Often, these questionnaires will include requests for information on incentives in the very early stages of a project, before a great deal of information on the project has been given. Naturally, the prospect would like responses to be as specific (and generous) as possible, while communities are very uncomfortable responding with specific offers. These questionnaires are often sent to allow the consultant to complete a screening study with similar information for a large number of communities and to screen out all but the top few candidates. The best strategy is not to leave these questions blank, since at this point the objective is usually to stay in the game. It is wiser to provide a response that identifies what you are legally able to do and not to do, at state and local levels, and to give a sense of what circumstances and conditions would allow you to provide various forms of incentives. Typically, a description of a state-funded training program and loan programs are not compelling answers, while descriptions of potential land cost reductions, infrastructure developments, tax exemption programs, and the like will be of interest.

Fair or not, your response to these initial questionnaires can cause you to be screened out of a project, but if that happens, it is usually not just because of incentive issues.

DOES MY COMMUNITY WANT THIS PROJECT?

At the foundation of any area's incentive strategy should be a well-defined set of potential tools and a set of guidelines on when and how to use those tools. The single most important element of a successful incentive strategy is the willingness and ability to walk away from a project if the price is too high. One of the highest profile examples of this behavior is North Carolina's decision to limit its offer to Mercedes once it felt it had reached a level of

support that was appropriate for the area. The second most important thing to remember is that the prices will be different for every area and for every project, and the benefits will also differ from project to project. Again, using the Mercedes project as an example, Alabama made a significantly more generous offer than competing states; however, their underlying economy was not as strong, and the potential benefits of long-term image and additional job creation was more critical to Alabama than to many of the competing areas.

In the best of all possible situations, the components of an incentive program are designed based on the needs or desires expressed by prospect companies, and lead to a win-win situation for the state, the community, and the company. In the real world, they are always heavily influenced by resource constraints and political constituencies. An investment approach can help to separate the incentive process from the political process, but it must be developed on a proactive basis; to expect to develop such a consensus in the heat of the hunt for a project is an invitation to failure.

Using an investment approach, the state or community should:

- **Quantify the benefits of the project**. The benefits of a project are often not as obvious as they may seem. A few years ago, a federal government project expected to provide several hundred jobs at average salaries of over $30,000 was being courted by a wide range of communities. The project was requesting significant incentive treatment, including provision of a facility free or at nominal cost. When communities began to document the potential benefits, however, they realized that most employees would be transferred in, so that there would be little actual job creation,

An "as of right" incentive is one, like industrial training or statutory tax exemptions, that is almost automatically available to any company meeting the criteria, as is often viewed only as a starting point for negotiations.

and since the entity was tax exempt, there would be little tax revenue to ultimately pay back the incentive award. Conversely, projects that may appear to have little benefit can actually turn out to be valuable contributors to the community, as is sometimes the case with call centers, whose significant investment in (taxable) furniture, fixtures, and equipment and (taxable) telephone usage is often overlooked.

- **Determine the desired payback period.** Ordinarily, a state and community should have a sense of how soon its investment will be paid back through tax revenues. The State of Virginia and the participating communities near Richmond, Virginia, have indicated that they believe their $85.6 million incentive package for Motorola's semiconductor factory will be paid back within three years of start-up. If the benefits and desired payback period are correctly determined, it is possible to solve for an appropriate level of investment. For most high profile projects, a three- to five-year payback period is desirable, although for high-image projects or for important retention projects, longer periods are often acceptable.

- **Consider alternative investments and their benefits.** Especially when faced with a large prospect requiring significant investment, communities must determine whether or not it is in their best interest to "put all their eggs in one basket"; sometimes landing one large project is not as desirable for a community as landing two or three smaller, more diversified new companies.

- **Determine the appropriate level of investment, and the components of that investment.** Communities will benefit, and companies will appreciate, an incentive proposal that summarizes the financial benefits of each type of program.

- **Refuse to exceed this level of investment, without corresponding increases in benefits.** Perhaps the most difficult rule to implement, the community must be prepared to "lose" a bad deal if the financial price is too high or to divisive for the business community as a whole.

By contrast, an incentive policy that is ruled by a political approach allows the desire to win, or the desire to "hold the line" to obscure the judgment of benefits and neglects to evaluate the project objectively. Worst of all, because the process is transformed into a win-lose proposition or a show-down, those who have staked reputations on the win leave themselves no room to back away from a project that has gotten to expensive to yield a net benefit to a community and no choice but to blame another community for unfair competition or a company for unbridled greed.

Quantifying the benefits of a project has always been one of the more difficult aspects of evaluating a prospect's attractiveness. There are many theories regarding the correct multipliers to use which will accurately predict the spin-off jobs and revenues generated by projects, each with their own rationale, and two-day courses are available through AEDC that deal solely with economic impact assessment. At the present time, however, there does not seem to be any one theory that will apply to every community and every situation. In the absence of specific, valid data, the best approach is to create a number of scenarios supported by research into other similar projects or companies wherever possible. The potential benefits of a project that should be considered include:

- Direct employment
- Indirect employment
- Property tax revenue
- Income tax revenue, direct and indirect
- Sales tax revenue, direct and indirect
- Bank deposits, direct and indirect
- Mortgage and construction lending
- Incremental home sales

Often, there are additional intangible benefits to a project, such as the improvement to the image or visibility of a community that often comes with publicity associated with new projects.

Equally important, the community must take on the responsibility of evaluating the potential costs of the project in areas such as utility capacity increases, increased demands on the school system, police and fire systems, and others. The impact statements often provided by prospects will not typically include this information, and it is not their responsibility to do so.

A successful incentive policy will not win all projects, but will win projects that are good for the state and good for the community. While the individual components will differ depending on the characteristics of the community, its economy, and its culture, the ruling elements behind the policy should be:

— Applicable to all types of projects of equal value.
— Contains a process for quantifying costs and benefits to the community (an impact model).
— Pre-set broad guidelines for investment and required return.
— Draws on benchmark research of business requirements and cost profiles.
— Displays a true understanding of competitive advantages and disadvantages.
— Contains a procedure for quick response and approval.
— Exists before the prospect calls.
— Allows the community to walk away from bad deals.
— Contains safeguards to protect the community's investment.

There is virtually no way to guarantee that the jobs projected by a prospect will materialize; as we have seen in recent years, companies cannot guarantee anything to their employees about their futures, much less make guarantees to communities. It is possible and prudent, however, to attempt to build in safeguards for the state's and community's investments. The most logical and acceptable form of safeguards are to tie incentive awards to successive levels of job creation and investment, and to pay them out over time.

WHO IS MY COMPETITION?

In many cases, companies or consultants may share with you the identity of competitor locations, particularly if the project is in its final stages. In other cases, they may share only the location of the company's headquarters or the location where the project originated. Do not make the mistake of assuming that your only competition is the place that the company is relocating or expanding from—if that location's cost structure and operating conditions were ideal, the company wouldn't be looking for another location.

More often than not, however, a company or consultant won't directly let you know who your competition is, other than to imply that they are locations that are extremely attractive and extremely aggressive. It is still possible, however, to make some assumptions about the states or cities that are also under consideration. Depending on the type of project, for example, the state of Washington will often compete with Oregon, California, Utah, Arizona, and Colorado. Cities tend to compete with others than have similar air access levels, cost structures, university resources, or are of similar size. One mayor of a mid-sized Midwestern city identified twelve communities that the city regularly competes with for the type of projects it targeted as desirable and engaged a consultant to research the type of incentive programs that those cities have available and have used in the past. In the absence of specific, verifiable information, it is better to research a broad range of possibilities.

The single most important element of a successful incentive strategy is the willingness and ability to walk away from a project if the price is too high.

HOW DO I STACK UP AGAINST MY COMPETITION BEFORE INCENTIVES ARE CONSIDERED?

Once any information about the identity of competing locations is determined, competitive research is a critical step in determining whether or not a project is winnable and what strategy might be most effective. Economic developers are trained and rewarded to present their areas in the most positive light possible, but a true assessment of competitive advantage requires absolute objectivity. By the time serious consideration is being given to your state or community, most communities are roughly equivalent with regard to issues such as air access, transportation logistics, and general labor availability and costs. These are not issues that can usually be directly influenced by incentives, although a company may be induced to choose an area with higher labor costs, if savings in real estate costs and taxes can make up the difference. Key issues at this point tend to center around site and building cost and readiness, taxes, and labor skills. In the case of a relocation that involves transferring a large number of people, relocation costs themselves can also be critical. Much of this information, such as tax rates, is publicly available and can be assembled and compared to the "home court" situation. If the company's specific taxable income, purchases, or other information is not available, model a typical situation, perhaps using information from an existing employer of similar size, to discover the order of magnitude of the cost advantage or disadvantage. Site or building readiness is particularly crucial, since many projects are already behind schedule by the time they begin. For this reason, a site that is not yet under control or graded or fully served with roads and utilities represents not only a potential cost liability, but a potential time delay.

Don't expect to be able to assembly a perfect comparative analysis, because perfect information won't be available. One the other hand, don't make the mistake of not doing any comparative research at all just because it won't be perfect and complete.

HOW DO THEIR INCENTIVES STACK UP AGAINST MINE?

In most cases, a competing community's economic development organizations will not respond to questions regarding their incentives when a specific project is up for grabs. There are sources, however, that can help you to understand what another state or community may offer. Competitive research consists of two elements: finding out what a state or community is legally able to do, and finding out how they have actually behaved in other situations. For states, the single best source documenting incentive programs is the *Directory of Incentives for Business Investment and Development in the United States*, published by the National Association of State Development Agencies. This is a valuable resource; however, it is important to remember that incentive programs are changing every day, and this directory is not published every year, so it is only a starting point. Industry publications such as *Business Facilities*, *Area Development*, and *Expansion Management* regularly feature profiles of states and cities that highlight incentive programs, particularly new programs. The best resources, however, are computer databases of local and regional newspapers and industry publications. Basic databases are available through consumer-oriented services such as America On-Line, Compuserve, and Prodigy; Compuserve at this time provides the best access to business-oriented publications and newspapers, often through their premium services such as Knowledge Index. Specialized databases or direct access to local newspapers are available on the Internet, or through Knight-Ridder's Dialog Information Service. Access to this information may not be free, but with efficient search techniques it can be valuable and cost effective. The objective of these searches is to get information regarding the way competing states and communities have handled project incentives in the past, and to look for confirming evidence regarding assumptions that have been made about competitive advantages and disadvantages. Coverage of these types of issues is often available in articles announcing new relocations and expansions and announcing new incentive programs. Other articles that provide interesting insight into the corporate perspective are available through publications aimed at corporate financial officers, treasurers, and CEOs.

The ultimate goal of competitive research is to gather as much information as possible to determine the strength of your community, so that an informed decision can be made regarding the level of investment that is prudent and necessary to make.

HOW DOES THE NEGOTIATION TAKE PLACE?

The classic picture of a negotiation comes to us from either treaties or car sales, but usually involves some face-to-face contact, the purpose of which is specifically to negotiate price or conditions. In reality, the process is rarely that clean or well-organized. Often, the initial round of negotiation consists of a written request for proposal, detailing the company's needs and requests, and hopefully providing background on job creation and investment; but in some cases, the request may be a verbal "tell me what you can do." Follow-up questions for clarification often takes place over the phone. Ideally, for the benefit of the community and the client, there should be a single point of contact and a single document summarizing the state, community, and private sectors positions, so that the company can see a bottom line impact.

When face-to face negotiations are called for, it is important to maintain the primary point of contact, regardless of who else is introduced. Often the person with the most impressive title or political position is not the best representative, particularly if he or she is not the best equipped to answer specific questions. There is a role for people in a position to express the community's interest and general assurances, but there must also be individuals involved who can deal with the details.

Another key element of incentives is the influence of timing on decisions. Often, the ability to close a deal quickly and decisively will win a project. Recently, RR Donnelley chose to build a $102 million new printing plant in the Roanoke, Virginia, area not only because the environment and the incentive package was attractive, but because the state and the community were able to assemble a specific package of incentives and commit to them quickly, while their competition was still talking in vague terms about what might be available.

WHERE ARE WE GOING?

Will companies stop asking for incentives of some type? Probably not. Will states and communities stop giving incentives to expanding and relocating companies? Probably not. There have been repeated situations of governors challenging one another to stop providing incentives, but to date no one has been willing to go first and risk losing jobs to the states that do not participate in non-compete agreements. Recently, a lawsuit was filed in North Carolina by a private citizen asking the courts to rule on the constitutionality of providing any incentives to a private entity (company) that is funded by public funds (tax dollars). The lower courts ruled in favor of the plaintiff, finding that there was a violation of the constitution and a direct benefit to the private entity. However, upon appeal to the state Supreme Court, the ruling was overturned. On a 5 to 2 vote, the Court found that such expenditures, "while providing incidental private benefit, serve a

Economic developers are trained and rewarded to present their areas in the most positive light possible, but a true assessment of competitive advantage requires absolute objectivity.

*Will companies stop asking for incentives or some type?
Probably not.
Will states and communities stop giving incentives
to expanding and relocating companies?
Probably not.*

primary public goal." That overarching public purpose, the Court said, justifies efforts by localities to shore-up job pool and tax base by doing such things as purchasing land for industrial concerns, providing training, and giving money for training to new or existing businesses. The challenge against the use of incentives to attract business in this case was both common and understandable. However, what is even more interesting is that the stated aim of this challenge is to achieve rulings in states across the country, or at the federal level, that would limit the ability of states and communities to make their own decisions regarding these issues, at a time when the trend in national politics is toward more state and local control.

The North Carolina case is not the only time that communities have been challenged on their use of incentives, nor is it likely to be the last. In its ruling, the North Carolina Supreme Court noted that about 46 states had such laws that had withstood similar legal challenges. It is unrealistic to assume that everyone in a community will always understand circumstances faced by economic developers or the decisions they make.

If we assume that companies will continue to be interested in incentives, and states and communities will continue to address that interest, there are a number of interesting challenges in the future. One of the principal arguments that has been used to justify awarding incentives to any given project has been its ability to create jobs and generate tax revenue. A project's desirability is typically measured by the magnitude of its investment and the number of full-time, permanent jobs with benefits that are created. The challenge for the future

will be to structure incentive programs that address the impact created by companies that use nontraditional staffing strategies, the so-called networked businesses or virtual corporations. Many business experts are predicting that the model corporate organization in the future will contain only a small core of full-time permanent employees, supplemented by much larger cadres of temporary workers and outsourced services. Today, we do not typically "credit" a project with job creation unless the company is the direct employer; this approach may have to change if alternative staffing becomes the rule rather than the exception. Our traditional assumptions used in multiplier models hold that indirect employment resulting from a project generally consists of lower paid jobs than direct employment; in the case of employers who make heavy use of temporary agencies, the reverse may be true. If the aim is to create jobs, does it really matter which payroll the employee is on? Can we really say, in today's and tomorrow's environment, that a job on a corporate payroll is more secure than one with a corporation through a temporary or staffing agency?

A second challenge will come from the projection that much of the new job growth will come from small to mid-sized companies, and therefore from projects that are smaller, at least at the beginning. Small businesses and "lone eagle" entrepreneurs are also expected to be strong growth niches and will require new focus. Their need for access to low-cost capital should lead to a renewed interest in incubators, small business programs, and venture capital corporations, perhaps with public investment. It would not be surprising to see a ranking among the best cities to start a business gain the same prestige as a ranking among the best cities for business.

A third challenge will be to design incentive programs that respond to the borderless view of geography prospects hold. The positive economic impacts of a project are felt well beyond the boundaries of the city or county where it locates, and strides are now being made to share the costs of investments and incentives required to attract these projects. Prime examples are the experiments in revenue sharing from multi-county industrial parks in South Carolina and Georgia. Although they have had their growing pains, as all new endeavors do, they merit the time and energy to perfect, and offer a way for rural and poorer areas, in particular, to effectively leverage their resources.

SUMMARY

Each community and state must decide for itself whether or not they believe in incentives and how to decide which projects they are willing to invest in. Certainly, there may be some projects "lost" if a competing community offers more, but in many cases different cost profiles mean that an incentive package is the only way to equalize operating costs. As an economic development professional, however, the most important thing is to understand the competitive position of the area without incentives, and to understand the community's attitude. If education of the community and the leadership is required, either to change attitudes or to make people aware of the consequences of prevailing policies, it should be an ongoing, proactive process, and not something that takes place surrounding a specific project.

About the Author.....Kate McEnroe

Kate McEnroe is president of Kate McEnroe Consulting, a full-service economic development agency. Kate was formerly with PHH Fantus, one of America's leading economic development consulting firms. Throughout her career she has focused on the effective use of incentives in the economic development/site selection process. Ms. McEnroe can be reached at 770.333.6343.

INCENTIVE IMPACT CHECKLIST ✓

PROJECT TITLE: _____   **PROJECT NUMBER:** _____

Corporate Investment	(1)	_____
Jobs (FTE)	(2)	_____
Average Annual Salaries	(3)	_____

		Local	**State**
Property Taxes	(4a)	_____	_____
Sales Tax	(4b)	_____	_____
Personal Income Taxes	(4c)	_____	_____
Corporate Income Taxes	(4d)	_____	_____
Other Taxes _____	(4e)	_____	_____
Other Taxes _____	(4f)	_____	_____
TOTAL: (5)	_____	(6) _____	

Local Incentive Package	(7)	_____
State Incentive Package	(8)	_____
TOTAL: (9)	_____	

Public/Private Ratio [Line 9 ÷ Line 1]   _____

Incentive Dollars/Job Created [Line 9 ÷ Line 2]   _____

Incentive Dollars/Annual Wages [Line 9 ÷ Line 3]   _____

Locally Leveraged Investment [Line 7 ÷ (Line 8 + Line 1)]   _____

Local Break Even Analysis [Line 7 ÷ Line 6]   _____

State Break Even Analysis [Line 8 ÷ Line 5]   _____

Project Break Even Analysis [Line 9 ÷ (lines 5 + 6)]   _____

NOTE: This summary checklist is provided by the editors, not Kate McEnroe Consulting. It is not intended to take the place of a formal impact analysis, which is highly recommended. However, it will serve as a guideline for gathering information, and it may give a thumbnail comparison of investment to incentive.

INCENTIVE CHECKLIST ✓

PROJECT TITLE: _____   PROJECT NUMBER: _____

FACILITY INCENTIVES	*One Time Value*	*Annual Value*
Zoning Changes	_____	_____
Free/Discounted Land	_____	_____
Land Lease	_____	_____
Free/Discounted Building	_____	_____
Building Lease	_____	_____
Equipment Lease	_____	_____
Infrastructure Improvements:		
Water	_____	_____
Sewer	_____	_____
Gas	_____	_____
Electric	_____	_____
Project Financing (Savings over Market Rate)	_____	_____
Job-Related Incentives:		
Job Creation Tax Credits	_____	_____
Pre-Employment Screening	_____	_____
Pre-Employment Training	_____	_____
On-the-Job Training	_____	_____
Tax Incentives:		
Tax Abatements	_____	_____
Foreign Trade Zone Savings	_____	_____
Enterprise Zone Savings	_____	_____
Payments in Lieu of Taxes (PILOTs)	_____	_____
Other Incentives:		
Discounted Utility Rates	_____	_____
Corporate Relocation Incentives	_____	_____
Discretionary Funds	_____	_____
Other: _____	_____	_____

       TOTAL VALUE OF INCENTIVES   _____
       (discounted to present year)

       INCENTIVE $ PER JOB CREATED   _____

       INCENTIVE $ AS % OF
       CORPORATE INVESTMENT   _____

CHAPTER 13

BECOMING THE CHOSEN ONE

Audrey Taylor
President, Chabin Concepts Inc.

Florence Chadwick could see nothing but a solid wall of fog. Her body was numb, as she had been swimming for nearly 16 hours. Alongside Florence in one of the boats were her trainer and her mother. They told her it wasn't much farther, but all she could see was the fog. With half a mile to go, she eventually quit and asked to be pulled out of the water.

*Still thawing her chilled body several hours later, she told listeners that if she had seen land she might have made it. It was not her fatigue or even the cold water that defeated her. It was the fog. **She was unable to see her goal.***

Two months later, she tried again. This time, despite the same dense fog, she swam with her faith intact and her goal clearly pictured in her mind. She new that somewhere behind the fog was land and this time she made it! In September of 1952 she not only became the first woman to swim the Catalina Channel, she beat the men's record by two hours!

——— o ———

This chapter deals with everything associated with the time between the site tour and the selection or elimination of your community. Like Florence Chadwick, your success during the period becomes a function of your ability to focus on the goal of closing the sale. It is your ability to visualize a successful site selection decision partnered with the continual follow-through that will make you successful in economic development marketing.

PROSPECT WOOING

The process of community marketing is much the same as that of selling any other product. You have already segmented the market and selected those categories of buyers that offer the greatest opportunities for your community. You have identified a list of specific companies and individuals within these market segments. You have defined the benefits your community provides these industries or this particular prospect. Now you need to close the sale.

Becoming the chosen one is a building process. You promote market strengths and sell benefits. You must build trust and confidence with the prospect that you can deliver the benefits your community offers. Remember the three reasons CEOs buy from salespeople:

1— The salesperson knows the company and industry.
2— The salesperson is thorough in every detail and time sensitive.
3— The salesperson has built trust and the product provides a benefit to the CEO.

The prospecting process began with the first contact at which you determined the prospect's interest in a possible location in your community. You have now made the short list of a prospect. Now is an excellent time to go back and review:

- ► the specific needs of the prospect
- ► the time frame of the proposed project
- ► client profiles
- ► industry-specific data
- ► the sales team roles and responsibilities
- ► project follow-through checklists

PROSPECT SPECIFIC NEEDS

Did you get all the information for this project that everyone needs to close this deal? Review all the notes from previous meetings. Have you addressed everything? Is there something you missed? Did someone hear something else the prospect wanted? What were their top three needs? Have you sufficiently addressed those so you can win this project? No matter what, always highlight the benefit the community provides on any decision element of the project. Review the specific needs and the benefits your community can offer, such as real estate costs, infrastructure, labor quality and availability, taxes, regulatory

environment and processing time, and overall quality of life.

ESTABLISH TIME FRAME OF THE PROPOSED PROJECT

Review with the prospect their time frame targets, such as the selection of the location, groundbreaking, and start-up for operations. This will help you plan. Your team can prepare time charts to show they can meet the time frame of this project on every element involved in the decision-making process. This impresses prospects that you fully understand the development and location process.

DETERMINE WHO IS THE CLIENT

How you approach the next phases of selling your community is determined by the type of client. The pitch may be different if it is the owner, an employee who will not move with the project, an employee who will move with the project or a consultant/site selector. Understand the prospect (both company and individual). Define their motivation. Understand what is important to this prospect. You want to present yourself as a professional solely with the goal in mind of helping them succeed with their site decision. Your job is to provide the prospective buyer with the information needed to make that decision. Knowing what information is needed by a prospect in a specific industry is a plus. This is a reflection that you care about their business and have taken time to do your homework.

Prospects come in all shapes, sizes and forms. Although sales efforts try to reach the decision maker, they often end up dealing with another individual in the company or even a site selection consultant. You must quickly discern the decision-level position or motivation of this individual. What are the hot buttons or services you can provide for this person to keep them dealing with your office and give your community a fair chance? Generally speaking, you will find yourself working with either the decision maker or the decision influencer.

DECISION MAKER—This individual will commonly be making the move with the company. Decision makers are typically very interested in lifestyle, improvement, or retention in their quality of living—and in making a profit. They approach the site selection process as they would purchase a home. This is a major commitment to them, because they want their company to be successful and want a great lifestyle. These types of prospects are more receptive to a cordial hosting and assistance in the process. Pitch quality, employee productivity and loyalty; provide facts and figures but in a more personal manner than with a corporate operation. Find out more personal "hot buttons" so you can influence the decision with peers already in the community with the same opinions.

DECISION INFLUENCER—The individual handling the site search is not the decision maker but will be analyzing information and making a recommendation first on site profitability and secondarily on quality of life. Typically this person will not be moving with this facility, so selling them on the community is not as important as providing accurate, bottom-line facts in a format they can use in their presentation on your behalf. Clearly identifying and highlighting the long-term benefits of the location is of greatest value to this prospect.

INDUSTRY PROFILES

In your targeting process you obtained information on the industry as a whole. Use this—remember, information is power. A prospect is always impressed with a professional who knows the product but who also knows their industry and is sensitive to the trends and issues they are facing. Gathering industry specific data can be accomplished by:

▶ Hiring a consultant (professionals, universities, interns) to conduct studies.
▶ Joining trade associations.
▶ Subscribing to industry-specific magazines.
▶ Holding focus group meetings with industries in your community.
▶ Preparing an industry profile (see Checklists in Chapter 5, pages 77-84).

How you approach the next phases of selling your community is determined by the type of client.

SALES TEAM ROLES AND RESPONSIBILITIES

Who is the team that will help you sell? Who do you need at the table to close this project? What are their roles and responsibilities? Who specifically is going to handle site development, financing, employee recruitment and training, relocation assistance, tracking, lobbying, and project coordination?

Site Development—Is this site ready for development? What is going to be required to issue a building permit? Team members should include planning, public works, air pollution control, engineer, and economic development staff.

Financing—How is this project going to be financed? Will the community provide financial assistance? Is there need for working capital, capital assets, real estate or building financing? How much of the project is site development costs? Are there community mechanisms to assist in site development financing? The biggest questions are: Who will work with the prospect to package the financing, and what programs are available for this project?

Employee Recruitment and Training—The project coordinator should obtain the type and number of employees needed for the start of operations, their skill requirements, projected employment needs after start-up, and any training that may be needed. The job training representative should prepare a package that specifically addresses the prospect's labor requirements, outlining the process to recruit employees for their interview process; this should include an assessment of individuals prior to interviews, a place to hold interviews or testing, estimated number of skilled or trainable respondents expected from a recruitment process, previous recruitment efforts (within last year), customized or on-the-job training to be offered, and the value of that training.

Relocation Assistance—Do you have a local firm that can handle relocations for the company? If not, do you know of one that could assist the company? You need to know what they can do for a company and use them when needed.

Lobbying—It is very common to have a certain amount of lobbying to bring a project to closure. Usually, the project team will need to convince local decision makers why certain incentives are critical to a project. This is a commonplace activity for economic development professionals. In larger deals, it is not uncommon to need legislation passed at the state level. The passage of legislation will require a great deal of lobbying by the project team and may require the hiring of professional lobbyists to get the project funded.

Project Coordination—Who will be responsible for keeping this project moving forward? Who will coordinate information, calling team meetings, etc.? Who will do the presentation, and who will be the point person with the prospect? That usually is you! Always give the mayor or city manager the opportunity to "present" the community's offer. You are responsible for keeping everyone on track, completing their information, being prepared to meet

with the prospect, and ensuring information gets to the prospect.

FOLLOW-UP SCHEDULE AND CHECKLISTS

The importance of follow-through cannot be overstated. You must schedule follow-up calls, meetings, and contacts. Everyone on the team should know the schedule and be prepared with their information if you need it for the prospect. Always be available to answer questions or to get answers to questions. The capacity to respond quickly and precisely to request for information on any aspect of the business climate demonstrates professionalism and competence—traits that argue well for a favorable future working relationship. Return telephone calls immediately; if you will be out of the office, call within 24 hours. If the prospect has requested confidentiality when calling, do not leave your name or phone number. Offer to call back at a more convenient time, or say, "It's just a personal call." Also, when sending material to confidential clients, send it in a plain brown envelope marked PERSONAL AND CONFIDENTIAL. Be sure to deliver information requested when you promised it.

Keep your team informed of your prospect contacts and any results from your follow-up. Things they may need, additional information the clients need, and any key changes need to be communicated immediately. You need to work as a team.

PROSPECT TRACKING SYSTEMS

You should have a prospect file system that enables you to record and track each contact and to maintain regular communication with a prospect from initial contact to eventual disposition. The size and scope of your program will dictate the form that this system will take, but off-the-shelf software programs, such as ACT!, Goldmine, and Telemagic, are inexpensive (less than $200), easy to install, and will save you time and worry. (Besides, they will automatically do your monthly reports.)

With the ACT! database, for example, you can maintain client records; set identification criteria; prepare reports; do word processing

> *Your prospect file system should enable you to record and track each contact and to maintain regular communication with a prospect from initial contact to eventual disposition.*

and mail merge; maintain address lists and time logs; and set call, meeting, and action dates that automatically remind you when action is needed on a project. You can schedule a standard follow-up process and due date for each phase of the project. This will help you manage the project as well as keep in contact with the prospect. The program is available in network form so any member of the team can input to a prospect file. (Sample demo screens of the ACT! program can be found on pages 194-196.)

The key to landing a prospect is: follow-up—follow-up—follow-up! Schedule your contact in your client tracking system, and when the date arrives decide if you should call, write a letter, or send a personal note, a clipping, or a fax. Be sure to gauge the prospect, respect his or her wishes, and be helpful. Address any needs immediately, remove any hurdles that could constrain the development of this project, use your influence, and call on people to help you facilitate the project.

RESPECTING CONFIDENTIALITY

Part of understanding the prospect is respecting confidentiality. Typically in the initial stages of a site or facility search, prospects prefer to conceal their identity. There are legitimate reasons for this, and it is unwise to probe for information not needed at that time. However, the community is entitled to certain facts which can usually be given without endangering the prospect's need for secrecy. The community has the right to know the nature and size of the intended operation in order to determine how it will fit into the community's development plans. Coordination and cooperation from all agencies and organizations in the prospecting arena will help to

avoid an instance where an exaggerated desire to maintain secrecy, or the issue of "who gets the credit," results in the loss of an opportunity because the community presentation was unnecessarily faulty or incomplete in some way.

In cases where the prospect does not require secrecy, it may be highly desirable to let your development team members know of the exact nature of the proposed project, since this will tend to put a stop to unfounded rumors that can seriously damage the entire operation. The matter of secrecy is one of balance and usually serves the interests of the community as well as the prospect. Telling the whole county the name of a prospect before the final agreement is reached is actually an invitation to competition from other communities. Confidentiality is also needed to protect the prospect, as there may be some danger in upsetting employees at existing plants until they have been informed that a new plant is pending.

THE PROPOSAL

The nucleus of the proposal should address your prospect's specific needs and specially present industrial site and building opportunities. Many of the facts can be in boilerplate form. The key is to make it look customized and show the benefit and value of your community. The information about sites and buildings should be assembled in terms of the specific needs of the company. The site/building data should have a consistent format and look. To make the strongest impression, use colored photos of buildings, colored copies of plat maps, and black and white aerial photographs of sites.

PREPARING YOUR PROPOSAL

In preparing to meet with a serious prospect, a professional proposal is a good sales tool. The presentation should be determined based on your assessment of the previous meetings and information the prospect has received. It is assumed by this point the prospect has received the initial response piece and the economic profile. Before preparing the formal presentation, determine what will be most important for the prospect at this point. Also determine if this proposal needs to be made in duplicate copies for other decision makers of the company. Many times the individuals gathering the research are not necessarily making the decision.

There are several options for the presentation to the prospect. The specific circumstances of the prospect's inquiry, time frame and expectations will define the best type of proposal. There are basically three methods for proposal presentations: **informational letter**, **letter proposal**, and **formal prospect proposal**. Remember, "off-the-shelf" material (economic profile, community data, business climate factors) should not be considered as part of a proposal; these are informational and research pieces only.

INFORMATIONAL LETTER

When a prospect needs only a few items of additional information, answer the specific questions by providing an informational letter. The purpose of the letter is to show that your community is interested in the company, to demonstrate your ability to answer questions quickly, and to encourage follow-up conversations so that a more complete proposal can be prepared.

Time: *Send the letter almost immediately (within 48 hours) after speaking with the prospect.*

Contents: *Include specific answers to the prospect's questions.*

Length: *Limit the letter to no longer than two pages, preferably one.*

Attachments: *Include attachments that support points made in the letter—professionally typed excerpts or fact sheets, maps, graphs, charts and pictures. Bind the attachments neatly, or place them in a pocket folder. Highlight in yellow any particular information in the attachments that answer the prospect's questions.*

Action-Oriented: *Request further contact in the letter.*

Follow-up: *Make a follow-up call to the prospect within one week to confirm receipt of information, inquire if additional information can be sent, obtain additional information on the project, or request an appointment.*

LETTER PROPOSAL

When a short but significantly impressive message is to be delivered to the prospect, prepare a letter proposal. The purpose of the letter is to encourage and possibly influence the prospect to consider the community more seriously.

Time: *Send the letter as soon as possible after speaking with a prospect—no later than one week.*

Contents: *Answer any questions the prospect may have had, and propose specific advantages, incentives offered by the community, and quantitative benefits of locating in the community.*

Length: *Limit the letter proposal to no more than three to four pages.*

▶

Attachments:	Keep attachments to a minimum, and use them only to highlight any points being made. Including material from other sources adds credibility to proposal, e.g., a newspaper testimonial from other companies.
Action-Oriented:	Call for further contact and action in your letter.
Follow-up:	Place a follow-up call within two to three days of sending the letter. Determine if additional information or a formal proposal can be prepared. Try to obtain additional information on the project if it is needed.

FORMAL PROSPECT PROPOSAL

The formal prospect proposal is a complete report highlighting all of the issues and answers to the prospect's questions. At this point, you should have all the details of the proposed project.

The purpose of the prospect proposal is to provide a formal presentation of all material pertinent to the prospect's location decision. The prospect proposal should be clearly organized and written and be a document which the prospect can present to other decision makers.

Time:	Send the prospect proposal with the same urgency as any request from the prospect, or within a specified time agreed to by both parties. To show the urgency you have given the proposal, send it marked CONFIDENTIAL via overnight mail.
Contents:	Consider the proposal a formal presentation of the community and what it has to offer. Answer any specific questions the prospect might have, emphasize the advantages offered by the community, and identify specific sites or buildings with pertinent data. Graphically display quantifiable benefits of the community and any incentives that will be offered.
	Your formal prospect proposal should be customized to the prospect. Focus on specific needs: sites and/or buildings; labor, productivity, and training programs; and economic incentives. Present information in graphic format: maps, charts, tables, illustrations, and photographs. Also include a one- or two-page executive summary. (See page 190 for sample table of contents.)
Length:	The formal prospect proposal should be 15 to 30 pages but no longer than 80 pages. It must be organized, page-numbered, and have a table of contents so the prospect can easily find any information.
Format:	Use three-ring binders, either with preprinted covers or clear-view covers for customization. The binder should have tabbed sections for easy reference.
Attachments:	Any attachments to the formal proposal should be included in the appendix. The documents should be clearly marked and referenced in the body of the proposal as well as in the appendix. Highlight items of interest to the prospect with a yellow marker for easy reference.
Action-Oriented:	The letter of transmittal should be from an influential individual (mayor, chairman of the board, president), requesting a meeting to discuss the proposal.
Follow-Up:	Make a follow-up call two days after sending the package to check on receipt, ask about additional information required, and attempt to schedule appointment or visit to your community.

In preparing the proposal, focus on the facility and operational needs of the business, not on what a great community it is located in. If the name of the prospect is known and presentation is to be made to him or her directly, a personal visit or delivery of the proposal to the prospect is most preferred. The personal factor is highly important, and face-to-face meetings designed to place the negotiations on an easier and more friendly basis work the best. If appropriate, a personal visit by the mayor to present the proposal will make the best impression.

FORMAL PROSPECT PROPOSAL — A Sample

Following is one example of what to include in the three-ring binder you submit as your formal prospect proposal:

TABLE OF CONTENTS	
EXECUTIVE SUMMARY	Two-page executive summary outlining proposal, or graphic presentation of benefits.
ACCESS TO MARKETS	Graphic presentation of location; maps; distance charts
ORIENTATION MAP	of the community which highlights industrial, residential, and commercial areas.
LABOR	— Graphic presentation of labor availability.
	— Productivity charts.
	— Survey of local industries.
	— Wage comparison charts.
SITES/BUILDINGS	— Master vicinity or area map with sites highlighted.
	— Aerial photograph of sites or buildings.
	— Plat maps and site/building details.
	— Environmental clearances.
TRANSPORTATION	— Map of all transportation routes.
	— Public transportation route maps.
	List of all transportation companies and contacts, including UPS and Federal Express.
FINANCING	List of financing programs and their advantages.
UTILITIES	List of companies that will be involved with project, including names of contacts and phone numbers. If appropriate, include rate sheets and quantify any benefits.
SUPPLIERS/SERVICES	Pertinent supplier information can be taken from *Industrial Demographic Inventory*.
DEVELOPMENT GUIDE	Outline, graphic form, showing timelines of permitting process.
REFERENCES	List of existing businesses to be offered.
BUSINESS CLIMATE	Attitude of government, public investment; brief story.
QUALITY OF LIFE	— Cost of living comparison chart.
	— Current housing guides usually published by local realtors.

Focus only on those items that are of most importance to the prospect for decision making. If the detailed community data is completed, excerpt this information directly from the computer database. The presentation package should attempt to convey any specific information requested from the prospect, identified labor cost, and attempt to show the benefit the community provides for these factors. Do not include the entire site inventory; only include information on sites and buildings the company is looking for with as much detail as possible about service to any of those sites. Emphasize any incentives that might be provided for their location in the community.

*The matter of secrecy is one of balance . . . .
Telling the whole county the name of a prospect
before the final agreement is reached is actually
an invitation to competition from other communities.*

CLOSING THE SALE

Whatever the system, the key to success lies in a professional approach that conveys sincere interest in each prospect and a level of integrity that is unquestioned. The act of signing the deal works itself out—there is no consistent or pat method. Once you feel the deal has been struck, the commitments that the community is willing to make should be consolidated with the prospect's proposed project and drawn up into a letter of intent. This puts the discussion into writing and helps to focus the position of each party involved in the deal.

Often, on larger deals, the letter of intent is matured into a memorandum of understanding (MOU), which details the responsibilities of all parties involved in the deal. In the MOU, the community will identify which incentives it will provide and quantify—to the degree possible—the value for each. Other parties such as the county and state will detail their participation also. The company will outline its commitments in terms of capital investment, job creation, and salaries to be paid. Frequently, modern MOUs will entail specific performance levels and deadlines to be executed by all parties. If these activities are not met by the prospect, the community will have the ability to retract a portion of the incentive package.

If the community fails to meet their commitments, the prospect is relieved of certain performance levels they have previously committed.

ANNOUNCING YOUR SUCCESSES

One of the hardest issues in the final hours of the project is deciding exactly when to announce its successful closure. Toward the end of a deal, the project team has often grown to such a size that a great number of people are involved in bringing it to closure. Each of these players has worked diligently to bring the project to closure and each will need to be recognized for their contribution. If you announce the project too early, you may cause the prospect to select another community (this has happened often in economic development). If you announce the project too late, someone else in the community may do it for you and in an unprofessional manner.

The announcement should be made by the elected officials of the community and company, not the economic developer. Regardless of how much work you put into the project (for which you should receive credit), the deal only closes when you receive the elected officials' approval and endorsement. Their role in the community is to handle public matters. See to

*The announcement should be made by an elected official
of the community, not the economic developer. . . .
The deal closes only after you receive the company's
and elected officials' approval and endorsement.*

it that they step to the front of the line at press time and take credit for the success.

The other members of the team should also be recognized. It may seem hard to understand, but you must downplay your role in the process. The other members of the team will know how hard you worked and will have developed a professional respect for your skills and performance. That recognition will carry you a lot farther than any of the press headlines you may be tempted to steal at press time.

A press packet needs to be prepared for the press conference. In it, you should include:

- a formal press announcement
- a question-and-answer piece
- quotes from key project participants
- a statement from the prospect
- a profile of the prospect's company

These pieces should be included in a press folder and handed out to media personnel when they arrive at the conference. Larger projects often have some kind of memento involved in the press announcement as well. Silver shovels are commonly used for ground breakings. Lucite-covered "tombstones" of large financial packages are common as well.

If the project is large, it probably has been tracked in some form or another by the media as it has developed. This will bring regional, state, and possibly national media to the press conference. However, for most projects this will be the exception, not the rule. To get the greatest exposure for your announcement, schedule the press conference for early afternoon. This will help to ensure that it appears on the evening news, instead of being reported on the midday edition. To make sure that any nonattending media get the information, have a staff member fax your formal press announcement to all media sources you want to know about the success.

Although there are some generalities that apply to all projects, there is very little consistency in the type and number of activities that occur between the site tour and the successful closure and announcement of a project. Each will find its own path to success, guided of course by the skillful hands of a competent economic developer.

If there is any one characteristic that seems to traverse all projects and types of organizations, that characteristic is follow-through. To some, the profession of economic development appears to be one of glamour and glory. To those who succeed at this profession, it is merely a process of working closely with the prospect, providing accurate and detailed information, and consistently removing the roadblocks to a successful site selection in their community. The best economic developers are people who follow through with high-potential clients and ensure that everything they need to decide in favor of their community is presented to them. Your ability to adopt and apply these skills will be directly proportional to your success rate in creating new investment in your service territory. Hang in there!

About the Author.....Audrey Taylor

Audrey Taylor has prepared marketing and industrial recruitment plans, strategic plans, and enterprise zone applications for more than 30 communities in California. In 1989, she was recognized as Woman of the Year by the California State Legislature. In 1993, Ms. Taylor was appointed by the California Trade & Commerce agency to TeamCalifornia, an advisory council made up of public and private economic development professionals. In 1995, Governor Pete Wilson appointed her to the Rural Development Council. Ms. Taylor has more than 16 years of experience in economic development. She can be reached at 916.345.0364.

BECOMING THE CHOSEN ONE CHECKLIST ✓

PROJECT TITLE: _____   **PROJECT NUMBER:** _____

SITE DEVELOPMENT

Name	Phone	Activity	Deadline

FINANCING

Name	Phone	Activity	Deadline

EMPLOYEE RECRUITMENT AND TRAINING

Name	Phone	Activity	Deadline

RELOCATION ASSISTANCE

Name	Phone	Activity	Deadline

LOBBYING

Name	Phone	Activity	Deadline

PROJECT COORDINATION

Name _____   _Phone_ _____

ACT!
COMPUTERIZED CLIENT TRACKING SYSTEM

The ACT software program is designed to manage clients and prospects. This program enables managers to successfully execute business sales and recruitment plans, aid in business retention programs, and measure benefits. The ACT program is a state-of-the-art client management system that allows for the collection of data specific to each client. Its key features are:

- Client Records
- Call, Meeting, and Action Dates
- Identification Criteria
- Word Processing
- Reports
- Time Logs

CLIENT RECORDS

ACT client records include all essential information ranging from name, address, phone and fax numbers to sales and employment figures. User-defined fields are also available to identify specific information.

Trade show and advertising response leads are received and viewed by the director who marks the companies that match the targeted industries of the community. The leads are then input into the ACT program by staff. Special "fields" are used for tracking information such as: square footage and acreage requirements, SIC code, industry, product, source of lead, expansion plans, location dates, etc. This information can usually be found in the trade show contact log.

CALL, MEETING, AND ACTION DATES

ACT allows for each client to be scheduled for a "Call," "Meeting," or "Action." A date, time, and objective for the call or meeting is included. Each day the manager can "call up" the day's schedule of prospects to contact.

When the initial information on a lead is entered into the program, the client is marked to receive an introductory letter from the manager. In this letter the manager indicates that he or she will contact the client again on a specific date, usually within 30 days. When the letters are drafted by the manager and input into the ACT word processing system, the secretary places the indicated follow-up date in the "Call" field as a reminder to the manager to call the client on that specific date.

During the follow-up telephone conversation any action that may be required, such as information to be researched and forwarded to client, is noted in the "To Do" field along with a due date. Specific technical information requested on sites is forwarded, via memo, to the city's economic development director for action. When contact is made with an existing company, the pertinent data is gathered by the director through meetings and phone conversations and entered into the system. The secretary marks the client record for a three-month follow-up date. Any contact made or information received on the company during this time is noted by the director in the client record.

Through the report writing function, the secretary generates a to-do list which includes all contacts and actions scheduled for the next 30 days. This ensures a timely follow-up to all client requests.

IDENTIFICATION CRITERIA

Classes and Flags are user-defined fields that can identify the company's industry (class) and specific product (flag). Classes are identified by an alphabetic code (A for Agriculture, B for Banking, etc.). A rating field is used to indicate the importance of the prospect. The manager marks new leads according to the immediacy of a move or status of decision-making. For example, a "__" rated client is actively looking for a new or additional location; a "__" rated client has indicated interest in a new location within the next two to three years; a "__" rated client is an initial contact, currently being qualified. Status indicates the type of client: advertising lead, trade show lead, direct contact, retention, expansion, financing, etc.

WORD PROCESSING

Personalized documents and letters are produced with the ACT word processing system. The director composes letters and, from the client listing, indicates which clients are to receive a letter. The secretary then "marks" each client record identified by the director and merges them with the letter to compose a very detailed, specific direct mail campaign. These mail campaigns are used in conjunction with the "Call" field to prompt the director to make the appropriate follow-up calls. This provides a complete tracing of all contacts made and information sent to prospective companies.

REPORTS

The eight predefined, standard reports included in the ACT software provides the user with the ability to generate reports and lists that are sorted by various key information, depending on the specific information requested by the director, agency, city, etc. In addition, a custom report generator creates additional, very specific reports. Any combination of data can be sorted and presented to exact specifications.

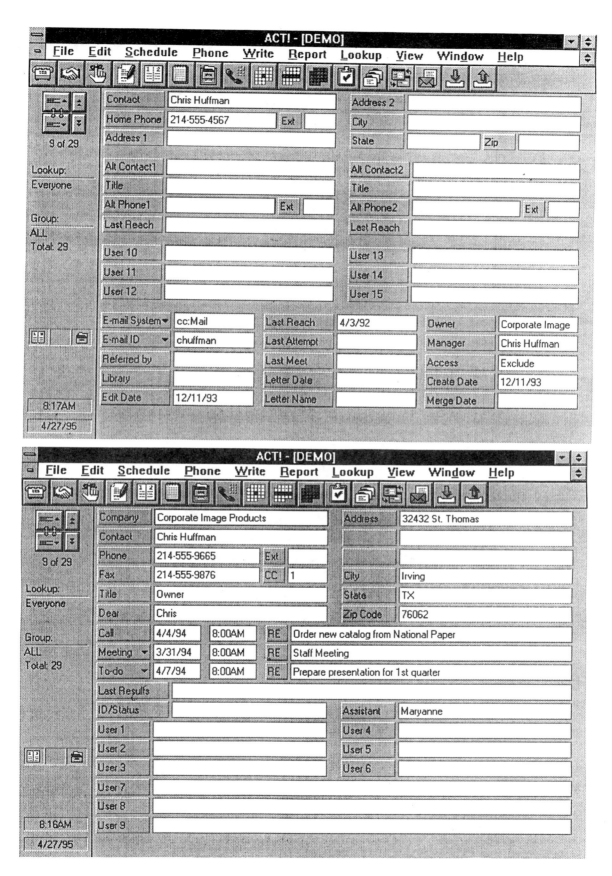

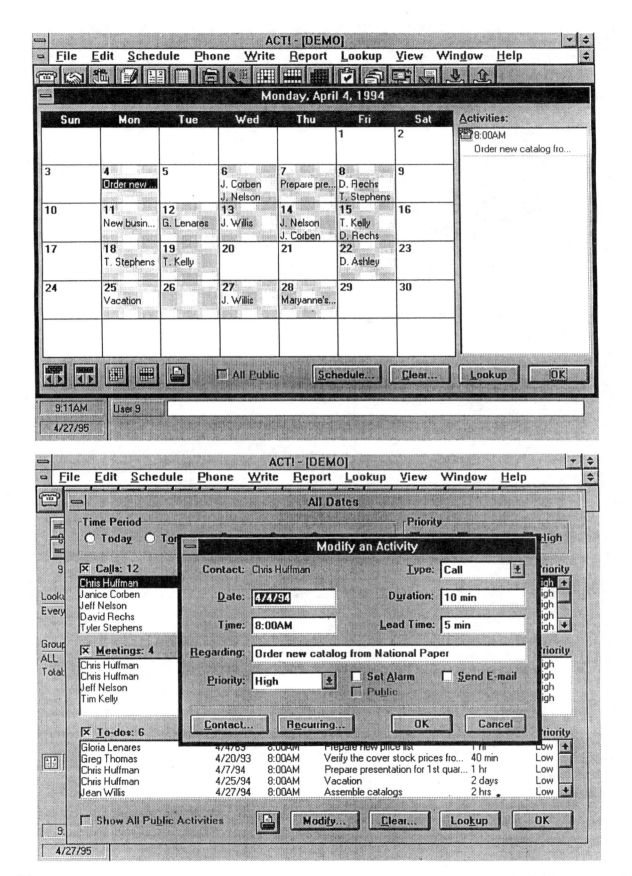

CHAPTER 14

PROJECT REVIEW

Rick Weddle
President, Toledo Regional Growth Partnership

In the beginning God created the heaven and the earth. And God saw everything that He made. "Behold," God said. "It is very good."

And on the seventh day God rested from all His work. His archangel came then unto Him asking, "God, how do you know that what you have created is very good? Toward what mission was your creation directed? What were your goals? What are your criteria for what is 'very good'? On what data do you base your judgement? Aren't you a little close to the situation to make a fair and unbiased evaluation?"

God thought about these questions all that day and His rest was greatly disturbed. On the eighth day, God said, "Lucifer, go to hell."

———o———

It has often been said that economic development is too simple for most people to understand. For some crazy reason, people seem to think that large or important problems or issues must necessarily have complex or complicated answers. When it comes to basic economic development processes, that concept is simply untrue. When it comes to the economic development site location process, we tend to complicate matters by attempting to explain why development occurs and where companies tend to locate by using and sometimes abusing almost every analytical process except the most important one. That is customer feedback or, simply put, just asking the customer why. That is what the project review process is all about: finding out the real reasons why companies locate where they do.

Unfortunately, the process of learning why companies do what they do and translating that information into actionable knowledge is not as easy as it sounds. It does require organization, discipline, and a little hard work on the part of the economic development practitioner. Consequently, a systematic and organized approach to securing and assessing customer feedback is recommended. Such a structured approach will be referred to in this chapter as a **project review**.

As you examine the project review process, keep in mind the following questions:

— What is a formal economic development project review process?

— Why is customer feedback from the review process so important?

— What are the different types of reviews that should be conducted?

— What can be learned from a systematic review process?

— How should an effective project review process be organized?

— What do you do with, and how do you use, the project review findings?

If all this seems too obvious and logical, then you're getting the point. Effective project reviews are simply the process of getting inside the customer's thought processes to identify and understand the rationale for their decision making. Then it is about putting the information or knowledge gained to use, either in improving your handling of future projects or correcting disadvantages so as to be more competitive the next time around. Let's take a look at what a project review really is and is not.

As a customer feedback mechanism, the project review process is helpful with securing important market information so you can better understand what exactly it means to you and your community. It is, therefore, a key learning process essential to planning and implementing effective economic development programs and activities. A good project review process will provide you with three key insights:

Market Intelligence—a systematic project review process covering all projects in aggregate will generate essential information regarding customer preferences, site selection and elimination factors, and the relative desirability of your various prod-

uct offerings, community resources, and attributes.

Project-Specific Knowledge—critical insight into your community's competitive posture can be gained by conducting detailed reviews of specific projects. You can learn a great deal about the relative competitiveness of both how you manage the process and what you have to sell.

Competitor Information — project reviews, both company-specific and in aggregate, will reveal important competitor information. From the review, you should be able to clearly document just who your top competitors are by project type and how they compare to your community's offerings. Moreover, you can see how their recruitment process compares to what you are doing.

It is also important to remember what a project review is not. It should not be considered as a mechanism for fixing or assigning blame or fault when a project goes wrong or the community fails to attract a particular company location. Unfortunately, this is often the chief reason a project-specific review is undertaken. We've all seen examples of a project that goes wrong and places an elected official or the economic development staff under fire. There is a tendency in economic development to blame the economic development staff for failures that, more often than not, are due to fundamental competitive disadvantages that are beyond the ability of anyone to control or impact over the near-term. Of course, if there is a staff failure or management process problem, it should and will be uncovered in a valid project review process. The problem is that when finger pointing, fault finding or blame shifting is the principal reason for undertaking a project review, then blame tends to be laid, regardless of the real reasons,

Effective project reviews are simply the process of getting inside the customer's thought processes to identify and understand the rationale for their decision making.

at the feet of the economic development or sales staff. Attempts to document community competitive disadvantages after you are already under fire make you look defensive and appear as lame excuses at best. The only way to avoid such negative situations is to put a formal project review process with standardized procedures in place well in advance of recruitment losses or trigger incidents. In fact, a formal review process can minimize and, in some cases, prevent finger pointing and fault finding because everyone knows a formal structured process is likely to reveal and disclose the real underlying reasons for recruitment failures.

When things go well and you have just landed a new facility location, remember that the project review process is not merely a public relations tool or mechanism to give credit or glory to those who helped make the project a success. To be sure, giving credit and rewarding those who have helped is an important aspect of the process. It is not, however, the primary reason and should not overshadow the real purpose of learning how to improve the process and do better the next time around.

WHY CUSTOMER FEEDBACK IS IMPORTANT

Remember that your "next best customer" will, for the most part, have a profile just like your "last best customer." Sadly, many economic development practitioners don't get this point. They are too busy trying to manipulate detailed and sophisticated targeting models (based on a consultant's analysis of generalized industry operating requirements compared to a cursory review of your community's resources and attributes) to take the time to stop,

look, and listen to their marketplace. The best source of economic development intelligence and near-term targeting information is right there before your eyes. It is direct customer feedback. It is the best source of market intelligence for two simple reasons. First of all, it is the straight truth from the customer—unfiltered and unaltered. It may, in fact, be the only real truths you will hear, because almost everyone but the customer has a vested interest in the local development process and necessarily speaks from that perspective. Secondly, it is readily accessible and there for the taking. It lies in your files, records, recollections, conversations, and direct marketing experiences with previous and current customers or clients. It lies in the findings, conclusions, and opinions of those firms that have already considered your community and either located a facility or eliminated your community from further consideration. It is a gold mine of information. But like a gold mine, the value lies beneath the surface. In order to benefit, you must work to extract it. You must find a way to dig out—or mine—this valuable source of market data and information.

IMPORTANT FINDINGS FROM THE PROJECT REVIEW PROCESS

Let's turn now to look at just what type of valuable information or key findings you may expect from a formal structured project review process. As already noted, project reviews generally take two forms. They are:

- Ongoing systematic reviews of all projects in aggregate, and
- Project-specific reviews conducted on a case-by-case basis.

A formal review process can minimize and, in some cases, prevent finger pointing and fault finding because everyone knows a formal structured process is likely to reveal and disclose the real underlying reasons for recruitment failures.

The direct information to be gained through these two separate types of project review processes is similar but different. An ongoing review process will yield more generalized information that is highly useful in guiding the targeting of your program and the focus of your marketing efforts. Collected in aggregate form, such information is easily compared to note trends and common practices. Verification of customer trends and site location practices can help you to segment general target industry groupings and concentrate your marketing resources where they will yield the best results.

On the other hand, project-specific reviews do not generate comparative data. Rather, they provide accurate customer feedback regarding specific and detailed elements of the site location process. Company-specific project reviews will give you a clear and valid picture of the relative competitiveness of both your community's product offerings and your economic development management processes. Such detailed information is very valuable in formulating strategies and action plans needed to address specific competitiveness and/or program management issues and concerns.

CONDUCTING ECONOMIC DEVELOPMENT PROJECT REVIEWS

As noted above, two types of project review processes are recommended. A comprehensive economic development program should have an organized process in place to conduct both ongoing aggregate project reviews and the more detailed company-specific project reviews. Failing to organize such simple customer feedback mechanisms is like trying to fly blind when you don't have to. Conversely, operationalizing the process of surveying your customer base lets you operate with real time market information and may create a distinct competitive advantage for your community and your program. Let's take a look now at what it takes to begin such an important customer feedback program.

Establishing an Ongoing Project Review Program

The economic development process is rarely managed so as to collect important market intelligence needed to effectively guide current and future program efforts. In planning marketing programs we tend to follow published information about target firms and decision-maker practices. We also tend to make quite a few assumptions that may or may not prove to be accurate. In the sales management process, we are usually too busy trying to get on to the next deal to take the time to put meaningful data collection and analysis programs in place. One way to avoid this situation is to establish a regular procedure for reviewing all projects, both successful and unsuccessful. It is recommended that this procedure involve a formal structured customer or client survey conducted at least twice annually.

Depending on the number of projects involved, the survey can be conducted either by telephone or by mail. Although more time consuming, the telephone survey is more highly recommended. Mail surveys may be better suited for surveying a large audience. The telephone survey is much better suited for a smaller audience, because it is more accurate and provides you with a controlled response rate. Direct telephone contact also enables you to probe for customer feedback in a more open-ended manner. Whether you use the mail or telephone approach, the process involves developing a standardized customer feedback questionnaire, rigorously surveying as many customers as possible, compiling the data in an understandable format, and then putting the information gained to good use.

Customer feedback, no matter how valid or accurate, does you no good while sitting in a pile on your desk. To be valuable, it must be utilized effectively.

Project Review Questionnaire Design

Considerable attention and thought needs to be given to the design of the project review questionnaire. A word of caution is due here: Many economic developers attempt to collect too much detailed information. Consequently, clients or customers are reluctant to answer such detailed questionnaires. Moreover, once the information is acquired in such detail, meaningful analysis is quite complicated and is often shelved until there is "more time to do the job right." Customer feedback, no matter how valid or accurate, does you no good while sitting in a pile on your desk. To be valuable, it must be utilized effectively.

A straightforward questionnaire that involves very simple but essential customer feedback points is all you need to yield valuable market intelligence. To this end, open-ended questions often are the most effective. While each development program should customize the list of questions for their own particular market needs and requirements, questions will typically be grouped in four specific areas:

— *Why was our community initially considered?*
— *Why was our community eliminated?*
— *Why was the successful community selected?*
— *What could have been done to change the site selection decision?*

WHY WAS OUR COMMUNITY INITIALLY CONSIDERED?

While this may seem elementary, few if any economic developers routinely ask this question to customers or clients. Even fewer fully understand exactly why their community is considered in the marketplace by various types of clients. Most economic developers have a good understanding of site selection factors and the relative importance these factors hold in company location decisions. What many don't understand is that their particular community is often considered for reasons that may not appear on such standardized surveys.

For example, the December 1995 issue of *Area Development Magazine* published the tenth annual survey of site selection factors. This survey indicated that labor cost was the number one rated factor in final company site location decisions. Few experienced practitioners would dispute this finding. Even so, the chief reason a particular company initially considered your community for a project location will rarely be simply "labor cost." More often than not, the initial reason for consideration may be more closely linked to more obvious factors as:

- Available building that appeared to meet initial requirements.
- All communities of a certain size in a particular market area or along a particular transportation corridor were considered.

This doesn't mean that labor costs or other key location factors aren't important. It means that companies do things for a wide variety of reasons that often don't show up on published surveys or reports. It also means that while labor costs are vitally important in being eventually chosen as the winning location, it may not be the most important reason that companies consider your community in the first place. It follows that you can't be selected as a winning site if you aren't considered in the first place. The key with this line of questioning is to better understand what you can do to be considered initially. You want to find ways of becoming "top of mind" and, therefore, short-listed for initial consideration.

WHY WAS OUR COMMUNITY ELIMINATED FROM CONSIDERATION?

This question goes to the foundation of your community's overall competitive posture. In other words, what are the principal barriers to your success in locating new business and industry? Once again, you will be likely to find that the reasons you are frequently eliminated may or may not track directly with published information regarding site selection factors or objective assessments of your community's strengths and weaknesses. Since reasons for elimination may include both product and process issues, you should probe for open-ended answers here. Let the customer open up and speak to you entirely from the customer's point of view. This can be particularly insightful. Responses to this question cover a wide range of issues but could reveal:

- The available building didn't really fit (especially if that was the only reason you were being considered in the first place). Perhaps it was the right size and cost but didn't meet the company's requirement for image or wasn't in good enough condition and would require extensive repair.

- The company was concerned about your community's ability to meet their labor availability requirements within their desired or intended cost range. Other factors that looked good on paper didn't meet expectations or compare favorably with competing locations after more detailed analysis. For example, you may have failed to submit adequate information to enable the company to fully assess the cost, time frame, or other factors in detail and caused them to miss a deadline in their decision-making process.

WHY WAS THE SUCCESSFUL COMMUNITY SELECTED?

You may be surprised to learn that the reason the successful community was selected may not be directly tied to why communities were considered in the first place or why your community was eliminated. It is not that these factors aren't related, but rather that the process of site elimination and selection varies greatly from company to company and involves a great many variables, all weighed to fit the particular company's requirements. Frequently, in response to this question you will be provided with a generalized answer that blends a number of variables together leading to a bottom line operating cost conclusion. Even so, you can find out important strategic information if you probe for open-ended responses. You may be surprised to learn answers such as some of the following:

- The successful community had an available building that closely met the company's requirements and gave them a considerable time and capital cost advantage.

- A recently approved incentive package in the successful community's state provided a substantial operating cost advantage.

- The winning community's recruitment approach tipped the balance in some unique or unanticipated way.

Note the consistent references to "available buildings" in each of the above question areas. I have long felt that an available building inventory is highly underrated on most site location factor surveys. To be sure, on balance, it is only one of many factors. However, my experience suggests that as many as 85 percent of business/industry clients begin their search by looking for an available building. So when it comes to being considered by such clients, an available building is perhaps the most important factor. This is the kind of significant customer feedback you need to be gathering from your customers in your community.

It follows that if you are staying close to your customer—and your competitors—you shouldn't find yourself surprised by who is frequently beating you on recruitment deals. The key here is to probe for new trends and stay tuned to market changes that will affect future location projects. Be sure to listen and learn.

As many as 85 percent of business/ industry clients begin their search by looking for an available building.

WHAT COULD HAVE BEEN DONE TO CHANGE THE SITE SELECTION OUTCOME?

This question will help you learn if, in fact, anything could have been done to change the location decision outcome. In the vast majority of instances you will be told that either there was nothing you could have done to change the outcome or the things that could have been changed were beyond your ability to impact within the project decision time frame. Even so, you should probe with open-ended questions to learn all you can about exactly what would have made a difference. Sometimes you will be surprised. Always you will end up better informed and better focused on what you could do better next time.

DESIGNATING SURVEY RESPONSIBILITY and DECIDING WHO TO SURVEY

For consistency purposes, it is recommended that survey responsibility be designated to either one person, a group, task force, or committee that can carry through on a regular schedule. The key here is to provide both consistency and credibility, especially if the survey is being conducted by telephone. You may want to assign the responsibility for managing the process to someone in an administrative position that is not directly involved in the sales management or client handling process. This, of course, depends entirely on the size of your staff and human resource capacity.

Deciding who to survey is equally important. A comprehensive survey process will survey all customers or clients on both successful and unsuccessful projects. This will be needed to generate balanced information that will be of real use in guiding future program direction.

The survey effort should be directed to the principal individual with whom the economic development effort had direct contact. This individual is not only a key member of the site location team, but also the person in the best position to critique your efforts and your community's relative competitive posture. If he or she is unavailable or unwilling to participate, attempt to get the feedback from someone else directly involved in the location process. Direct involvement is essential, because, as you will find out, published reasons for considering and/or eliminating communities and selecting the eventual winner are usually not the only reasons. In many instances, they are not even the most important reasons. You have to cut through the public relations spin and try to find the underlying rationale.

Survey experience indicates that the optimum timing for conducting surveys is six to nine months after the final decision was made.

The timing for an ongoing survey process will have a direct impact on the accuracy of the information gained. Experience suggests that survey efforts conducted immediately following an unsuccessful project rarely have the accuracy or candor of later surveys. The principal reason for this is that the company may think you are still in the sales mode and are still trying to impact the project outcome. Also, all elements of the final location may not be complete and the company's focus is on wrapping up and getting the deal done, not on helping you understand what went wrong or what you could have done better. Survey experience indicates that the optimum timing for conducting surveys is six to nine months after the final decision was made. That is long enough for most of the project location work to be fully under way and quick enough so that memories remain valid.

Often you will find that, after such an interval, the lead member of the site selection team will be very candid and quite helpful in responding to your questions. This is especially true if you approach the questioning as a part of a structured process and assure that the information provided will be reported only in aggregate form, thus providing a measure of confidentiality. It is important to note that nobody will be candid about telling you where you failed or where your community is non-competitive if they think their name will end up in the newspaper. It is not good for them, you, or anyone for that to happen. If it does happen, don't expect to do any repeat business with the firm anytime soon.

COMPANY-SPECIFIC PROJECT REVIEWS

Company-specific reviews differ from ongoing reviews in a number of ways. First, they are almost always conducted individually and soon after the project decision is made, rather than at some future time when a group of firms may be surveyed. Secondly, they are typically conducted for the express purpose of either learning what went wrong (and how it can be corrected or avoided next time) or what went right (and how it can be improved upon in the future). And finally, company-specific project reviews are sometimes conducted in an effort to conduct a cost-benefit analysis of a particular project. Or in other words, did the community provide too much, too little or just the right amount to the company, in terms of financial incentives? Such an assessment can prove helpful in selling the project to the community.

POLICIES AND PROCEDURES FOR CONDUCTING PROJECT REVIEWS

Since company-specific project reviews are frequently conducted at the end of an unsuccessful project, it is important to establish a standard set of policies and procedures or guidelines within which the project review will be conducted. Project review procedures should govern when and on what type of projects a full review will be conducted, who should be involved in the process, how the facts of the project will be compiled and verified, and how the findings or results will be reported or communicated to the public. Debating and adopting such procedures in advance of an actual project review will assure an orderly and productive process.

THE PROJECT REVIEW TEAM

In order to establish credibility of the project review process, the project review team should involve both those involved in the particular project and also those stakeholder groups who, although not directly involved, have a direct stake or interest in the economic development process. Representatives of those involved in the process typically include members and representatives of the recruitment team. Other stakeholder groups that may be included in the process are elected officials, public sector staff, economic development agency board of directors, organized labor, and citizen or neighborhood groups directly impacted or affected by the project.

Remember that involvement of stakeholders in the project review process is not just to secure their input and oversight of the process. If conducted correctly, the project review process will develop strategic information about the community's relative competitive posture. It is, therefore, an extremely important community leadership educational tool.

Written Chronology of Events

Project review processes must be correctly focused or the review team may tend to ramble from issue to issue. An important starting point for focusing discussion and review is the chronology of events associated with the project under review. Remember that, after the fact, it is sometimes difficult for laypersons to understand why certain action steps were or were not taken. Putting events into chronological order will help to make sense of the process. It will also help to guide discussion along the project decision timeline so as to better understand the process from the customer or client's point of view. (See "Case Study: The Relocation of Harper's Furniture," page 95.)

COMPANY PARTICIPATION AND INVOLVEMENT

If possible, involve the company in the review process. It adds credibility to the overall effort and helps focus and guide discussion. If the recruitment effort was unsuccessful, be prepared for the company to decline to openly participate. In these instances you may try to talk to the company privately to explain the process and solicit its indirect involvement and participation.

If the recruitment process was successful, you will be more likely to secure company participation. This is especially true if the company needs your help in selling certain aspects of the project to the community. Such matters may include resolving zoning issues, coordinating transportation improvements, accomplishing utility line extensions, monitoring financial incentive compliance, and assimilating management into the community. In these instances, company participation will be likely. Their candor, especially on negative matters, may be severely limited.

Project Review Meetings

As soon as the chronology of events has been prepared, send it to the recruitment team members for review and comment. Make certain you have all the events and dates correct before sitting down to review the project. It can be quite embarrassing and damaging to your credibility if substantive corrections to the chronology have to be made or noted in the midst of the initial review meeting. It is recommended that a community leader who is supportive of the economic development program be secured to chair the project review meeting. While it is essential that the review be conducted at an arm's length from the recruitment team, it is equally important that it be conducted in a friendly environment, if at all possible.

Written Summary of Findings

The project review process will culminate with the preparation of a written summary of findings. In most instances this report will be in summary form, omitting many of the details covered through the general assessment process. The summary should, however, cover and describe the following informational points and key findings:

► The purpose of the project review.
► A listing of those involved in preparing the project review.
► A description of the economic development project including the various roles and relationships of different recruitment team members in the project.
► A summary of the key factors involved in the site location process.
► A brief summary or overview of the chronology of events.
► Key reasons the community was eliminated (on unsuccessful projects).
► Key reasons the community was selected (on successful projects).
► A cost-benefit analysis of the project (on successful projects) that examines the level of direct financial incentives provided in comparison to the direct and indirect financial return to the community.

A summary of action steps (if appropriate) is recommended. The action step summary should identify and address any product or process disadvantages and the appropriate actions, both near- and long-term, needed to improve the community's competitive posture.

MANAGING COMMUNICATIONS

The project review process is not complete until the results, findings and conclusions are communicated to key stakeholder groups. It is, therefore, important that you develop a specific communications strategy and plan. The plan should address both internal and external, or public, audiences. Remember that an important aspect of the project review process is community education, hence the significance of a solid communications plan.

The communications plan is essential in those instances where you have been unsuccessful in recruiting a large showcase project. This is true regardless of whether the failure is due to either a community resource disadvantage or a specific failure/limitation in the economic development management process. In either instance, you want to do more that just respond to the criticism regarding the problem or failure. You want to turn the project review into a learning exercise and try to focus on either what the community needs to do over the long-term to correct the resource disadvantage or on what you are doing immediately to correct the management problem and make sure it doesn't happen again.

Remember that the public and the media find it difficult to follow long, detailed explanations. But a project review report is just that—a long and detailed explanation of a situation for which most people will seek a simple explanation. They will want to know why you won or lost, who gets the credit or blame, and what is going to be done next. Therefore, your communications plan should attempt to focus on one or two compelling issues or message points that further your overall communications objective. Your communications objective should link to the reason the report was prepared and focus, if possible, on future action.

Your communications plan should be prepared in conjunction with the project review team's work so that consensus will exist with regard to both the message and the delivery of the message. In other words, you need to make sure, to the extent possible, that everyone on the project review team is in general agreement and supportive of the overall communications message.

PUTTING WHAT YOU LEARN
TO EFFECTIVE USE

Now that you have collected all this information, what are you going to do with it? That depends entirely on what you have learned. Don't assume that everyone will see the project review findings and immediately understand their implications or even know what to do with the information gained. It is important that you establish direct communication links to both community leadership and economic development marketing and sales staff.

Community leaders need to be regularly apprised of the ongoing information flow from the project review process. In doing so, you will be helping to educate leadership regarding the need to constantly improve your community's competitive posture. You will be creating an awareness that the economic development program success is, in large part, dependent upon the community's ability to provide what prospective companies require from the marketplace. This education process should focus on segmenting the information into two areas: what can and cannot be changed. For example, while it is impossible to alter the distance to key markets, you might succeed in increasing market presence and economic development success by building a speculative building tailored to a particular industry segments requirements. Just as you can't directly impact the cost of labor, you can provide specialized training programs, on-the-job training subsidies, and a host of other program initiatives that may serve to improve relative competitiveness. Again, the key is not just what you learn from the process, but what you do with what you learn.

The communications plan is essential in those instances where you have been unsuccessful in recruiting a large showcase project.

The most important near-term use of information gained from the project review process may be in the areas of industry targeting, marketing program focus, and sales management. Comparing the customer feedback to other industry targeting data should provide important insight into how general industry groups can be better segmented and thus understood. Identifying the reasons yours and other communities are initially considered can help fine-tune marketing programs to reach target firms with the correct images and messages. Understanding why and how you frequently are eliminated from further consideration will help you revise your sales management processes to remain alive in the site location process. Again, getting close to your customers and understanding their decision processes more fully will pay real dividends over time.

---

*About the Author.....*Rick **Weddle**

Rick Weddle is President of the Toledo Regional Growth Partnership, the lead economic development agency for Toledo and the 10 counties that comprise Northwest Ohio. Under Mr. Weddle's leadership, the Partnership has achieved an unprecedented combination of regional cooperation, job creation, and new capital investment. Simultaneously, Mr. Weddle has spearheaded the evolution of the RGP into a progressive, private, nonprofit organization. Prior to his tenure at the RGP, Mr. Weddle served as President and CEO of the San Joaquin Partnership and Business Council of Stockton, California; President of North Carolina's Winston-Salem Business, Inc.; and Vice President of the Metro Tulsa Chamber of Commerce Economic Development Division in Tulsa, Oklahoma. Mr. Weddle serves as Chairman of the Education Board and as an elected member of the Board of Directors of the American Economic Development Council. He can be reached at 419.252.2724.

PROJECT REVIEW CHECKLIST ✓

PROJECT TITLE: _____ PROJECT NUMBER: _____

WHY WAS OUR COMMUNITY INITIALLY CONSIDERED?

_____
_____
_____
_____
_____

WHY WAS OUR COMMUNITY ELIMINATED?

_____
_____
_____
_____
_____

WHY WAS THE SUCCESSFUL COMMUNITY SELECTED?

_____
_____
_____
_____
_____

WHAT COULD HAVE BEEN DONE TO CHANGE THE SITE SELECTION DECISION?

_____
_____
_____
_____
_____

PROJECT REVIEW CHECKLIST ✓

PROJECT TITLE: _____ **PROJECT NUMBER:** _____

PROJECT TEAM:

Name	Organization	Key Role
_____	_____	_____
_____	_____	_____
_____	_____	_____
_____	_____	_____

KEY FACTORS INVOLVED IN SITE SELECTION/REJECTION:

a) _____

_____

b) _____

_____

c) _____

_____

d) _____

_____

e) _____

_____

CHRONOLOGY:

Date	Activity
_____	Project initiated by our organization
_____	_____
_____	_____
_____	Project closed as successful/unsuccessful

COST BENEFIT ANALYSIS:

$_____ Private investment

$_____ Incentives

$_____ Ratio

ABOUT THE EDITORS

Until 1993, Maury Forman and Jim Mooney didn't know the other existed. Through a chance meeting triggered by Jim's first book, *Doing the Deal: A Developer's Guide to Effective Incentive Utilization*, they began to discuss ways in which they could advance the economic development profession. With Maury's background as an academic and Jim's background as a practitioner, they decided to combine their skills to produce a handbook that people would not only read but use in their recruitment practices as well.

"The Race to Recruit" started in mid-1995 as a workshop coordinated by the Washington State Department of Community, Trade and Economic Development. The purpose of the workshop was to view business attraction as a process whereby each step would be mastered with an understanding of how to utilize basic economic development skills.

The success of the workshop led the two to believe that a more lasting document was necessary to serve not only their constituents but others as well. Their intent was to limit the amount of theory typically found in other business recruitment books and, instead, provide useful tools for the practitioner in the form of questionnaires and checklists.

In order that the book not be dominated by practices in either editor's state, they set out to identify some of the most successful people in the field of economic development throughout the United States. *The Race to Recruit: Strategies for Successful Business Attraction* is the result of many years experience that includes successful and unsuccessful recruitment efforts by the skilled practitioners who contributed to this publication.

Dr. Maury Forman is Program Manager for education and training for the Washington State Department of Community, Trade and Economic Development. He is the creator and course director for the Northwest Economic Development Games and serves on the American Economic Development Council's Education Committee. He has a Ph.D. from New York University. Maury can be reached at 206.464.6282.

Jim Mooney is Principal of Business Development for Northern Indiana Public Service Company (NIPSCO), the largest combined utility in the state of Indiana. He is responsible for European, automotive, and food processing marketing for his service territory, the northern third of the state of Indiana. Jim has a Masters degree in development administration from Michigan State University. He is certified in economic development finance through the National Development Council and is a candidate for certified economic developer status through the American Economic Development Council. Jim can be reached at 219.647.5127.

NOTES